Around the World, Around Our Town

Recipes from San Pedro

Around the World, Around Our Town

Recipes from San Pedro

Edited by
Dolores S. Lisica

Illustrated by
Leo Politi

FRIENDS OF THE SAN PEDRO LIBRARY
San Pedro, California

San Pedro Library

Friends of the San Pedro Library, Producer of *Around the World, Around Our Town: Recipes from San Pedro*, is a non-profit support group for the San Pedro Regional Library, a branch of the Los Angeles Public Library. Chartered in 1972 with six founding members, we number close to 400 members. Our original goal was a new facility, and we feel that we did help our community achieve that goal. All proceeds from this book will be used to purchase books to expand and enrich the San Pedro Library collection.

Additional copies of this book may be ordered from Friends of the San Pedro Library, 931 South Gaffey Street, San Pedro, CA 90731.

CONTENTS

*A particular thank you to an artist who believed in
us and shared his creative gifts with our community,*

LEO POLITI

INTRODUCTION

One of the basic similarities of all mankind is food, which ironically is also one of the main indications of diversity. Diversity in food has found a happy home in San Pedro, California. Immigrants from all areas of the world (24 are represented here) have introduced strange and wonderful tastes to their American friends and neighbors.

In return, the immigrants were taught the pleasures and joys of American food, primarily through the nagging of their children who had tasted their first chocolate cake and couldn't wait for the next taste.

Many of the recipes which appear here have been passed from generation to generation and this makes their first appearance in print. While these recipes have been home-tested over many years, none of them are immutable (except for cakes and especially the chocolate cake on page 237). Do experiment, try substitutes, add or omit seasonings. The important thing is to prepare a dish that you, your family, and guests will enjoy.

A sincere thank you to all of the volunteers that have devoted hours and hours to typing and proofreading over and over again: Betty Di Masi, Sean Flynn, Nancy Hedges, Janet Edwards Johnson, Gladys Kidwell, Chris Lisica, Jr., Margaret Litman, Virginia Manzella, Sue Munio, Kathy Rogers, Ann Rumery, Gay Ryan, Ruth Shannon, and Selma Streicher. Our comprehensive index was compiled by Gay Ryan and Selma Streicher. Thank you to all the excellent cooks and restaurants who have contributed recipes.

A special thank you to Robert Miles and Teri Stewart; they added a much needed professional touch to the editing and production of *Around the World, Around Our Town: Recipes from San Pedro*.

Appetizers and Beverages

APPETIZERS AND BEVERAGES

ARTICHOKE LOAF

Cut bacon into small pieces and fry in large skillet. Add parsley, onion, and garlic and sauté. Add artichokes and seasonings. If dry, add olive oil. Sauté about 20 minutes.

Beat eggs, add cheeses and bread crumbs and combine with artichoke mixture; mix thoroughly.

Pour into two 9 x 4 inch greased loaf pans and bake at 350 degrees for 30 to 45 minutes.

Refrigerate several hours.

To serve, slice thinly and arrange on platter.

May be served as an appetizer or vegetable side dish.

Serves 10 to 20   *Pamm Vuoso*

3/4 pound bacon
1 cup parsley, minced
3/4 cup chopped onion
8 cloves garlic, minced
4 cups cooked artichokes or 5 jars
    marinated artichokes
2 tablespoons oregano
2 tablespoons sweet basil
2 tablespoons thyme
salt and pepper to taste
olive oil, if needed
12 eggs, beaten
1-1/2 cups Parmesan cheese, grated
1 cup shredded cheddar cheese
1 cup bread crumbs

AVOCADO DIP

Mix all ingredients together until well blended.

Serve with corn chips or potato chips.

Tip: Place avocado pit in dip to keep it from turning brown.

Helen Homen

2 medium avocados, mashed
1 small tomato, peeled and finely
    chopped
1-1/2 teaspoons grated onion
Tabasco to taste
salt and pepper to taste
1 tablespoon lemon or lime juice

CHILI CHEESE DIP

Cook over low heat until cheese is melted and sour cream is blended in.

Keep warm in fondue or chafing dish.

Serve with mini-tacos or corn chips.

June Gwartney

1 can chili con carne (without beans)
1 cup (approx.) grated cheddar cheese
1/4 cup (or to taste) sour cream or
    cream cheese

CLAM DIP

2 cans (8 ounce) minced clams,
    drained (retain juice)
1 package (8 ounce) cream cheese,
    softened
1/2 cup dry sherry
Worcestershire sauce
paprika

Reserve liquid from clams. Finely chop the clams.

Thin the softened cream cheese with sherry and clam juice. Add a dash of Worcestershire sauce and the clams and mix well. Chill.

Flavor improves if made at least 1 or 2 days in advance.

To serve, sprinkle paprika on top.

Yield: 1-1/2 to 2 cups   *Jacqueline P. Smith*

DILL WEED DIP

1 cup sour cream
1 cup mayonnaise
1 teaspoon lemon juice
1 teaspoon Worcestershire sauce
1/4 cup Parmesan cheese
2 tablespoons dill weed
1 tablespoon parsley
grated onion
fresh cracked pepper

Mix all ingredients and let stand in the refrigerator at least 1 hour.

Especially delicious with raw broccoli, carrots, mushrooms.

Vicki Boutté

HOT CRAB DIP

3 packages (8 ounce) cream cheese
1/2 cup mayonnaise
2 teaspoons dry mustard
1/2 teaspoon garlic powder
1/2 teaspoon onion salt
1/2 tsp. seasoned salt
2 tablespoons powdered sugar
3/4 pound or 2 cans crab meat

Mix first seven ingredients together until well blended over low heat or in a double boiler. When well blended and heated through, add crab.

Serve in fondue or chafing dish to keep warm.

Serve with cubed French bread.

Helen Homen

MEXICAN LAYER DIP

Layer ingredients, in the order listed, on a round platter with tortilla chips around the border.

Holly Hulett

1 large can spicy refried beans (or homemade refried beans)
1 cup sour cream
4 avocados, mashed or your favorite guacamole dip
1/2 of 8 ounce jar of Ortega green chili picante sauce
2 or 3 tomatoes, diced
1 bunch diced green onions
grated cheddar cheese
chopped black olives

VEGETABLE DIP

Mix all ingredients together.

Chill.

Serve with raw vegetables such as celery and carrot sticks, cucumber slices or sticks, cauliflower and broccoli pieces, sugar peas, tender green beans, radishes, and cherry tomatoes.

Selma Streicher

2 cups whipped cottage cheese
1 tablespoon horseradish
1/4 cup chili sauce
1/4 cup mayonnaise
1/2 teaspoon garlic salt
1/2 teaspoon onion
1/2 teaspoon salt

BOURBON APPETIZER FRANKS

Combine brown sugar, catsup, and bourbon in a saucepan. Bring to boil.

Slice frankfurters into bite-size pieces. Add to sauce and heat through.

Pat Trutanich

1 cup brown sugar
1 cup catsup
1 cup bourbon
frankfurters

QUICK APPETIZER BALLS

1 cup biscuit mix
1 cup shredded cheddar cheese
1 pound bulk sausage

Combine all ingredients. Using your hands, work all ingredients together until blended. Shape into small, walnut-size balls.

Place on broiler pan and bake at 350 degrees for 20 to 30 minutes.

Yield: 4 dozen   *Pat Trutanich*

CHEESE BALLS

4 packages (3-ounce) cream cheese,
    softened
6 ounces blue cheese, softened
6 ounces cheddar cheese spread
2 tablespoons grated onions
1 teaspoon Worcestershire sauce
1/8 teaspoon Accent
1 cup finely ground pecans
chopped parsley

In a bowl, cream the cheeses with the Worcestershire sauce and Accent. Add onions and mix well.

Form into two cheese balls. Roll in pecans and then in parsley.

Wrap tightly in plastic wrap. Refrigerate.

Yield: 2 cheese balls   *Laura Divona*

CHEDDAR CHEESE BALLS

1/2 pound butter or margarine
1 pound sharp cheddar cheese, grated
2-1/2 cups flour
1/8 teaspoon salt

With fork or hands, mix butter and grated cheese, then add flour and salt. Mix thoroughly.

Form into balls the size of walnuts. Can be stored in refrigerator or freezer until baking time.

Bake 15 minutes at 350 degrees. Serve warm.

Variation: Wrap 1 teaspoon dough around a small stuffed green olive, covering it completely. Bake as above.

Helen Homen

CHOPPED LIVER

Broil liver. Hard boil eggs.

Put all ingredients, except Miracle Whip, through the meat grinder. If food processor is used, consistency will be more like a paté.

Mix in the Miracle Whip and chill.

Selma Streicher

2 pounds calves liver, sliced 1/2 inch thick
3 to 4 hard boiled eggs
1 to 2 small onions
1 teaspoon seasoned salt
salt, to taste
2 tablespoons Miracle Whip

SOUDZOUKAKIA
Wine Dipped Meatballs

Greece

In a bowl, mix all the ingredients, except the wine.

Shape into small balls and roll in the wine.

Fry in vegetable oil or shortening until they are brown.

They may be served plain or in a tomato sauce.

Mrs. C. J. Petrofanis

1 pound ground beef
2 eggs
1 cup bread crumbs
dash of cinnamon
salt, pepper to taste
2 cloves garlic, chopped fine
1/2 teaspoon cumin
Red table wine

NONI'S PIZZAS

Let pizza dough rise. Break off 1-inch pieces and flatten with hands. Fry in hot oil until brown. Drain on paper towels.

In a saucepan, sauté garlic in olive oil until golden. Add tomato sauce, oregano, capers, salt, pepper, and sugar. Cook for 45 minutes on low heat.

Spoon small amount of sauce on fried pizzas and sprinkle with grated cheese.

These little pizzas are a favorite of my family. They are very popular wherever I bring them.

Noni Caterina Cuomo

1 pound pizza dough
oil for frying
1/2 cup olive oil
1 large clove garlic, minced
1 can (1 pound) tomato sauce
1/2 teaspoon oregano
1 tablespoon capers
salt and pepper
1 teaspoon sugar
grated Parmesan cheese

BROILED SEAFOOD-STUFFED MUSHROOMS

15 to 20 large mushrooms
1 can (6-ounce) crab or 1 can
    (4-ounce) shrimp, drained
1/4 cup seasoned bread crumbs
1/4 cup thinly sliced green onions
1 large clove garlic, pressed
3 tablespoons mayonnaise
1 teaspoon lemon juice
1/4 teaspoon white pepper
1/4 teaspoon Tabasco sauce
1/4 cup melted butter

Wash and dry mushrooms. Remove and chop stems.

Grind crab or shrimp in food processor or blender. Add mushroom stems, bread crumbs, green onions, garlic, mayonnaise, lemon juice, white pepper, and Tabasco sauce. Process until blended.

Stuff mushroom caps with seafood mixture. Drizzle with melted butter and broil until lightly browned.

Serve immediately.

Dolores Lisica

COLD SPINACH APPETIZER

2 packages (10-ounce) frozen,
    chopped spinach
3 tablespoons butter or oleo
1 small onion, chopped
1/4 cup mushrooms, sliced
4 eggs
1/4 cup bread crumbs
1 can (10-3/4 ounce) cream of
    mushroom soup
1/8 teaspoon basil
1/8 teaspoon oregano
1/8 teaspoon white pepper
1/4 cup grated Monterey jack cheese

Thaw spinach and drain well. Press out as much liquid as possible. Melt butter in frying pan. Add chopped onion and sliced mushrooms and cook until limp.

In a medium bowl, beat eggs. Stir in bread crumbs, mushroom soup, basil, oregano, white pepper, drained spinach, onion-mushroom mixture, and 2 tablespoons of the cheese. Stir to blend.

Pour into greased 9-inch square baking pan and sprinkle with the rest of the cheese.

Bake uncovered at 325 degrees for about 35 minutes, or until set.

Chill and cut into 1-inch squares. May be served as a vegetable side dish.

Jacqueline P. Smith

EASY CHOPPED HERRING

Remove black skin from herring.

Place herring, bread, white wine, diced onion, and apple in food processor, and pulse 2 or 3 times. Do not over-process. Add liquid from herring or more wine if needed. Add sugar to taste.

Garnish with grated yolk.

May be refrigerated up to 1 month.

Selma Streicher

1 jar (16-ounce) herring tidbits in wine sauce
1 slice rye or pumpernickel, crust removed
1/2 cup white wine
1 small onion, diced
1 small apple, peeled, cored, and cut up
1 to 2 teaspoons sugar (optional)
1 hard cooked egg, yolk only

HERRING IN SOUR CREAM

Cut herring into bite-size pieces.

Place a layer of herring at the bottom of a refrigerator (or other type) dish, approximately 8 inches in diameter and 3 or more inches high. Cover with layer of sour cream. Next cover with a layer of thinly sliced onion. Continue layering until the herring is gone.

Mix together the sugar and juice and pour over the top layer of herring and pat over the herring and sour cream.

May keep for 2 weeks in the refrigerator.

Selma Streicher

1 jar (16-ounce) herring tidbits in wine sauce (do not use the onions that come in the jar)
1 small carton sour cream
1 small onion, thinly sliced
1/2 teaspoon sugar
2 tablespoons juice from jar

TUNA SPREAD

Beat cheese until smooth.

Gradually add sour cream, stirring until mixture is thoroughly blended.

Drain and mash tuna, then stir into cheese/sour cream and mix well.

Add horseradish, Worcestershire sauce, minced onions and garlic, chervil, salt, and pepper, and blend until smooth.

Serve as spread for crackers or mini-slices of bread.

Yield: 1-2/3 cups

Pat Trutanich

1 package (8 ounce) cream cheese, softened
1/2 cup dairy sour cream
1 can (6-1/2 or 7 ounce) tuna, drained and mashed
1 tablespoon prepared horseradish
1 teaspoon Worcestershire sauce
2 tablespoons onion, minced
1 clove garlic, minced
1 teaspoon chervil
1/2 teaspoon salt
dash of pepper

DILLY BACON-STUFFED EGGS

10 bacon slices, diced and cooked
    crisp
12 hard-cooked eggs
1 package (3 ounce) cream cheese,
    softened
1/2 cup sour cream
1/2 teaspoon dill weed
1 tablespoon capers
watercress (optional)

Dice bacon slices, cook until crisp, and drain on a paper towel.

Hardboil eggs, then shell and halve each lengthwise. Remove yolks and place in a small bowl; mash with a fork and set aside.

In a larger bowl, beat cream cheese until fluffy. Blend in mashed egg yolks, sour cream, dill, capers and bacon.

Generously fill egg whites with yolk mixture. Garnish each with a sprig of watercress, if desired.

Chill overnight.

Kathy Rogers

CHICKEN DRUMMETTES

1 package regular Shake & Bake
1 teaspoon garlic powder
1/8 cup sesame seeds
1/4 cup grated Parmesan cheese
2 packages chicken wing drumettes
    (14 in a package)

Combine Shake & Bake, garlic powder, sesame seeds, and Parmesan cheese in a plastic bag. Shake to blend together.

Shake 4 drumettes at a time to coat with mixture.

Bake on cookie sheet at 400 degrees for 35 minutes.

Serve warm or cold. Great for children, as well as for an appetizer.

Giovanna Mannino

GOLDEN CHICKEN NUGGETS

Bone chicken breasts; remove skin. Cut each breast half into 6 to 8 nuggets, about 1-1/2 inches square.

Combine bread crumbs, cheese, MSG, salt, and herbs.

Dip each chicken nugget in melted butter, then in crumb mixture. Place in a single layer on foil-lined baking sheets.

Bake in hot oven at 400 degrees for 10 minutes.

Chill until ready to use. Great appetizers!

Yield: 4 to 5 dozen   *Esther Marovich*

4 whole chicken breasts
1/2 cup unseasoned fine dry bread crumbs
1/4 cup grated Parmesan cheese
2 teaspoons MSG (optional)
1 teaspoon salt
1 teaspoon dried leaf thyme
1 teaspoon dried leaf basil
1/2 cup butter or margarine, melted

MARINATED CHICKEN WINGS WITH BATTER
Hawaii

Disjoint chicken wings and place in refrigerator dish or bowl.

Beat eggs. Add cornstarch, flour, sugar, salt, MSG, green onions, garlic, and sesame seeds. Mix well and pour over chicken wings.

Note: For more batter, double the recipe.

Soak overnight in refrigerator.

Deep fry in hot oil.

Serves 6 to 8   *Sue Inouye*

4 pounds chicken wings, disjointed
2 eggs
8 tablespoons cornstarch
4 tablespoons flour
2 tablespoons sugar
1 tablespoon salt
1-1/2 teaspoons ajinomoto (MSG)
2 stalks green onions, sliced thinly
2 cloves garlic, pressed
1 tablespoon sesame seeds

PAPER WRAPPED CHICKEN

1 whole chicken breast
1 tablespoon rice wine
1 tablespoon soy sauce
2 slices ginger
1 tablespoon oil
1/2 teaspoon salt
1/2 teaspoon sugar
2 to 3 green onions, cut in 1-inch
    slices

Skin and bone the chicken breast and cut into 1 inch squares, (1/2 inch thick).

Mix thoroughly with rice wine, soy sauce, ginger, oil, salt and sugar, and marinate overnight.

Wrap 1 piece of chicken and 1 piece of green onion in a small piece of foil (parchment squares can be used instead of foil). Repeat until all chicken is used.

Bake at 450 degrees for 15 minutes. Can be fried 5 minutes in 350-degree oil and drained on paper towels.

Variations: Any of the following ingredients may be added to each individual packet:

1 teaspoon minced Chinese parsley
1/4 teaspoon 5 flavors seasoning
2 tablespoons oyster sauce
sprig parsley
1/4 teaspoon sesame oil
1 tablespoon catsup
1/2 teaspoon hoisin sauce
sliver of ginger
piece of smoked ham (1-inch square, 1/2 inch thick)

Helen Homen

On Maple Beer

"To four gallons of boiling water, add one quart of maple syrup and a small table-spoonful of essence of spruce. When it is about milk warm, add a pint of yeast; and when fermented, bottle it. In three days it is fit for use."

—*The Young Housekeeper's Friend*, 1845

WRAPPED CHICKEN LIVERS No. 1

Marinate chicken livers in soy sauce and brandy for 30 minutes.

Halve water chestnuts. Halve slices of bacon.

Wrap 1/2 chestnut and 1/2 liver in 1/2 slice of bacon. Secure with toothpicks.

Broil 4 to 5 minutes.

Serve with sweet & sour sauce, if desired.

Sweet & Sour Sauce:

Combine all ingredients in a medium saucepan. Bring to a boil, stirring frequently. Simmer until thickened and clear.

Helen Homen

1 pound chicken livers
3 teaspoons soy sauce
3 teaspoons brandy
2 cans (5-ounce) water chestnuts
sliced bacon
sweet & sour sauce

Sweet & Sour Sauce

1 tablespoon cornstarch
1/3 cup vinegar
6 tablespoons brown sugar
1 tablespoon melted plum jelly
1/2 teaspoon salt
5 tablespoons catsup
2 teaspoons grated horseradish
1 teaspoon lemon juice

WRAPPED CHICKEN LIVERS No. 2

Cut chicken livers in half and place in a bowl.

Cut each water chestnut into 3 pieces. Place in bowl with chicken livers.

Pour teriyaki sauce over livers and chestnuts. Refrigerate about 4 hours, then drain.

Cut bacon slices in half. Wrap each half around a piece of chicken liver and a piece of water chestnut. Secure with toothpicks. Roll in brown sugar.

Broil, turning occasionally, 3 to 4 inches from heat for about 10 minutes, or until bacon is crisp.

Serve with sweet & sour sauce (see recipe under Wrapped Chicken Livers No. l), if desired.

Teriyaki Sauce:

Combine all ingredients; mix well, and pour over livers and water chestnuts.

Helen Homen

6 chicken livers
4 water chestnuts
teriyaki sauce
6 slices bacon
brown sugar

Teriyaki Sauce:

1/4 cup salad oil
1/4 cup soy sauce
2 tablespoons catsup
1 tablespoon vinegar
1/4 teaspoon pepper
2 cloves garlic, crushed

NORMA'S PÂTÉ

2 tablespoons butter
2/3 cup minced onions
1-1/4 pounds sausage meat
3/4 pound chicken breasts, deboned
    and cubed
1/2 pound chicken livers
1 cup fresh white bread crumbs
1 egg
1/3 cup cream cheese
1 medium clove garlic, puréed
2 to 3 tablespoons brandy
1 tablespoon salt
1/4 teaspoon ground allspice
1/4 teaspoon ground thyme
1/4 teaspoon ground bayleaf
1/4 teaspoon pepper

Sauté onions in butter till lightly golden; cool.

Purée all the ingredients together in a food processor, or put them through the fine blade of a meat grinder, then beat in a large mixing bowl to blend.

To check seasoning, sauté a spoonful in a frying pan, let cool, and taste. Correct seasoning as necessary; use a little more seasonings if necessary, since pâtés are served cold.

Pack mixture into a well buttered, 1-1/2 quart baking dish or loaf pan, cover with buttered wax paper, then with foil, allowing only 1 inch of overhang. Set baking dish in a larger pan and pour enough boiling water in the latter to come halfway up the pâté pan.

Bake in the middle level of a 350-degree oven for 1-1/4 to 1-1/2 hours. When meat is pressed, juices should be pale yellow with just a trace of pink color.

Remove from pan of water and let cool for an hour.

Drain juices, then cover pâté, using a similar pan or board or clean brick that fits inside; weight it down, using something such as cans of food as weights.

When completely cool, drain out juices again and refrigerate. Flavor will be best after one or two days of refrigeration.

Norma Doskow

PICKLED GREEN PEPPERS

Pickling Liquid:

Combine all above ingredients and bring to a boil.

Pickled Green Peppers:

Halve peppers, remove seeds. Add peppers to pickling liquid in batches. Boil for 3 minutes; remove from water, drain, and cool. Reserve liquid and cool thoroughly.

Place cooled peppers in a 2-pound glass jar with a tight-fitting lid. Add peppercorns and garlic, cover with cold cooking liquid, and refrigerate. Pickles will be ready to eat in a few days; will keep for several weeks if refrigerated.

Maria Čudič

Pickling Liquid:

1-1/2 cups white vinegar
1-1/2 cups water
2 tablespoons salt
2 tablespoons sugar
1 chili pepper
1/2 cup salad oil

Pickled Green Peppers:

3 lbs. bell peppers, halved and seeds removed
2 peppercorns
2 cloves garlic, whole

KOSHER STYLE PICKLES

Place cucumbers in a layer in the crock, add a layer of dill and garlic, and cover with grape leaves or corn husks. Repeat several times with remaining material.

Place the masonite disc (or dinner plate placed upside down) over the top so as to not disturb the layers of pickles.

Make a brine of the salt, vinegar, and water and pour over the batch.

Place rock on masonite (or plate) and cover with a towel.

It is advisable to seclude the crock in a cool place, such as the garage, where the garlic will not stink up the house.

After one week, taste a fresh pickle every one or two days until they "pop in your mouth." It may take as long as two weeks.

When they reach the "delicatessen endpoint," place the pickles in small glass jars. Strain the brine, dilute it with an equal volume of water, and pour it over the pickles. Seal.

Jackson Menze

1 5-to-10-gallon crock (not previously used for wine or beer)
4 to 5 dozen pickling cucumbers
10 to 15 fresh heads of dill or 5 ounces of dried dill
20 cloves of garlic, coarsely peeled and crushed
60 to 80 grape leaves or corn husks
1 disc of perforated masonite to fit in crock (a heavy dinner plate will do)
2 pounds pickling salt
2 pints cider vinegar
4 gallons water
1 rock, approximately 5 pounds, to hold down masonite (or plate)

PICKLES TODAY

7 cups pickling cucumbers, sliced
1 green pepper, sliced
1 cup onion, chopped
2 tablespoons salt
little water
2 cups sugar
1 cup vinegar
2 teaspoons celery seed

Mix cucumbers, green pepper and onion. Sprinkle with salt and a little water. Let stand for 2 hours.

Drain.

Mix sugar, vinegar, celery seed. Pour over cucumbers.

These are ready to eat.

Carole Haagenson

BANANA-PINEAPPLE CRUSH

Philippines

1 can (46 ounce) pineapple juice
5 to 6 ripe bananas
1-1/2 cups calamansi nectar
    (lemon-lime)
2 cups sugar
4 cups water
4 bottles (36 ounces each) of 7-Up

Blend or mash bananas into pineapple juice.

Mix Calamansi nectar with sugar and water; mix together with pineapple mixture. Freeze.

Before serving, mash with fork and serve 1 part mixture with 1 part 7-Up.

Eloise Knoll

CITRUS PUNCH

1-1/2 cups sugar
10 cups water
1 can (6 ounce) frozen orange juice
1 can (6 ounce) can frozen lemonade
3/4 teaspoon almond extract
1 teaspoon vanilla
1 quart 7-Up

Bring sugar and 2 cups of water to a boil to dissolve sugar.

Cool and add other 8 cups of water, orange juice, lemonade, almond extract, and vanilla. Mix well, then freeze if you desire a slush.

Stir occasionally while freezing.

At time of serving, add 7-Up.

Yield: 1 gallon   *Bernice Cunningham*

LIMEADE PUNCH

Put ice cubes in a punch bowl.

Pour limeade and club soda over ice cubes and stir to mix.

Yield: 24 portions   *Jacqueline P. Smith*

ice cubes
2 cans (6 ounce) frozen limeade
1 large bottle club soda

LEMON VARIATIONS

Lemon Ice:

Boil water and sugar together for 5 minutes. Add lemon juice. Cool and freeze.

Fresh Lemonade:

Mix all ingredients and pour over ice. Add a maraschino cherry and a bit of cherry juice to make pink lemonade.

Lemonade Syrup Base:

Dissolve sugar in boiling water. Add lemon peel and juice. Store in covered container in refrigerator.

To make one glass, use 1/4 or 1/3 cup syrup base with 1-3/4 cups cold water. Add ice cubes and stir.

To make one pitcher, combine base with 5 cups cold water. Add ice cubes and stir. Add thin lemon slices, if desired.

Carole Haagenson

Lemon Ice:

4 cups water
2 cups sugar
3/4 cup lemon juice

Fresh Lemonade:

juice of 1 lemon
1-3 tablespoons honey or sugar
3/4 glass water
maraschino cherry and some cherry
    juice

Lemonade Syrup Base:

1/2 cup boiling water
1-1/2 cup sugar
1 tablespoon lemon peel
1-1/2 cup lemon juice

MINTED ICED TEA

Boil the water and sugar for 10 minutes.

Add tea and mint and steep for 10 minutes.

Strain and add the lemon juice.

Refrigerate.

Yield: 2 quarts   *Jacqueline P. Smith*

2 quarts water
1-1/4 cups sugar
1/3 cup loose black tea
mint leaves
juice of 2 lemons

KAMPER'S HOT CHOCOLATE

8 quarts dry powdered milk
6 to 9 ounces non-dairy creamer
1 pound powdered sugar
16 ounces sweetened cocoa mix
   (Nestle's Quick)

Mix all ingredients thoroughly. Store in an air-tight container.

To make hot chocolate, use 1/4 cup mix to 3/4 cup hot water.

Eloise Knoll

ITALIAN EGG NOG

2 egg yolks
1 tablespoon sugar
3/4 cup milk
1/4 cup coffee

Put the egg yolks in a cup and add the sugar. Using the handle of a tablespoon, mix until fluffy.

Add heated milk and hot coffee.

Frances DiMeglio

ENGLISH EGG NOG

6 eggs, separated
1 cup sugar
1 pint cognac
1 cup light rum
2 quarts half & half
1/2 cup powdered sugar

In a large bowl, beat yolks until thick. Add sugar, beating until light. Slowly stir in cognac and rum. Add 1-1/2 quarts half & half and 3 unbeaten egg whites, beating until well combined.

Beat remaining 3 egg whites until foamy. Gradually add powdered sugar, beating well after each addition until soft peaks form.

Gently stir egg whites and remaining half & half into egg yolk mixture.

Refrigerate covered until ready to serve.

Steve & Janice Miller

DANDELION WINE

This recipe was given to me by the mother of a friend who used it during prohibition.

Wash dandelions and place in a crock. Cover with 1 gallon boiling water and let stand overnight.

Drain, put the dandelions in a large pot, add water to cover and boil 10 minutes.

Cool to lukewarm.

Return to crock. Add the softened yeast, lemon slices, orange slices, raisins and sugar. Cover the crock with cloth and let stand for 3 weeks to ferment.

Skim, strain and bottle. DO NOT CORK for at least a week.

Jacqueline P. Smith

1 gallon boiling water
4 quarts dandelions, mashed
1 yeast cake, softened in a little water
2 lemons, sliced
2 oranges, sliced
1-1/2 cups raisins
3 pounds sugar

SANGRIA

Mix juice of lemons and oranges with sugar.

Strain over ice in punch bowl.

Add red table wine.

Yield: 16 to 20 punch cup servings

Helen Homen

juice of 8 lemons
juice of 2 oranges
1 cup sugar
ice
2 large (4/5 quart bottles) red table wine

HOT MULLED WINE

In a large saucepan, dissolve sugar in water. Add lemon peel and cloves. Boil 15 minutes.

Add burgundy or claret. Heat gently. Do not boil.

Serve hot in preheated mugs or cups.

Garnish each with cinnamon stick to use for stirring.

Yield: 20 servings   *Helen Homen*

1 cup sugar
4 cups water
peel of 1/2 lemon (may substitute orange peel)
18 whole cloves
2 bottles (4/5 quart) California burgundy or claret
cinnamon sticks

COFFEE LIQUEUR

1 jar (2-ounce) instant coffee (not freeze-dried)
4 cups water
4 cups sugar
1 bottle (2 ounce) vanilla extract
1 quart or fifth vodka

In a saucepan, mix coffee and water. Add sugar, heat, and boil for 5 minutes.

Let cool.

Add vanilla and vodka. Stir to mix.

Let stand 2 weeks or more.

Helen Homen

ICEBREAKER PUNCH

2 cups light rum
3/4 cup dark rum
1 cup Galliano liqueur
3/4 cup passion fruit syrup
1/2 cup lime juice
1 quart lemonade
2 quarts orange juice
ice
1 thinly sliced orange (optional)

Combine all ingredients, except ice and orange slices. Stir thoroughly in punch bowl.

Add ice and serve.

Orange slices may be floated on top of punch.

Yield: 35 4-ounce servings   *Dolores Lisica*

CHAMPAGNE PUNCH #1

ice (10 pounds)
1 bottle champagne
1 bottle white wine, such as chablis
1 bottle pale dry ginger ale
1 bottle sparkling water
1/4 to 1/2 cup Cointreau

Place ice in large punch bowl. Pour all ingredients over ice, mix, and serve.

Bernice Cunningham

CHAMPAGNE PUNCH #2

1/2 gallon wine, white or rosé
2 quarts ginger ale
1/3 quart Southern Comfort
2 quarts champagne
ice

Mix first 3 ingredients in a large punch bowl, adding champagne last.

Add ice and serve.

Virginia Mulligan

Salads

SALADS AND DRESSINGS

CALIFORNIA GREEN AND GOLD SALAD

Salad:

Tear lettuce into bite-size pieces and place in salad bowl.

Peel, remove seeds, and cut both avocado and oranges into bite-size pieces. Put in bowl with lettuce and mix.

Put salad dressing on salad and toss.

Variation: You may substitute chopped apples, dates, and walnuts for avocado and oranges.

Dressing:

Place salad dressing into a 1-cup measuring cup. Fill remainder of cup with topping and gently stir together.

This dressing is very good with all kinds of fruit salads.

Carole Haagenson

Salad:

**Lettuce, bite-size pieces
1 avocado, peeled, seeded, bite-size pieces
2 oranges, peeled, seeded, bite-size pieces**

Dressing:

**4 tablespoons salad dressing (such as Miracle Whip)
Reddi-Whip Topping**

MANDARIN SALAD

Sweet-Sour Dressing:

Make sweet-sour dressing by shaking listed ingredients together in a tightly covered jar and refrigerate for at least 2 hours.

Salad:

Cook almonds and sugar over low heat, stirring constantly, until sugar is melted and almonds are coated. Cool and break apart. Store at room temperature.

Tear lettuce and romaine into bite-size pieces. Place in a large plastic bag. Add celery and onions. Pour sweet-sour dressing into bag. Add orange segments, plus chicken (if desired). Close bag tightly and shake until all ingredients are well coated. Add almonds and shake again.

Do-ahead tip: Before dressing is added, bag of salad greens can be closed tightly and refrigerated up to 24 hours.

Serves 6   *Bitsy Lauro*

Sweet-Sour Dressing:

**1/4 cup vegetable oil
2 tablespoons sugar
2 tablespoons vinegar
1 tablespoon snipped parsley
1/2 teaspoon salt
dash of pepper
dash of red pepper sauce**

Salad:

**1/4 cup sliced almonds
1 tablespoon plus 1 teaspoon sugar
1/4 head lettuce
1/4 bunch romaine
1 cup celery, chopped
2 green onions with tops, thinly sliced
1 can (11-ounce) mandarin orange bite-size pieces 1 cup cooked chicken breasts, cut in chunks (optional)**

BEET SALAD

Estonia

1 salted herring
3 beets, boiled in jackets
6 potatoes, boiled in jackets
2 hard-boiled eggs
1/2 onion, minced
4 dill pickles
2 cups roast beef
2 apples

Dressing:

1 cup sour cream
1 teaspoon mustard
1/2 teaspoon sugar
1/4 teaspoon pepper
2 tablespoons vinegar

This salad is a must on a smorgasbord table. The beets give the salad its pink color.

Soak the herring overnight in a bowl of cold water. Then clean off salt and chop it into small pieces.

In separate saucepans, boil beets and potatoes. When done, peel and dice.

Hard-boil the eggs.

Mince the onion.

Chop eggs, pickles, roast beef, and apples into 1/2 inch cubes.

Combine all ingredients in a large bowl.

Blend all of dressing ingredients and pour over salad ingredients. Mix well, serve.

Aino Lauri

CLAIRE'S CARROT SALAD

4 green onions, diced
2 large stalks celery, diced
1/2 medium green pepper, diced
2 cans julienne carrots
1/2 cup sugar
1/2 cup oil
1/2 cup vinegar

Dice onions, celery, and pepper and place in a salad bowl.

Add carrots and mix well.

Mix sugar, oil, and vinegar and pour over vegetables. Marinate overnight.

Note: Will keep in refrigerator for 2 weeks or more.

Claire Grainger

CARROT PENNIES

Pare and slice carrots; cook until tender. Drain and cool.

Into a medium bowl place the salt and mustard; beat in a little of the oil to blend; add remaining oil and sugar, vinegar, Worcestershire sauce, and soup, and beat again to blend. Add carrots (and bell peppers and onions, if desired). Cover tightly and chill overnight.

Recipe may be doubled or halved. Any marinade left over may be refrigerated and used as dressing for a green salad.

Serves 12 to 16   *Betty Spence*

5 cups (2 pounds) carrots, pared and sliced
1 teaspoon salt
1 teaspoon prepared mustard
1/2 cup salad oil
3/4 cup sugar
3/4 cup cider vinegar
1 teaspoon Worcestershire sauce
1 can (10-3/4 ounces) condensed tomato soup, undiluted
chopped bell pepper (optional)
chopped onion (optional)

NORTHERN BEAN SALAD

Wash the cooked beans thoroughly in running water. Drain and place in salad bowl.

Chop pickles, onions, and celery, and set aside.

Whip the minced garlic, mustard, salt, pepper, and vinegar in a small bowl; pour in the oil gradually, and beat until thick and smooth. Pour over beans and mix well.

Add pickles, onions, celery, sour cream, and mayonnaise, and mix well.

Mildred Davis

1 pound great northern beans, cooked
1 cup chopped sweet pickles
1 cup onions, chopped
1 cup chopped celery
2 teaspoons garlic, minced
2 teaspoons prepared mustard
1 teaspoon salt
black pepper
2 tablespoons red wine vinegar
6 tablespoons salad oil
1 cup sour cream
1/2 cup mayonnaise

PEA VERDE SALAD

Shred lettuce; dice onion, celery, and water chestnuts.

Layer ingredients, in the order shown, into a 2-quart serving bowl. Cover with plastic wrap and refrigerate overnight.

Toss just before serving.

Vicki Boutté

2 cups shredded lettuce
1 cup diced green onion
1 cup diced celery
1 cup diced water chestnuts
1 package (8-ounce) frozen baby peas
1 cup mayonnaise
Parmesan cheese to cover

PATLICAN SALATASI
Eggplant Salad

2 medium eggplants
juice of 2 lemons
1 small onion, chopped finely
    (or 1/3 cup scallions)
1 teaspoon salt or salt to taste
1 small tomato, chopped fine
    (optional)
1/2 cup green pepper, chopped fine
    (optional)
1 small clove garlic, mashed
    (optional)
1 tablespoon to 1/4 cup olive oil
garnish: parsley (chopped) or
    lemon slices and tomato slices

Begin by roasting the eggplants. The best way is over the flame of a gas stove. Place each whole, unskinned eggplant on the burner grid and turn the flame on to medium high. You want the entire eggplant skin to become black and burned, and the inside to be soft. This will take about 45 minutes and you will want to turn the eggplant 3 to 4 times so that as much of the skin as possible becomes charred. (The skin may pop, but don't worry.) If you do not have a gas stove, broil the eggplant under the broiler, turning frequently.

Remove the eggplant from the fire and place on a flat plate. Slice in half lengthwise and scoop out the soft fleshy part, putting it into a bowl immediately with the lemon juice. Get as little of the charred skin as possible, but when you have scooped out the flesh, pour any juices which have accumulated on the plate into the bowl. Mash well with a fork; add onions, salt, and, if you wish, the tomato, green pepper, and/or garlic. Mix in enough olive oil—1 tablespoon to 1/4 cup—to make the mixture a nice consistency. Cover and chill well. Garnish with chopped parsley or slices of lemon and tomato.

Serve it as a salad on a bed of crisp romaine lettuce, or as a dip for crusty bread. Wonderful on a picnic!

Roasting the eggplant gives an elusive, smoky flavor to this unusually delicious dish.

Yield: 2 cups   *Ruth Hamren*

SPINACH BACON SALAD
With Poppy Seed Dressing

Rinse spinach thoroughly in cold water and remove stems. Combine in a salad bowl with lettuce, bacon, and cottage cheese.

Dressing.

Combine dressing ingredients and mix well. Pour over salad and toss.

Serves 8   *Steve & Janice Miller*

2 pounds spinach, leaves only
2 heads red leaf lettuce
1 pound bacon, fried crisp & broken
    in bits
1-1/2 cups large curd cottage cheese

Dressing:

1/2 cup sugar
1 teaspoon salt
1 teaspoon dry mustard
1 tablespoon poppy seeds
1 tablespoon onion juice
1/3 cup cider vinegar
1 cup salad oil

RAW SPINACH SALAD

Dressing:

In a small saucepan, mix all dressing ingredients and heat over low flame until sugar is dissolved (don't boil).

Cool before pouring over salad.

Salad:

Rinse spinach thoroughly in cold water and remove stems. Drain and place in salad bowl with bean sprouts.

Cook bacon, drain on paper towels, and crumble onto salad.

Hard-boil eggs, shell and slice; add to salad.

Slice water chestnuts and onion, and add to salad.

Toss salad ingredients, then pour dressing over them.

Nancy Hedges

Dressing:

1/2 cup oil
1/2 cup sugar
1/4 cup catsup
1/4 cup wine vinegar
2 tablespoons Worcestershire sauce

Salad:

1 pound raw spinach, leaves only
3/4 cup fresh bean sprouts
6 slices fried and slightly crumbled
    bacon
2 to 4 hard-boiled eggs, sliced
1 cup water chestnuts, sliced
1 small onion, sliced thinly

MARINATED ZUCCHINI SALAD

5 medium zucchini, sliced thinly
1 head cauliflower, in small florets
1 red onion, chopped or sliced in rings
1 green pepper, chopped
1 teaspoon parsley, chopped
1 small jar pimiento, chopped, or
    1 large red pepper, chopped
3/4 cup sugar

Marinade:

3/4 cup salad oil
1/2 cup red wine vinegar
1/2 cup cider vinegar
2 tablespoons sugar
1 tablespoon salt
1 teaspoon celery seed
1 teaspoon mustard seed

Wash zucchini, slice thinly, and place in salad bowl.

Wash cauliflower, cut into small florets, and add to salad bowl.

Chop onion or slice in rings, then add to salad.

Chop green pepper and parsley and add to salad.

Drain the pimiento, then chop and add. Or, if red pepper is used, chop and add.

Toss all vegetables to mix well. Then add sugar and mix again.

Marinade:

Place all ingredients in a small saucepan. Bring to a boil, then pour over vegetables. Let stand overnight at room temperature. Refrigerate to chill.

Drain before serving and reserve marinade for use later as a dressing on a tossed salad.

Emmy Ruud

SHRIMP SALAD

1 large loaf of thinly sliced bread
butter
1/2 cup yellow onions, chopped
1/2 cup green onions, chopped
4 to 5 hard-boiled eggs, chopped
1/2 cup celery, chopped
1 cup shrimp (fresh cooked)
1/4 cup mayonnaise

Remove crust from sliced bread; lightly butter each slice, then cube and place in a container which can be sealed.

Chop yellow and green onions and add to bread. Seal container and refrigerate overnight.

The following day, add eggs, celery and shrimp to bread and onion mixture. Toss lightly with mayonnaise, chill and serve.

Serves about 15   *Sharon E. Hand*

FUMI SALAD

First, mix all dressing ingredients and set aside.

Chop the cabbage and onions and combine in a bowl. Break the uncooked Top Ramen noodles into the bowl; add dressing. Mix well and let stand at least 3 hours or longer.

Before serving, add toasted sesame seeds and almonds to mixture and toss lightly.

Serves 12   Clara Love

Dressing:

6 tablespoons rice vinegar
1 cup salad oil
2 tablespoons sugar
salt and pepper
2 Top Ramen seasoning packets
    (from packages listed below)

Salad:

1 head cabbage, finely chopped
8 green onions, chopped
2 packages Top Ramen (pork flavor)
8 tablespoons roasted sesame seeds
8 tablespoons slivered, blanched
    almonds (toasted)

ITALIAN CHEF'S SALAD

In a large salad bowl, combine all salad ingredients and toss lightly.

Combine dressing ingredients in a small jar and shake well.

Pour dressing over salad and toss lightly.

Serves 6 to 8   Jacqueline P. Smith

1 Italian salami (12-ounce), cubed
1 small can sliced black olives
1 jar (6-ounce) marinated artichoke
    hearts
12 cherry tomatoes, halved
6 green onions, sliced thinly
1/4 pound cheese, diced (Swiss, Jack
    or Mozzarella)
1 avocado, diced
1 head lettuce, washed and torn
    into pieces

Dressing:

1/3 cup salad oil
3 tablespoons wine vinegar
1/2 teaspoon salt
dash pepper
1 clove garlic, minced

LUCY'S CHICKEN SALAD

2 chicken breasts or drumstick
    and thigh
1/3 package rice noodles
8 won ton skins
1/2 head of lettuce
1 teaspoon prepared mustard
1/4 teaspoon Chinese five spices
    powder, or to taste
1 teaspoon sesame oil
1 teaspoon rice vinegar
2 tablespoons soy sauce
3 tablespoons toasted almonds,
    chopped finely
1/2 cup green onions, finely sliced
1/2 teaspoon salt
vegetable oil for frying

Place chicken in a pot and cover with water. Simmer for 20 minutes. When done, remove meat from bones. Drain on paper toweling to prevent spattering when frying.

Deep fry the rice noodles in hot vegetable oil. Remove them from the oil when they "explode" and drain them on paper toweling.

Cut won ton skins into 1/8-inch strips and deep fry in the same oil.

Fry chicken for 5 minutes. Drain and cut into slivers, skin and all, to make about 2 cups.

Shred lettuce and make a bed for the salad on a medium sized platter.

Mix the chicken meat, mustard, five spices powder, sesame oil, rice vinegar, soy sauce, almonds, green onions, and salt. Add the crisp-fried won tons, noodles and mix gently. Don't toss or it will get soggy.

Serves 4   *Selma Streicher*

HAM AND TURKEY SALAD

1 large red apple, sliced (unpeeled)
1 tablespoon lemon juice
4 cups diced turkey (or chicken)
2 cups diced ham
1 cup halved lichee nuts
1 cup slivered almonds, toasted
1-1/2 cups mayonnaise
2 teaspoons soy sauce
1-1/2 teaspoons curry powder
salad greens

Core and slice (but do not peel) apple. Place in a 2-1/2 quart bowl, then coat with lemon juice.

Dice cooked turkey and ham and add to apple.

Halve lichee nuts and sliver and toast almonds and add to salad, reserving a few to use as a garnish.

In a separate bowl, combine mayonnaise, soy sauce and curry powder. Add to salad and mix. Refrigerate overnight, or for several hours.

Turn out onto salad greens and garnish with more almonds and lichee nuts.

Serves 6 to 8   *Jacqueline P. Smith*

TOSTADA SALAD

Brown beef over a low flame, breaking it into pieces with a fork. Add onion and season (salt, pepper, garlic powder, basil) to taste during latter part of cooking time. Remove meat to a plate covered with paper towels so excess fat can drain. (After cooling, meat may be refrigerated until salad preparation time.)

Place meat, avocado, beans, lettuce, cheese and tomatoes into a large salad bowl and mix gently.

Just before serving, add half of the chips (broken) and the dressing. Toss. Serve with remaining chips on the side.

Emma Roublow

1-1/2 pounds ground beef
1 bunch green onions, chopped
salt
pepper
garlic powder
basil
1 avocado, peeled & chopped
1 or 2 cans (16-ounce) kidney beans, drained
1 head red-leaf lettuce, washed, drained, broken
2 cups shredded cheddar cheese
3 or 4 medium tomatoes, cut in small pieces
1 large bag tortilla chips, unsalted
Italian or bacon salad dressing

CURRY DRESSING

In a large bowl, combine all ingredients and mix well.

Use as a dressing on tossed salad or lettuce wedges or sliced avocados.

Eloise Knoll

1/2 pound shrimp or lobster, shredded
1/2 teaspoon onion salt or juice
1 teaspoon Worcestershire sauce
1-1/2 teaspoons prepared mustard
1 cup mayonnaise
1 teaspoon paprika
1 tablespoon lemon juice
dash Tabasco
1 teaspoon curry powder

ROQUEFORT CHEESE DRESSING

Mix all ingredients except cheese together and blend well.

Add crumbled cheese and mix.

Store in tightly covered jar in refrigerator until ready to use.

Jo Luz

1/2 pint mayonnaise
1/3 pint sour cream
3 to 4 tablespoons buttermilk or milk
garlic salt or powder (to taste)
1/2 teaspoon Worcestershire sauce
hot sauce (Tabasco) to taste
1/2 teaspoon lemon juice
4 ounces Roquefort or blue cheese, crumbled

MACARONI SALAD

1 pound cooked macaroni
1/2 pint mayonnaise
1/2 pint Best Foods Sandwich Spread
1 medium green onion or 1/4 Spanish
    onion, minced
2 small sweet pickles, chopped
2 small or 1 medium carrot, grated
2 medium celery sticks, sliced
1 to 2 tablespoons chopped parsley
1 to 2 tablespoons sugar
1-1/2 inch wedge bell pepper,
    chopped
24 chopped ripe olives
24 chopped green olives
1 can pimiento, minced

Cook macaroni according to package directions. Drain, rinse, and set aside in a large bowl.

Chop and add all other ingredients to the macaroni. Mix well.

Serve immediately or refrigerate.

Mildred Davis

MAKE AHEAD SALAD

3/4 cup (6 ounces) salad macaroni
1 small head lettuce
1/2 cup diced celery
1/2 cup chopped onion
1/2 cup chopped green pepper
1 package (10-ounce) frozen peas,
    thawed
2 tablespoons sugar
1/2 teaspoon salt
1-1/2 cups mayonnaise
1/2 cup shredded cheddar cheese

Cook macaroni according to package directions. Drain. Rinse with cold water and drain again. Set aside.

Tear lettuce into small pieces and place in a 9 x 13-inch glass dish. On top of lettuce, place one layer each of pasta, celery, onion, green pepper, and peas, in that order.

In a separate bowl, blend sugar, salt, and mayonnaise, and spread over vegetables. Sprinkle with shredded cheddar cheese.

Cover and chill overnight.

Serves 8 to 10   *Pat Trutanich*

THOM'S ORZO SALAD

Greece

Boil orzo in liquid for 6 minutes, drain and cool. Place in a large bowl.

Add bell pepper, olives, parsley, capers, crab meat, shrimp, salt, pepper, and cayenne pepper with orzo; mix well.

Blend in mayonnaise.

Chill and serve.

Ann Rumery

1 cup rosemarina orzo (Greek pasta)
1-1/2 cups liquid—clam juice or
    chicken broth or water
1 red bell pepper or Anaheim pepper
black olives
green olives with pimientos
1/4 cup parsley, minced
capers to taste
1/4 pound crab meat
1/4 pound cooked and shelled shrimp
salt and pepper
cayenne pepper
1/2 cup mayonnaise

PASTA SALAD

Cook pasta per package instructions. Rinse, cool, and set aside in large bowl.

Chop tomatoes, bell peppers, celery, and onion, and place in bowl with pasta.

Add Italian dressing and Salad Supreme seasoning and mix well.

Refrigerate for several hours or overnight before serving.

Carole Haagenson

1 package (16-ounce) pasta
    (vermicelli, shells, or whatever
    you like)
several tomatoes, chopped
1 large bell pepper, chopped
3 stalks celery, chopped
1/2 Bermuda (purple) onion, chopped
1 bottle Italian dressing
2 tablespoons Salad Supreme
    seasoning

VEGETABLE AND PASTA SALAD

Cook macaroni according to package instructions. Rinse, drain, and set aside in a large bowl.

Combine all other ingredients except tomato and avocado. Mix well with macaroni.

Cover and refrigerate for 3 or more hours.

At serving time, stir in tomato and avocado.

Serves 10   *Karen Cressy*

1 cup medium shell macaroni, cooked
    and drained
2/3 cup Italian salad dressing
1/2 cup sliced zucchini
1/2 cup fresh mushrooms, halved
1/2 cup quartered, marinated
    artichoke hearts
1/2 cup broccoli florets, broken into
    bite-sized pieces
2 tablespoons chopped green onions
1 large tomato, cut in wedges
1/2 avocado, peeled and cubed

NINA'S POTATO SALAD

5 pounds fresh, white potatoes
8 eggs (+ 2 eggs for garnish)
1 teaspoon salt
2 stalks celery, finely chopped
1 medium onion, finely chopped
2 large dill pickles, finely chopped
1/2 cup sliced black olives
1 tablespoon vegetable oil
1 teaspoon salt
1 teaspoon prepared mustard
1 cup or more mayonnaise
salt and pepper to taste
paprika
1/8 cup black olives (garnish)

Rinse potatoes under cold water. Fill large saucepan with cold water and add 1 teaspoon salt. Add potatoes and eggs. Boil together until potatoes are tender and eggs are hard-cooked. Drain. Peel potatoes and shell the eggs.

Chop potatoes and 8 eggs into small pieces and put into large bowl. Add celery, onion, pickles, and 1/2 cup sliced olives. Add oil, salt, mustard and mayonnaise. Mix ingredients together thoroughly with large spoon until all are well blended. Additional mayonnaise may be added if consistency seems a little dry. Add more salt to taste, if desired.

To garnish, sprinkle with paprika or decorate with black olives and 2 sliced hard-cooked eggs.

May be served immediately.

Serves 12   *Anna DiMeglio*

PICKLED POTATO SALAD

6 large potatoes
5 eggs
1 small onion, diced
4 large sweet pickles, diced
1/2 cup sweet pickle juice
2 teaspoons prepared mustard
4 tablespoons Miracle Whip salad
    dressing
1 teaspoon celery seed
salt and pepper to taste
paprika

Boil potatoes in skins; peel and cube.

Hard-boil eggs. Peel and chop 3 of the eggs and mix with all other ingredients in large bowl.

Garnish with 2 remaining eggs, sliced.

Chill several hours or overnight.

Before serving, sprinkle with paprika.

Serves 10 to 12   *Char Arno*

APRICOT JELLO SALAD

Prepare gelatin per package instructions, except dissolve the marshmallows in the hot gelatin before adding any cold water.

Add cold water and refrigerate. When it begins to gel, fold in mashed bananas and drained crushed pineapple (reserve the liquid for use in topping). Refrigerate overnight.

Topping:

In a saucepan, cook sugar, flour, margarine, and pineapple juice until thickened. Remove from heat and add cream cheese. Let cool. Prepare Dream Whip according to directions on package, and add to topping mixture.

To serve, spoon topping over gelatin.

Mildred Davis

2 small packages apricot gelatin
1 cup miniature marshmallows
2 mashed bananas
1 can (16-ounce) crushed pineapple
    (reserve liquid)

Topping:

1 cup sugar
2 tablespoons flour
2 tablespoons margarine
1/2 cup pineapple juice
1 package (3-ounce) cream cheese
1 package Dream Whip

APRICOT SALAD

In a saucepan, combine pineapple and sugar. Bring to a full boil. Pour mixture into a large bowl. Add gelatin. Mix thoroughly and add cream cheese. Stir until cheese melts. Add ice water. Cool.

Add chopped celery and chopped nuts. Refrigerate until it starts to gel; fold in Cool Whip.

Pour into 9 x 13 inch glass pan. Refrigerate another 24 hours before serving.

Lucy DiMeglio

1 can (2-pound) crushed pineapple, in
    heavy syrup
1/2 cup sugar
1 package (3-ounce) peach or apricot
    gelatin
1 package (8-ounce) cream cheese
1 cup ice water
1 cup chopped celery
1 cup chopped pecans or walnuts
1 package (9-ounce) Cool Whip

FROZEN BANANA SALAD

2 cups sour cream
1 can (8-ounce) crushed pineapple
1 tablespoon lemon juice
1/2 cup chopped pecans
3/4 cup sugar
4 bananas, mashed
1 jar (8-ounce) maraschino cherries,
    quartered

In a large bowl, mix all ingredients well. Pour into a 9 x 9-inch pan. Freeze.

This salad will melt in your mouth. It's really delicious!

Serves 9   *Nancy Hedges*

CRANBERRY JELLO MOLD

1 package (6-ounce) raspberry Jello
1 can (15-1/2 ounces) whole
    cranberry sauce
1 can (13-1/2 ounces) crushed
    pineapple (undrained)
2/3 cup port wine (or water)
1/2 cup chopped walnuts
1 package (8-ounce) cream cheese,
    softened
1 cup sour cream

Dissolve Jello in 1 cup boiling water. Add the cranberry sauce, pineapple, port wine (or water), and walnuts.

Pour mixture into a gelatin mold and chill until firm.

Remove from mold and place on a serving platter.

Mix cream cheese and sour cream and spread on top of Jello. Chill again.

Lucy DiMeglio

ELIZABETH SALAD

1 small package lime Jello
1 small package lemon Jello
1/2 cup boiling water
1-1/2 cups sour cream
1 cup cottage cheese
1/4 cup milk
1 cup crushed pineapple, drained

Dissolve lime and lemon Jello in boiling water and let cool.

Mix sour cream, cottage cheese, milk, and crushed pineapple together. Fold into Jello and pour into 1-1/2 quart dish.

Refrigerate overnight.

Serves 8   *Kelly Hulett*

MELON MOLD SALAD
With Orange Juice-Lemon Yogurt Dressing

In a small saucepan, combine gelatin, sugar, and water. Stir over low heat until sugar and gelatin are dissolved.

Pour mixture into a bowl and stir in lemon-lime soda and orange liqueur. Stir well and chill until slightly thickened.

Dice cantaloupe and remove stems from grapes and fold into mixture.

Pour into a 1-1/2 quart mold. Chill until firm.

To make the dressing, mix yogurt and orange juice in a small bowl. Chill.

When ready to serve, dip mold into lukewarm water for a few seconds. Loosen edges with the tip of a knife, tap to loosen and invert onto a platter. Garnish with strawberry halves.

Serve spooned into lettuce cups with yogurt sauce spooned over each serving.

Serves 6 — *Nancy Hedges*

2 envelopes unflavored gelatin
1/3 cup sugar
1/4 cup water
3 cups lemon-lime soda
1/2 cup orange liqueur
    (Grand Marnier)
4 cups diced cantaloupe
2 cups stemmed, seedless grapes
1 cup lemon yogurt
1/4 cup orange juice
strawberry halves for garnish
    (optional)
1 head iceberg lettuce, cored, and
    separated into leaves

MOLDED LEMON SALAD

Make Jello according to package directions, except use only 1 cup water.

Dice celery and cucumber, and slice green onions thinly. Add to Jello.

Mix in lemon yogurt and Worcestershire sauce and chill to set.

This is very good with chicken.

Serves 4 to 6 — *Jacqueline P. Smith*

1 small package lemon Jello
1/2 cup diced celery
1/2 cup diced cucumber
1/4 cup green onion, thinly sliced
1 carton (8-ounce) lemon yogurt
dash of Worcestershire sauce

PEACE AND PLENTY SALAD

1 package (3-ounce) lemon Jello
1 cup boiling water
1 cup cold water or 1 cup pineapple
  juice
1 cup crushed pineapple
2 sliced bananas
1 cup miniature marshmallows
chopped nuts
1 package instant vanilla or lemon
  jello pudding
1 cup Cool Whip or whipped cream
sugar to taste
1 teaspoon vanilla
grated cheddar cheese

This recipe received rave reviews at the get-togethers of the Peace and Plenty Quilting group, based in San Pedro. It was given with love by Sally Medvidovich.

Dissolve lemon Jello in boiling water; add cold water or pineapple juice. Cool.

When it starts to thicken, add crushed pineapple, sliced bananas, marshmallows, and nuts. Refrigerate.

Mix package of instant pudding as directed. Put in refrigerator to thicken. Fold Cool Whip or whipped cream, sugar, and vanilla into pudding. Spread over set Jello. Grate cheddar cheese over all.

Serves 6 to 8 *Kathy Rogers*

TOMATO AND COTTAGE CHEESE SALAD

1-1/2 cups seasoned tomato juice
1 package lemon gelatin
1 tablespoon vinegar
2 tablespoons cold water
1-1/2 cups cottage cheese
2 tablespoons minced green pepper
1/2 cup diced celery
2 cups finely shredded cabbage
1/3 cup mayonnaise
salt to taste
1 tomato, sliced
1 hard cooked egg, sliced
watercress

Heat tomato juice and pour over gelatin to dissolve it. Add vinegar. Pour half of the mixture into another bowl. Add to it cold water; mix and turn into bottom of a ring mold. Chill until firm.

In a separate bowl, chill remaining gelatin until slightly thickened. Combine cottage cheese, green pepper, celery, cabbage, and mayonnaise, and fold into gelatin. Salt to taste. Turn into mold over firm gelatin. Chill.

To serve, unmold and garnish with tomato and hard-cooked egg. Decorate with watercress.

Ruth Shannon

ZIPPY MOLDED TOMATO SALAD

Stir gelatin, sugar, and 3/4 cup V-8 or Snap-E-Tom vegetable juice over moderate heat until gelatin dissolves.

Add 1 cup V-8, lemon juice, and salt and pepper. Chill until it begins to thicken.

Fold in shredded cabbage, chopped celery, sliced green onion and diced green pepper. Refrigerate until thickened.

This is attractive in a ring mold with chicken or tuna salad in the center.

Serves 4   *Jacqueline P. Smith*

1 envelope unflavored gelatin
1/2 teaspoon sugar
1-3/4 cups V-8 or Snap-E-Tom
    vegetable juice
dash lemon juice
salt and pepper
1/2 cup shredded cabbage
1/2 cup chopped celery
1-1/2 teaspoons sliced green onion
1-1/2 teaspoons diced green pepper

SHRIMP MOLD

Set cream cheese out so that it will be at room temperature when you are ready to use it.

In a saucepan, sprinkle gelatin over soup and heat until gelatin is dissolved. Cool.

Soften cream cheese with mayonnaise and cream. Add lemon juice. Mix, then stir into soup.

Fold in shrimp, celery, green onions, green pepper, pimiento, and mushrooms.

Pour into a 5 to 5-1/2 cup shrimp mold or decorative mold.

Refrigerate several hours.

Can be served as an appetizer with crackers or on a bed of lettuce as a salad.

Serves 10 to 20   *Pamm Vuoso*

1 package (3-ounce) cream cheese
1 can (10-1/2 ounces) condensed
    cream of mushroom soup
2 envelopes Knox gelatin
1/2 cup mayonnaise
1/2 cup cream
1 tablespoon lemon juice
3 cups cooked shrimp
2-1/2 cups chopped celery
6 green onions, chopped
1/2 cup green pepper, chopped
1 jar (2-ounce) diced pimiento
1 jar (2-1/2 ounces) sliced
    mushrooms

RASPBERRY JELLO MOLD

2 packages black raspberry gelatin
2 cups boiling water
3 cups cool liquid (juice from raspberries and water)
1 package frozen raspberries, thawed
1 small carton sour cream

Dissolve gelatin in boiling water. Add cool liquid and let set.

Stir in raspberries and let form.

Stir in sour cream and pour into mold. When sour cream is added, it looks lumpy, but that is okay! Chill.

Remove from mold and serve.

Selma Streicher

STRAWBERRY BANANA MOLD

4 packages strawberry banana gelatin
4 cups liquid, hot
1 pint sour cream
2 boxes frozen strawberries, thawed and drained
3 bananas
1 cup chopped nuts

Dissolve gelatin in hot liquid. Let cool.

Fold in sour cream. Refrigerate to gel slightly.

Remove and fold in strawberries, bananas, and nuts. Place in mold. Refrigerate.

Remove from mold and serve cold.

Selma Streicher

Soups

SOUPS

ALBONDIGAS SOUP

In a large pot, boil water with the bouillon cubes. Add tomatoes and juice; salt and pepper to taste. Slice and add the carrots, celery and zucchini.

In a skillet, brown onion and garlic in oil; add to soup.

Add chili powder.

In a bowl, mix the cooked rice, hamburger and egg. Form into 1-inch meatballs and brown in skillet.

Add meatballs to soup and simmer for 45 minutes.

Lucy DiMeglio

8 cups water
6 beef bouillon cubes
1 large can tomatoes and juice
salt and pepper to taste
4 carrots, sliced
2 stalks celery, sliced
2 zucchini, sliced
1 onion, sliced
2 cloves garlic
1 tablespoon chili powder
1/4 cup cooked rice
1 pound hamburger
1 egg
cooking oil

BEEF BORSCHT

Russia

Brown the beef in oil, a little at a time. Add water and simmer for an hour or two.

Add beets, tomatoes, onion, bouillon cube, lemon juice and sugar and simmer for another hour or two.

About 1/2 hour before serving add shredded cabbage, cubed potatoes, salt, and celery salt, and continue simmering.

Remove and discard the onion.

This may be served hot, or it may be refrigerated and served cold or hot the next day.

My husband's mother says that when she was growing up in Russia, borscht was a major part of their diet. The exact proportions depended on what particular vegetables happened to be in good supply in the garden on any given day. When they were lucky, they had a piece of beef for the pot; otherwise, it was a vegetable stew.

Margaret Litman

1 pound stewing beef, cubed
1 tablespoon cooking oil
water
1 can (1 pound) julienne beets
1 can (1 pound) tomatoes
1 onion, whole
1 beef bouillon cube
3 to 4 tablespoons lemon juice
3 to 4 tablespoons sugar
1/2 large head cabbage, shredded
2 to 4 potatoes, cubed
salt, to taste
celery salt (optional)

PEANUT BUTTER SOUP

1 quart rich chicken stock
3 ounces minced onion
3 ounces minced celery
8 ounces peanut butter
3 ounces butter
1 tablespoon flour
1 cup half and half
1/4 teaspoon pepper
1 teaspoon salt
4 teaspoons crumbled bacon or
    minced country ham

Simmer onions and celery in chicken stock for 40 to 50 minutes. Strain out onions and celery and discard. Stir in peanut butter until dissolved.

Melt butter; add flour and stir over low heat until blended. Add half and half; stir to combine. Add to soup and simmer for 15 minutes. Season with salt and pepper.

Garnish each serving with 1/2 teaspoon crumbled bacon or minced country ham.

Serves 8 to 10   *Jacqueline P. Smith*

PORTUGUESE SOPA

1 beef chuck or round bone roast
flour
2 tablespoons butter
2 tablespoons oil
1 teaspoon cumin seeds
1 teaspoon salt
pepper to taste
6 whole cloves
2 cloves garlic
1 cup red or rosé wine
1 cup water
6 small potatoes
1 head cabbage, quartered
sliced French bread

Dust roast with flour; brown on both sides in butter and oil. Add cumin seeds, salt, pepper, cloves, garlic, wine and water. Cover and simmer for 3 to 5 hours.

Add potatoes and cabbage the last 45 minutes of cooking. If needed, add more wine and water in equal parts.

Just before serving, remove meat to platter and arrange vegetables. Place slices of French bread in pot to soak up juices. Arrange bread around meat.

Jo Luz

STEAK SOUP

1/2 pound margarine
1 cup flour
1/2 gallon water
1 large carrot, sliced
1 medium diced onion
1 stalk celery, diced
1 package (6-ounce) frozen mixed
    vegetables
1 can (20-ounce) tomatoes
4 tablespoons beef granules
salt and pepper to taste
1 pound round steak
2 tablespoons margarine

Melt margarine. Stir in flour. Gradually add water. Stir until smooth. Add sliced carrots, diced onions, diced celery, frozen mixed vegetables, canned tomatoes, beef granules, and salt and pepper to taste.

Cut round steak into 1/2-inch cubes. Sauté in a skillet in 2 tablespoons of margarine until brown. Add meat to soup. Simmer for 1-1/2 hours, stirring frequently for first few minutes.

This soup freezes well.

Serves 6   *Virginia Wilcox*

THOMALINE'S ALBONDIGAS SOUP
Meatball Soup

Mexico

Mix meat, uncooked rice, salt, pepper, and beaten egg. Roll into balls. To make this easy, flour your hands before forming meatballs. Set meatballs aside.

Put 3 quarts of water into a soup pot. Add 1 teaspoon salt. Add tomatoes, onion, garlic, cumin, and celery, and bring to a boil. Add meatballs and simmer for one hour.

This recipe is especially good served with hot flour tortillas.

Serves 4 to 6   *Thomaline Aguallo Buchan*

1 pound hamburger or 1/2 pound
    each of ground beef and
    ground pork
1 cup uncooked rice
salt and pepper, to taste
1 egg, beaten
3 quarts water
1 teaspoon salt
1 cup whole canned tomatoes, or
    crushed fresh tomatoes
1 small onion, sliced
1 clove garlic, minced
1 teaspoon cumin
2 stalks celery, chopped (including
    leaves)

CHICKEN SOUP

Nigeria

Season chicken with salt and pepper; brown together with onions in oil in a large dutch oven.

Add water, tomatoes, tomato sauce, and pimiento and bring to a boil. Reduce heat and cook for approximately 30 minutes. Add turnips, carrots, leeks, cabbage, and yams, and simmer until done—about 20 minutes.

Remove chicken and vegetables. Blend the peanut butter into the broth and cook for about 5 minutes, stirring frequently. Stir in lime juice. Return chicken and vegetables to broth.

Serve hot.

Emma Roublow

l large chicken, cut up (discard neck
    and back)
2 teaspoons salt
1/2 teaspoon pepper
1/2 cup chopped onions
1/2 cup peanut oil
2-1/2 cups water
2 cups fresh tomatoes, chopped
2 tablespoons tomato sauce
1 pimiento, chopped
1/2 cup yellow turnips, diced
1/2 cup carrots, sliced
1/4 cup leeks, sliced
1 small head of cabbage, sliced
1 cup yams, diced
3/4 cup peanut butter
juice of one lime (optional)

RIŽI-BIŽI SUPA
Rice and Pea Soup

Yugoslavia

2 quarts chicken broth, homemade
    preferably
1 cup long grain rice
2 cups fresh or frozen green peas
salt and pepper, to taste
grated Parmesan cheese

Bring chicken broth to a rolling boil.

Add rinsed rice. Lower heat to a simmer, then cover and cook for about 15 minutes.

Add peas and simmer an additional 15 minutes, covered. Add salt and pepper to taste.

Serve garnished with grated Parmesan cheese.

Serves 6   Mary Lou Nizetich

WHOLESOME IRISH SOUP

3 pounds zucchini, unpeeled, cut into
    chunks
1/2 pound onion, cut into chunks
water
2 cubes chicken bouillon
2 cups milk

Cook the zucchini and onion in a little water until tender. Drain.

Put the vegetables into a blender and purée.

Return vegetables to saucepan. Add chicken bouillon and milk. Cook just until the mixture is heated through and the bouillon cubes are melted.

Serve with a sprig of parsley on top of each serving.

This soup developed during a summer of abundant zucchini in our vegetable garden. The healthy ingredients and bright green color influenced the name of this thick and fresh-tasting soup.

Serves 4 to 6   Carol Flaherty

On Soup

"Soup is economical food, and by a little attention may be made good with very small materials. All meat and bones for soup should be boiled a long time, and set aside until the next day in order that the fat may be entirely removed. Then add the vegetables, rice and herbs, and boil it from an hour to an hour and a half."

—*The Young Housekeeper's Friend*, 1845

HEARTY VEGETABLE SOUP

Combine carrots, celery, onions, chicken broth, salt, pepper, garlic, and bay leaves. Cook until vegetables are tender (about 20 minutes).

Add tomatoes and liquid, tomato sauce, zucchini, and squash. Simmer until squash is tender, about 30 minutes.

Yield: 5 quarts   *Delia Du Ross*

6 to 8 carrots, sliced
1 stalk celery, sliced
3 onions, diced
4 cups chicken broth
1 teaspoon salt
1/2 teaspoon pepper, or to taste
4 cloves garlic, chopped
5 bay leaves
2 cans (8 ounces each) tomatoes, diced
2 cans (8 ounces each) tomato sauce
2 large zucchini, sliced
4 yellow crookneck squash, sliced

WINTER VEGETABLE SOUP

Boil 2 potatoes until soft. Remove from water. Quarter 1-1/2 potatoes. Dice remaining 1/2 potato.

In a 3-quart sauce pot, put 1/3 of the salt pork, together with the dried peas, carrots, celery, and diced potato. Cover with water and bring to a boil on high heat. Reduce heat and simmer, covered, 45 minutes to an hour.

While this is cooking, sauté onion and remaining salt pork in a little oil in a frying pan. Add tomato sauce and simmer.

Sieve half of the pork and beans, together with quartered cooked potatoes, into simmering sauce pot. Add frozen and fresh vegetables, tomato mixture, salt, pepper, and remainder of pork and beans. Simmer until done, about 20 minutes or more.

I inherited this recipe from my mother. It probably dates from the 1920's, at least.

Serves 8 to 12   *Frances Munio*

1-1/2 small potatoes, quartered
1/2 small potato, diced
1 slice (3/8 x 4 x 2 inches) salt pork, diced
1/4 cup dried peas
1 carrot, peeled and diced
1 stalk celery, diced (including leaves)
1/2 small onion, diced
1 to 2 tablespoons oil
4 ounce tomato sauce
1 can (8-ounce) pork and beans
1/2 of 10-ounce package frozen mixed vegetables
any fresh cut-up vegetables you want, except those from the cabbage family
salt
pepper

OLD TYME BEAN SOUP

2 large onions, chopped
2 teaspoons paprika
1/2 cup vegetable oil
1 cup dried pinto beans
12 to 14 cups water or vegetable
    stock
1 teaspoon parsley
1 tablespoon celery seed
1 bay leaf
1 cup dried kidney beans
1 cup small dried lima beans
1 cup dried pink beans
1 cup dried yellow split peas
2 teaspoons dill weed
1 teaspoon salt
1 teaspoon oregano
several carrots, sliced thin
1/3 cup brown rice
1/3 cup barley
1 cup corn, canned, frozen, or cut
    fresh off the cob

Note: I like to soak my beans overnight, but do keep the pinto beans separate, as they need to cook longer. Throw away the excess soaking water.

Sauté onions and paprika lightly in oil.

Rinse pinto beans in cold water; add to 4 cups water or stock, parsley, sautéed onions, celery seed, and bay leaf. Cook for one hour in a large pot or roasting pan, partially covered.

To cooking pinto beans, add washed kidney beans, limas, and pink beans. Add 3 to 4 cups water. Continue cooking for another hour, partially covered.

Rinse split peas; then add peas, dill, salt, oregano, and carrots to the cooking beans. Cook for another hour. Add water when needed.

For complete protein add brown rice, barley, and corn at the time you add the split peas.

Betty Spence

SAUSAGE-BEAN CHOWDER

1 pound bulk pork sausage
2 cans (16 ounce) red kidney beans
1 can (1 pound 13 ounces) tomatoes,
    broken up
1 quart water
1 large onion, chopped
1 bay leaf
1-1/2 teaspoons seasoned salt
1/2 teaspoon garlic salt
1/2 teaspoon thyme
1/8 teaspoon pepper
1 cup diced potatoes
1/2 green pepper, chopped

Note: I use 1/2 pound each of hamburger and pork sausage instead of all sausage.

In a skillet, cook sausage until brown; pour off fat.

In a large kettle, combine kidney beans, tomatoes, water, onion, bay leaf, seasoned salt, garlic salt, thyme, and pepper. Add sausage. Cover and simmer for 1 hour.

Note: If you prefer macaroni to potatoes, use 1 cup uncooked macaroni.

Add potatoes and green pepper. Cook covered 15 to 20 minutes, until potatoes are tender. Remove bay leaf.

Serves 8 generously   *Helen Homen*

PAŠTA I FAŽOL
Macaroni and Bean Soup

1 pound dried pinto or kidney beans
4 quarts unsalted water
1 onion cut in chunks
1-1/2 pounds smoked ham hocks or
    leftover ham with meat left
    on bone
salt and pepper to taste
1-1/2 cups (approximately) elbow
    macaroni

Roux:

3 tablespoons olive oil
1 onion, chopped
3 tablespoons minced parsley
4 cloves garlic, minced
1-1/2 tablespoons flour
2 large tomatoes, peeled and chopped

Soak beans overnight in cold water.

Drain and add fresh water, onion and ham. Cook until tender—1-1/2 to 2 hours—or until beans are tender but not mushy.

When ham hocks are tender, remove and dice cooked ham and set aside.

Make roux.

Pour roux into bean soup and add diced ham. Add salt and pepper and cook an additional 20 to 30 minutes to blend flavors. Add macaroni and cook until pasta is done to your taste, about 12 to 15 minutes. Stir often.

Roux:

Heat oil in small sauce pan, add onions and sauté until golden brown.

Add parsley and garlic and continue sautéing. Sprinkle flour over mixture, stirring until completely absorbed and golden in color. Add tomatoes; stir often.

Serves 6 to 8   *Dolores Lisica*

MY MOTHER'S SPLIT PEA SOUP

ham bone
3 quarts water
2 cups (1 small package) dried split
    peas
2 teaspoons salt
1/4 teaspoon pepper
1 sliced medium onion
1/2 cup dried lentils (optional)
1-1/2 cups cooked, slivered ham
    (optional)

In a kettle, place ham bone (such as that left over from cooked shank), water, split peas, salt, pepper and onion. Mom always added 1/2 cup lentils with the peas. Simmer, covered, over low heat for 2-1/2 to 3 hours.

Remove bone from soup. Cut off any bits of ham and add to soup, along with 1-1/2 cups cooked, slivered ham (if you have it). Heat.

Serves 8   *Helen Homen*

LEČE I RIŽI SUPA
Lentils and Rice Soup

Yugoslavia

1 pound lentils, rinsed and culled
4 quarts cold water
1/2 cup olive oil
1 medium onion, chopped
1/3 cup minced parsley
4 cloves garlic, minced
1 heaping tablespoon flour
3 medium tomatoes, peeled and
    chopped
salt and pepper, to taste
3/4 cup uncooked, rinsed rice

Rinse lentils with cold water several times; discard all black lentils, bits of corn, or any other chaff.

Place rinsed lentils in a large 6-quart pot. Add cold water and cook over medium high heat. Skim when necessary. Stir regularly. Lentils should be soft in 45 to 60 minutes.

In a separate saucepan, heat olive oil; add chopped onions and sauté until they are limp and golden. Add parsley and garlic and sauté and stir until garlic is lightly browned. Sprinkle flour over mixture, stirring often until flour is absorbed. Add tomatoes, salt, and pepper. Cook an additional 3 to 5 minutes.

Add sautéed vegetables to cooked lentils. Salt and pepper to taste. Simmer for an additional 30 minutes. Adjust seasonings.

Rice is added 25 minutes before you wish to serve the soup. If you wish to freeze portions, do so before rice is added and adjust quantities of rice. When ready to serve frozen portions, melt over slow heat and bring to a boil. Add rice proportionately.

Serves 6 to 8   *Dolores Lisica*

OSMASHI
Soup

Japan

2 cups water
1 teaspoon soup base (chicken or
    Shumaza Dashi)
1 teaspoon soy sauce
1/3 cup chopped green onion
1/2 package tofu, cubed
salt to taste

In a saucepan, combine water, soup base, and soy sauce and bring to a boil.

Add green onion and bring to a low simmer.

Add cubes of tofu and simmer over very low heat for 5 minutes. Salt to taste.

Yoriko Mahdi

ONION CHOWDER FOR A BUSY DAY

In a deep saucepan or kettle, fry bacon until brown.

Add onions and cook until yellow.

Add water and potatoes. Cook 30 minutes, or until potatoes are tender.

Add milk, cream, salt, and pepper.

Mix flour and water together until smooth. Stir into soup. Boil 2 minutes, stirring frequently.

Serves 6   *Mildred Davis*

1/4 pound diced bacon
2 cups chopped onions
2 cups water
3 cups diced raw potatoes
2 cups milk
1/2 cup cream
2-1/2 teaspoons salt
1/4 teaspoon pepper
1 tablespoon flour
1 tablespoon water

SOUPE *de* CRESSON
Potato Leek Soup

France

Slice leeks thinly. Use white parts, plus 2 inches of the green).

Chop watercress finely; use only 2 inches from roots on up; discard roots and first 2 inches.

Peel potatoes and chop coarsely. Place in a large heavy saucepan with chicken stock, leeks, watercress, and salt. Simmer, partially covered, for 40 to 50 minutes, or until the vegetables are tender.

Purée soup in a blender; then pour back into the saucepan. Season soup with salt and pepper to taste. Stir in cream.

Before serving, return soup to low heat. Do not boil.

Garnish, when serving, with chives or parsley.

Eloise Knoll

1 pound leeks
3 tablespoons watercress
1 pound potatoes
3-1/4 pints chicken stock
1 teaspoon salt
fresh ground black pepper
1/4 pint heavy cream
3 tablespoons finely cut fresh chives
    or parsley

EASY SUMMER GAZPACHO

1 chicken bouillon cube
1 large can (48 ounces) tomato juice
1 cucumber
2 stalks celery
1 green bell pepper
3 tablespoons wine vinegar
3 tablespoons oil
dash Tabasco sauce
3 tablespoons dried onion
sprinkle garlic powder
salt and pepper to taste

In a large serving bowl, crush bouillon cube. Add tomato juice.

Dice skinned cucumber, celery, and bell pepper; add to tomato juice. Add wine vinegar, oil, Tabasco, dried onion, garlic powder, and salt and pepper to taste.

Chill. Serve.

Serves 6   Sean Flynn

RHODE ISLAND CLAM CHOWDER

1/4 pound salt pork, diced
2 large onions, chopped
3 cans (7-ounce) minced clams,
    undrained
2 bottles clam juice
pepper to taste
2 potatoes, diced
1 cup milk, room temperature
butter

This is a chowder for real clam lovers, being very basic in its ingredients. It is not authentic in that Quahogs are not available, but comes close using ingredients that are easily obtained here.

Fry salt pork in a large, heavy frying pan until very crisp. Remove and drain on paper towels.

Add onions to pork grease and fry until soft. With a slotted spoon, move onions from frying pan to a large kettle. To the kettle, add clams, clam juice, salt pork, and pepper to taste. Simmer 30 minutes. Cool and refrigerate overnight.

Next day, heat the clam mixture until simmering. Add potatoes and cook gently 12 to 20 minutes, or until potatoes are cooked. Add milk and heat just to warm.

Pour chowder into heated bowls, add a pat of butter to each bowl. Serve with oyster crackers.

Serves 4   *Jacqueline P. Smith*

SHERRIED CRAB SOUP

In the top of a double boiler, combine the asparagus soup, mushroom soup, and milk (or cream). Heat to a simmer, stirring occasionally.

Add crab meat, sherry, curry powder, salt, and pepper. Heat until piping hot.

Serve at once in heated soup bowls.

Variation: Substitute tomato and pea soups; 1-1/2 cans water for milk and sprinkle with cheese.

Serves 4 to 5   *Jacqueline P. Smith*

1 can (10-1/2 ounces) condensed
    cream of asparagus soup
1 can (10 1/2 ounces) condensed
    cream of mushroom soup
1 can evaporated milk or light cream
1 cup fresh or canned crab meat
1/2 cup sherry
1/8-1/4 teaspoon curry powder,
    optional
salt and pepper

SHRIMP BISQUE

Sauté the onions and celery in butter until transparent; remove and set aside.

Sauté shrimp until just pink, remove and set aside.

Return onion and celery to pan. Sprinkle flour over mixture. Slowly add the chicken broth and sherry.

After mixture starts to thicken, add cream, and salt and white pepper to taste, and heat on low flame. Add shrimp, sprinkle with nutmeg and serve.

Serves 6   *Margaret Spangler*

1/4 pound butter
1 medium onion, finely chopped
3 stalks celery, finely chopped
2 pounds medium shrimp, cleaned,
    deveined and chopped
3 tablespoons flour
1 can chicken broth
3 tablespoons sherry (optional)
1 quart light cream
salt and white pepper
dash of nutmeg

TEXAS SHRIMP GUMBO

2 tablespoons oil
1 large onion, chopped
3 stalks celery, sliced
2 cloves garlic, minced
salt, pepper, Accent, to taste
1 can (29-ounce) whole peeled
    tomatoes
1 large can water (use tomato can)
1 can (6-ounce) tomato sauce
2 pounds okra
2 pounds medium shrimp, rinsed,
    whole in shell
2 cups cooked rice

In a large saucepan, brown onions, celery, and garlic in oil. Add salt, pepper, and Accent to taste. Add tomatoes, water, and tomato sauce, and simmer for 45 minutes to 1 hour.

Pare tops of okra, being careful not to cut open so that the insides of the okra will leak out during cooking. Rinse shrimp, but leave whole in shell.

Add okra and shrimp and simmer an additional 15 minutes.

Serve over rice.

Serves 6   *Linda Lisica*

TOMATO SOUP

"Take two quarts of rich beef soup,—remove the fat and add an onion. Cut small, tomatoes enough to make three pints, stew them until they can easily be strained through a sieve or colander, and add to the soup. Put in salt and a little pepper, and, before serving, add a table-spoonful of sugar."

Copied from *The Young Housekeeper's Friend*, written in 1845.

Margretta Marshall

~Meats~

MEATS

BARBEQUE BEEF

Mix onions, seasonings, and water and pour over meat. Cover and bake 5 hours or longer at 300 degrees. If necessary, add more water.

Marvelous as an entrée or shredded for sandwiches. This makes the house smell so good as it bakes!

Nancy Hedges

6 pounds chuck roast or rump roast
8 onions, chopped
2 cups catsup
1 cup water
8 tablespoons barbecue sauce
2 teaspoons vinegar
2 teaspoons Worcestershire sauce
2 teaspoons Tabasco (optional)
salt to taste

CORNISH PASTIES

British Isles

Crust:

To make the crust, add 1/3 cup flour to 1/3 cup cold water, making a paste.

In a separate bowl, mix remaining flour and shortening; add paste and mix well.

Divide dough into 5 portions. Roll each portion out on a floured board to the size of a 9-inch pie pan.

Preheat oven to 350 degrees.

Filling:

On half of each 9-inch portion of dough, place 1/2 to 3/4 cup potatoes, 1/2 cup rutabaga, and a small amount of onion. Divide each meat into 5 portions. Place 1 portion of each meat on top of onion layer. Salt and pepper to taste. Top with butter.

Fold unfilled portion of dough over filled portion and crimp edges to seal. Cut 2 or 3 slits in top of each pastie to permit escape of vapor. Pastie is somewhat the shape of a half moon.

Bake at 350 degrees for 1 hour, or until crust is brown.

Yield: 5 pasties   *Dorice Madden*

Crust:

2 cups flour
2/3 cup plus 2 tablespoons shortening
1/3 cup ice-cold water

Filling:

4 medium potatoes, peeled and sliced
2 medium rutabagas (yellow turnips), peeled and sliced
2 medium onions, sliced
1-1/2 pounds round steak, cut into 1-inch pieces
1/2 pound lean pork, cut into 1-inch pieces
salt and pepper
5 walnut-size pieces of butter

BEEF WELLINGTON

Pastry:

4 cups flour
1 teaspoon salt
1/2 cup butter
1/2 cup shortening
1 egg
1/2 cup (approximately) ice water

Filling:

1 filet of beef
2 tablespoons cognac
salt and freshly ground black pepper
6 slices bacon
8 ounces paté de foie gras or chicken liver paté
3 or 4 truffles (optional)
1 egg, slightly beaten

Sauce Madeira:

1/2 cup chopped shallots
3 tablespoons butter
1/2 cup plus 3 tablespoons Madeira wine
1-1/2 cups brown sauce (or canned beef gravy)

Pastry:

Place the flour, salt, butter, and shortening in a bowl and blend with finger tips or pastry blender. Add the egg and enough ice water to make a dough. Wrap in wax paper and chill.

Note: Puff pastry may be used, but take care to roll it very thin. Brioche dough may also be used.

Filling:

Preheat oven to 450 degrees. Rub the filet all over with cognac and season with salt and pepper. Place the bacon over the top, securing with string, if necessary. Place the meat on a rack in a roasting pan and roast for 15 minutes for rare, or 20 to 25 minutes for medium. Remove from oven. Remove the bacon and cool roast to room temperature before proceeding. Spread the paté all over the top and sides of the beef. Cut the truffles into halves and sink the pieces in a line along the top.

Preheat oven to 425 degrees. Roll out the pastry into a rectangle (about 18 x 12 inches) one-quarter inch thick. Place the filet, top down, in the middle. Draw the long sides up to overlap on the bottom of the filet; brush with egg to seal. Trim the ends of the pastry and make an envelope fold; brush again with egg to seal the closure. Transfer the pastry-wrapped meat to a baking sheet, seam side down. Brush all over with egg. Cut out decorative shapes from the pastry trimmings and arrange down the center of the pastry. Brush the shapes with remaining egg. Bake for about 30 minutes or until the pastry is cooked.

Serve hot with Sauce Madeira or serve cold on buffet table.

Sauce Madeira:

Cook the shallots in 1 tablespoon butter until golden brown. Add 1/2 cup Madeira and reduce it by half. Add the brown sauce (or gravy) and cook for 10 minutes. Strain the sauce through a sieve and bring again to a boil. Turn off the heat and stir in the remaining cold butter. Stir until butter melts, then add remaining Madeira.

Jean Miner

RARE PRIME RIB ROAST

Preheat oven to 450 degrees. Place roasting pan in oven to heat.

Poke holes in the roast with potato parer and push in garlic slivers. Distribute evenly. Salt and pepper to taste. Place roast on end to sear for 20 minutes in the 450-degree heat. Turn to sear remaining end for another 20 minutes.

Lower heat to 400 degrees. Turn roast to rest on ribs and roast for an additional 30 minutes. Remove roast from oven. Allow to stand, ribs down, for 15-20 minutes before carving.

If beef gravy is desired, pour out all but 2 tablespoons of fat. Heat fat and add 1 tablespoon butter. Melt and then add 2 tablespoons flour. Stir until golden brown. Add 2 cups of beef broth, stirring with wooden spoon or whisk to remove lumps. Taste to adjust seasoning. Pour into heated gravy boat.

Dolores Lisica

3 rib or 4 pounds beef prime rib
3 cloves garlic, sliced in slivers
salt and pepper, to taste

Gravy: (optional)

1 tablespoon butter
2 tablespoons flour
2 cups beef broth

HONEY-GINGER BEEF RIBS

4 pounds beef short ribs, cut into pieces
1/2 cup honey
1 teaspoon Worcestershire sauce
1 teaspoon salt
1/2 teaspoon pepper
1/4 teaspoon Accent
1 tablespoon ginger
1 cup wine
2 cloves garlic, crushed
4 bay leaves
4 medium onions, sliced

Place beef ribs in shallow glass dish.

Mix all other ingredients, except onions, and spread over ribs. Top with onions. Cover and refrigerate 24 hours, turning ribs occasionally.

The next day, pour off marinade and set aside.

Brown beef in Dutch oven and drain off fat. Add marinade and onion to beef. Cover and cook in 350 degree oven until tender, about 2 hours.

Josephine Pittman

BEEF WITH GREEN PEPPERS

1 pound lean beef
1 tablespoon cornstarch
1 teaspoon sugar
3 tablespoons soy sauce
1 tablespoon dry sherry
2 medium green peppers
4 tablespoons vegetable oil
1/2 teaspoon salt
1 garlic clove, crushed

Cut beef into 2-inch strips, 1/4 inch thick.

Combine cornstarch and sugar; blend in soy sauce and sherry. Mix with beef and set aside.

Cut green peppers into 1-1/2 inch pieces. Pour 2 tablespoons oil into a skillet, set heat to high. Add salt then peppers, stirring constantly until peppers are dark green (about 1 minute). Remove peppers and spread on plate.

Add remaining oil to skillet with garlic and stir in meat. Cook 2 minutes, stirring constantly. Return peppers to skillet and mix well.

Serve immediately with fluffy rice.

Serves 2   *Vicki Boutté*

BEEF PICCATA

Pound slices of beef between pieces of wax paper. Dredge in seasoned flour.

Heat small amount of olive oil in skillet over high heat. Fry beef briefly on each side, just until browned. Add small amounts of remaining olive oil to pan as oil dries out. Transfer browned beef to plate and keep warm.

Add butter to skillet and scrape drippings from the bottom of the pan. Stir in lemon juice and parsley. Pour over beef.

Garnish with parsley sprigs and lemon wedges.

Serves 4   *Dolores Lisica*

1 pound beef eye of round, wafer-thin
4 tablespoons flour
1 teaspoon salt
1/8 teaspoon pepper
2 to 3 tablespoon olive oil
1/4 cup butter
2 tablespoons lemon juice
2 tablespoons minced parsley
parsley sprigs
lemon wedges

OYSTER SAUCE STEAK WITH MUSHROOMS
China

Heat butter in small saucepan, add mushrooms, and sauté lightly. Set aside.

Trim fat from steak and cut into 1-1/2 x 1-1/2 inch cubes.

Heat oil in wok or large heavy skillet; add cubed steak and fresh ginger. Brown the steak on high heat on all sides for about 2 minutes. Stir in oyster sauce and wine, stir to combine.

Add cold water to cornstarch; blend well.

Lower heat under wok, add cornstarch mixture and sautéed mushrooms, and stir until sauce is thickened. Taste and add salt if desired. Cut into cube of steak to check for desired degree of doneness.

Serve with steamed rice.

Serves 4   *Ling Y. Hsieh*

1 tablespoon butter
1/2 pound fresh mushrooms, whole
1-1/2 pounds spencer steak or filet mignon
1 tablespoon salad oil
3 to 4 slices ginger root
2 tablespoons oyster sauce
2 tablespoons sherry or dry white wine
1 tablespoon cornstarch
3/4 cup cold water
1/4 teaspoon salt (optional)
steamed rice

CALIFORNIA CASSEROLE

2 pounds tenderized round steak
flour
paprika
1/4 cup oil
1 can small cooked pearl onions
1 can cream of chicken soup
1 can water (or liquid from onions)

Butter Crumb Dumplings

2 cups flour
4 teaspoons baking powder
1/2 teaspoon salt
1 teaspoon poultry seasoning
1 teaspoon celery seed
1 teaspoon onion flakes
1 tablespoon poppy seed
1/4 cup salad oil
1 cup milk
1/4 cup butter, melted
bread crumbs

Coat steak with flour and paprika; brown in oil. Place in casserole. Add onions, reserving liquid to add to chicken soup.

Heat chicken soup in skillet used to brown meat. Add water or onion liquid to soup; bring to a boil. Pour soup over meat in casserole.

Bake, uncovered, for 45 minutes at 350 degrees, or until meat is tender.

Top with butter crumb dumplings. Bake at 450 degrees for 25 to 30 minutes.

Butter Crumb Dumplings

Sift together flour, baking powder, salt, poultry seasoning, celery seed, onion flakes, and poppy seeds.

Add salad oil and milk and stir until just moistened.

Drop a rounded teaspoon of dough into a melted butter to coat, then roll in bread crumbs. Repeat until all dough is used.

Serves 6 to 8   *Betty McKinney*

MARINATED SHORT RIBS

8 pounds lean short ribs
salt and pepper
2 cups olive oil or vegetable oil
2 cups zinfandel wine or fruit juice
2 tablespoons dried flaked or fresh
    minced parsley
6 cloves garlic, crushed
2 bay leaves, ground
2 teaspoons sage

Have butcher cut through rib bones in 2 or 3 places, leaving meat intact.

Rub ribs with salt and pepper. Place in bowl.

Cover with marinade made of oil, wine, parsley, garlic, bay leaves and sage. Let stand for 24 hours in marinade prior to barbeque.

Remove ribs from marinade; drain 3 to 4 minutes.

Place on grill over hot coals at elevation to cook slowly with frequent turning. Leaving the bone ribs in one piece means fewer pieces to turn. Baste often with remainder of marinade.

Serves 8   *Helen Homen*

FRAN'S GOULASH WITH POPPYSEED NOODLES

Goulash:

Brown steak in oil.

Add onions and celery. Brown lightly.

Add remaining ingredients and simmer 1 or 2 hours until meat is tender.

Poppyseed Noodles:

Mix flour and salt. Add beaten eggs. (Note: If you want your noodles to have more color, add a few drops of food coloring to the eggs.) Mix well, then knead dough a few times.

Roll to desired thickness on a well floured board. Sprinkle with flour and roll as for a jelly roll. Cut in desired width. Unroll cut noodles and let dry for about 20 minutes.

Cook in boiling, salted water. Drain. Add butter and poppyseed. Mix gently.

Serves 6   *Fran Henderson*

Goulash:

1-1/2 pounds round steak, cut into
   serving pieces
1/3 cup cooking oil
1 large chopped onion
1 cup chopped celery
1-1/2 teaspoons salt
dash pepper
2 tablespoons Worcestershire sauce
1/2 teaspoon sweet basil
1 tablespoon parsley
1 large can tomatoes
1 cup water (add more as needed)
1 can (8-ounce) tomato sauce
2 cloves minced garlic
1 bay leaf
pinch of thyme
pinch of marjoram

Poppyseed Noodles:

1 cup flour
1 teaspoon salt
2 beaten eggs
yellow food coloring (optional)
2 tablespoons butter
2 tablespoons poppyseeds

NORTHERN ITALIAN SPAGHETTI SAUCE

1 pound sautisa, or home made
    Italian sweet sausages
1 onion, finely chopped
10 to 15 sprigs fresh parsley, finely
    chopped
1 clove of garlic, minced
few sprigs fresh rosemary
1 pound ground sirloin, or lean
    ground beef
salt and pepper to taste
garlic powder
1 can (6 ounce) tomato paste
1 can (8 ounce) tomato sauce
2 bay leaves
1 tablespoon sauterne or white wine

Cut sautisa into 5- or 6-inch strips. Brown in a heavy frying pan which has been sprinkled with salt. Cover and cook on low. The sausage will seep water and grease as it cooks. When this liquid has evaporated, the sausage is done.

Mix onion, parsley, garlic, and rosemary and set aside.

Salt, pepper and garlic powder the ground beef. Spoon half of the onion mixture into the beef. Mix. Form into 2-inch balls (8 or 9 meatballs) and brown in oil in a high-sided saucepan. Add a pinch more salt. After the meatballs have browned on one side, add the remaining onion mixture to brown with the meat. Let simmer, but watch to prevent burning.

In a small bowl, dilute tomato paste with 2-1/2 tomato paste cans of warm water. Mix until smooth and add to meatballs. Add a little water to rinse bowl and add to sauce. Stir. Add tomato sauce and 1-1/2 tomato sauce cans of water. Add salt, pepper, and garlic powder to taste. Add bay leaves and wine. Add fully cooked sausages. Cover and simmer on low for 2 to 3 hours.

Serve, with Italian spaghettini and Parmesan cheese, as a side dish with roast beef, Italian green beans, sour dough rolls, Italian pastries, green salad, red wine, and antipasto.

Serves 8 to 10   *Frances Munio*

POT ROAST AND SPAGHETTI SAUCE

Yugoslavia

Using a potato parer, make slits in pot roast; wrap garlic slivers in small piece of lean bacon and insert into pot roast. Salt and pepper pot roast and spareribs.

Heat 1 tablespoon of the olive oil in cast iron skillet and brown meat. When browned, remove from skillet and set aside.

Add chicken broth and water to pan drippings; heat slowly, scraping bottom of skillet.

In a large, heavy-bottomed pot, heat remaining olive oil and minced bacon; add chopped onions, and sauté until golden brown. Add ground beef, breaking up clumps of meat. Add all measured seasonings. Stir regularly until hamburger is browned.

Add pot roast and spareribs to browned onions and hamburger. Add minced parsley and pressed garlic; stir to mix evenly. Add flour, stirring constantly until absorbed. Pour wine over meat in pot, stir until evaporated. Add chopped tomatoes, cook 5 minutes. Add tomato sauce. Pour broth, water, and drippings over meat mixture, simmer on medium low heat for approximately 1 hour or until pot roast and spareribs are tender. Stir often.

Cook pasta or njoki (see page 188), drain well and mix with sauce. Slice pot roast, arrange on platter and cover with additional sauce.

Serves 8 to 10   *Dolores Lisica*

2-1/2 pounds pot roast (round bone, 7-bone or rump roast)
6 cloves garlic (1 cut in slivers and 5 pressed or minced)
2 strips lean bacon, 1 strip minced
1-1/2 pounds spareribs, cut in 6 pieces
salt and pepper to taste
1/3 cup fine olive oil
1 can (14-1/2 ounces) chicken broth
1 can water (or more if needed)
3 medium onions, chopped finely
2-1/2 pounds beef, ground twice
Seasonings:
   2 teaspoons salt
   1 teaspoon Accent (optional)
   1 teaspoon allspice
   1/2 teaspoon white pepper
   1/4 teaspoon black pepper
1 large handful of fresh parsley, minced
2 tablespoons flour (optional)
2/3 cup wine (half marsala & half white wine)
3 medium tomatoes, chopped
1 can (8-ounce) tomato sauce

ITALIAN SEASONED POT ROAST

2 tablespoons fat
4 to 5 pounds chuck or blade bone
    roast
1 clove garlic, chopped finely
2 cans (8-ounce) tomato sauce
1 /2 teaspoon salt
1/4 teaspoon black pepper
1/4 teaspoon oregano
1/2 cup apple juice and 1/4 cup cider
    vinegar, or 3/4 cup wine
1 can (2-ounce) whole button
    mushrooms
1/4 cup chopped parsley
2 tablespoons cornstarch
2 tablespoons water

Melt fat in a heavy dutch oven. Place the pot roast in the pan and brown on all sides.

Combine garlic, tomato sauce, salt, black pepper, oregano, apple juice, and vinegar. Pour sauce over the browned meat in the dutch oven. Add mushrooms and parsley. Cover and heat slowly for 2 to 2-1/2 hours, or until meat is fork tender.

When roast is done, remove and place on a warm platter.

To make gravy, add 1/2 cup water to meat drippings in pan. Mix well. Make a paste of 2 tablespoons cornstarch and 2 tablespoons water. Heat the sauce in the pan to boiling. Slowly blend in cornstarch paste. Heat again to boiling.

Spoon hot gravy over each serving of pot roast.

Serves 6   *Helen Homen*

LITTLE POT ROASTS
With Peas

Have butcher score steak.

Spread steak with mustard on one side. Cut crosswise into 4 equal portions and sprinkle with salt.

Cut 4 pieces of carrot, each as long as meat is wide. Roll each in a piece of meat, mustard to the inside. Fasten with toothpicks or string.

Brown meat rolls on all sides in hot shortening. Drain.

Mix liquid from peas with catsup. Pour over meat. Cover tightly. Simmer 1-1/2 to 2 hours or until fork tender, replenishing liquid if needed.

Make gravy, if desired.

Serve with hot seasoned peas.

Serves 2   *Helen Homen*

1-1/2 pound flank steak
1 tablespoon prepared mustard
1 teaspoon salt
**1 or 2 slender whole carrots, scrubbed
    well or pared**
2 tablespoons shortening
1 can (17-ounce) peas
1/4 cup liquid from peas
1/4 cup catsup

PICCADILLY POT ROAST

Dredge the roast in a combination of 1 tablespoon flour, 1 teaspoon salt, and 1/4 teaspoon pepper.

In a large pan, brown meat in cooking fat. Pour off drippings.

Add water and vinegar to roast and sprinkle with dill seed. Cover tightly and cook slowly 2-1/2 to 3 hours, or until tender.

Add remaining salt and quartered carrots and zucchini. Cook until vegetables are tender.

...eat and vegetables from pan. Add remain-
...ur to pan juices. Cook until thick. Add
...t through.

Helen Homen

**3 to 4 pounds beef blade or chuck
    roast**
2 tablespoons flour
2 teaspoons salt
1/4 teaspoon pepper
1 tablespoon cooking fat
1/2 cup water
1 tablespoon vinegar
1 teaspoon dill seed
5 carrots, quartered
1 pound zucchini, quartered
1 cup dairy sour cream
1 tablespoon flour

OVEN BEEF BURGUNDY

2 tablespoons soy sauce
2 tablespoons flour
2 pounds beef stew meat, or round
    bone roast
4 carrots, cut into chunks
2 large onions, sliced
1 cup celery, sliced thinly
1 clove garlic, minced
1/4 teaspoon pepper
1/4 teaspoon marjoram
1/4 teaspoon thyme
1 cup dry red wine
1 cup fresh mushrooms, sliced

Blend soy sauce with flour in a 2-1/2 to 3-quart casserole.

Cut meat into 1-1/2 inch cubes. Add to soy sauce mixture, and toss to coat the meat.

Add carrots, onions, celery, garlic, pepper, marjoram, thyme, and wine to the meat. Stir gently to mix.

Cover tightly and bake at 325 degrees for 1 hour.

Add mushrooms, stir gently, cover, and bake 1-1/2 to 2 hours longer, or until meat and vegetables are tender.

Serve with fluffy hot rice, noodles, or boiled or mashed potatoes.

Serves 4 to 6   *Lillian Peterson Drenckhahn*

BEEF STIR FRY

1/2 to 1 pound beef, cut into bite size
    strips
2 tablespoons oil
1 onion, sliced
1 green pepper, sliced
1 cup celery, sliced
1 cup cut green beans
fresh mushrooms, sliced
1 jar pimiento

Sauce:

2 tablespoons soy sauce
1-1/2 tablespoons cornstarch
1/2 to 3/4 cup water
1-1/4 cup white wine

Cut beef into bite-size strips; brown in oil.

Slice onion, green pepper, celery, green beans, and fresh mushrooms; add to beef and cook about 5 minutes, stirring regularly.

Combine sauce ingredients. Add to beef and vegetables. Cook about 10 minutes until beans are tender, but not mushy.

Add pimiento. Heat.

Serve with rice or Chinese noodles.

Serves 2   *Carole Haagenson*

JAPANESE STYLE HAMBURGER

Brown beef in a skillet, leaving meat in bite-sized clumps.

Dissolve cornstarch and salt in water; add to skillet and bring to a boil. Stir in noodles, cover and simmer 2 minutes.

Add vegetables. Bring to a full boil over medium heat, separating vegetables with a fork. Stir until sauce cubes are blended. Reduce heat, cover and simmer 3 minutes. Stir in soy sauce.

Serves 3   *Ida Tandy*

3/4 pound ground meat
2 teaspoons cornstarch
1/4 teaspoon salt
1 cup water
1 cup thin noodles
1 package (10-ounce) Bird's Eye brand Japanese style vegetables with sauce
2 tablespoons soy sauce

MEATBALLS AND ZUCCHINI

Meatballs:

Mix all ingredients together. Shape into 1-1/2 inch balls.

Fry in large skillet over medium heat, turning occasionally, until brown, about 20 minutes—or place in ungreased, covered, oblong 9 x 13-inch pan, and bake at 400 degrees until light brown.

Vegetables:

Add all vegetables to meatballs and mix well. Bring to boiling point and simmer for approximately 15 minutes or until vegetables are tender. Serve over noodles or rice or with garlic bread.

Serves 4 to 6   *Josephine Pittman*

Meatballs:

1 pound hamburger
1/2 cup dry bread crumbs
2 eggs, beaten
1 teaspoon salt
1 teaspoon pepper
1/4 teaspoon Accent (optional)
3 tablespoons chopped onion
1/4 cup milk
1 tablespoon flour

Vegetables:

5 small zucchini, cut in chunks
1 large onion, chopped
3 stalks celery, diagonally sliced in 1/4" slices
1 can (29 ounces) tomatoes
1 jar button mushrooms or 1 pound fresh
l large can pitted black olives
1 bell pepper, chopped
1 clove garlic, mashed
salt and pepper to taste

LIHAMUREKEPIIRAS
Meat loaf in Sour Cream Pastry

Sour Cream Pastry:

2-1/4 cups flour
1 teaspoon salt
12 tablespoons chilled unsalted
    butter, cut into 1/4 inch bits
1 egg
1/2 cup sour cream

Meat Filling:

4 tablespoons butter
3 pounds finely ground raw meat
    (beef, pork, ham, lamb, or veal
    or any combination of these)
3/4 cup or 1/4 pound finely chopped
    fresh mushrooms
1/3 cup finely chopped onions
1/4 cup finely chopped parsley
1 cup freshly grated cheddar or
    Swiss cheese
1/2 cup milk

1 tablespoon soft butter
1 egg, beaten
2 tablespoons milk

Sour Cream Pastry:

Sift the flour and salt together into a large chilled bowl. Drop the 1/4-inch bits of butter into the bowl. Working quickly, use your fingertips to rub the flour and butter together until they have the appearance of flakes of coarse meal.

In a separate small bowl, mix together the egg and sour cream and stir into this the flour-butter mixture, working with your fingers until you can gather the dough into a soft, pliable ball. Wrap the dough in wax paper and refrigerate 1 hour.

Meat Filling:

Melt the butter in a 10- to 12-inch skillet. When the foam subsides, add the meat to the skillet and cook, stirring occasionally, for 8 to 10 minutes, or until the meat loses its red color and any accumulated liquid in the pan cooks completely away. Add chopped mushrooms and cook over moderate heat, stirring frequently for 6 to 8 minutes, or until they are lightly colored.

Place cooked mushrooms and meat in a large mixing bowl. Add chopped onions, chopped parsley, grated cheese, and milk. Mix well and set aside.

Cut the chilled dough in half and roll out each half into a 6 x 15-inch rectangle, setting aside any scraps. Butter the bottom of a jelly roll pan with 1 tablespoon of soft butter.

In order to handle dough as little as possible, roll the dough lightly and loosely on the rolling pin. Then unroll it carefully into the pan.

Gather the meat mixture into a ball and place it in the center of the dough in the pan. With your hands, pat the meat into a narrow loaf, extending across the center of the dough from one end of the pan to the other.

Lift the second sheet of pastry over the rolling pin and gently drape it on the meat loaf. Press the edges of the 2 sheets together. Beat egg and mix in 2 tablespoons milk. Dip a pastry brush into the egg/milk mixture and moisten the edges of the dough. Press down on the edges all around the loaf with the back of a fork. The tines will seal the edges securely. Prick the top of the loaf in several places with a fork to allow steam to escape.

LIHAMUREKEPIIRAS
(Continued)

Preheat the oven to 375 degrees.

Gather together into a ball all of the excess scraps of dough and roll it out into a thin rectangle. With a pastry wheel or small, sharp knife, cut this dough into long, narrow strips. Brush the loaf with more egg and milk mixture and crisscross the pastry strips over the top of the loaf in an attractive pattern. Brush the strips with the egg/milk mixture and set the jelly roll pan in the center of the oven. Bake for 45 minutes or until the loaf has turned a golden brown.

Serve thick slices of meat loaf, accompanied by a bowl of cold sour cream and a side dish of lingonberries.

N. Mulligan

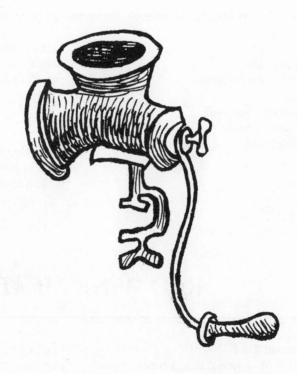

YVONNE'S MEATLOAF

1 pound round steak, ground
2 tablespoons melted butter
1 egg, slightly beaten
2 tablespoons chopped onion
1 cup coarsely broken crackers
1 cup milk
1 teaspoon salt
1/4 teaspoon pepper
2 hard cooked eggs, used whole
2 slices uncooked bacon
1 can (8-ounce) tomato sauce
1/2 cup water

In a large bowl, combine ground steak, melted butter, slightly beaten egg, chopped onion, crumbled crackers, milk, salt, and pepper. Put half of the mixture into a baking dish.

Place hard-cooked eggs on meat mixture. Cover with remaining meat and form into a loaf. Place uncooked bacon slices on top of loaf.

Bake at 350 degrees for 45 minutes.

Mix tomato sauce and water and pour over meatloaf. Continue baking for an additional 45 minutes.

Remove meatloaf from oven; let rest for 15 minutes before slicing.

Serves 4 to 6   *Yvonne Catte*

MEAT LOAF GWARTNEY

1 pound hamburger
1 cup bread crumbs
1 tablespoon parsley flakes
1 egg, beaten
1 medium onion, chopped
salt and pepper to taste
1 can (8-ounce) tomato sauce

Place hamburger in a large bowl. Add bread crumbs, parsley flakes, beaten egg, chopped onion, salt and pepper to taste, and tomato sauce. Mix well.

Place in a buttered baking dish and bake at 325 degrees for 1 hour.

Variations: 1 package dried onion soup mix may be used in place of onion and salt. 1/2 pound sausage may be substituted for 1/2 pound of hamburger.

Margaret Gwartney

RED WINE MEAT LOAF

2 pounds ground beef
1 package (1-3/8 ounces) dried onion
    soup mix
1 cup Burgundy wine
1 cup tomato juice
1 egg
bacon slices

In a large bowl, mix beef, soup mix, 1/2 cup wine, 1/2 cup tomato juice, and egg. Place in baking pan and top with bacon slices.

Bake at 350 degrees for 45 minutes.

Drain off fat. Add remaining wine and tomato juice. Bake an additional 15 minutes.

Serves 6 to 8   *Jacqueline P. Smith*

SLAV MACARONI GRAVY

Brown chopped bacon, onion, garlic, and parsley.

Add ground round, brown well, keep stirring.

Add tomato sauce, Boy-Ar-Dee sauce, consommé, and bouillon cubes. Add the cinnamon, nutmeg, allspice, pepper, and salt to taste. Cook for 2 hours on low flame, stirring occasionally.

Minnie Cvitanich

4 slices bacon, chopped
2 onions, chopped
3 cloves garlic, chopped
2 teaspoons flaked parsley (or 4 or 5 sprigs of fresh)
2 pounds ground round steak
2 cans (8-ounce) tomato sauce
1 can Boy-Ar-Dee sauce with mushrooms
1 can consommé
2 cubes chicken bouillon
1/4 teaspoon cinnamon
1/4 teaspoon nutmeg
1/8 teaspoon allspice
dash of pepper, salt to taste

KJOTTBOLAR
Meatballs

Sweden

Authentic recipes call for a mixture of beef, lean pork and veal, but one may prefer to use all beef or a combination of beef and pork.

Mix beef, pork, and veal together well.

Beat eggs and milk together and pour over bread crumbs. When crumbs are soft, mix with meat and work together well.

Sauté onions in margarine and add, together with spices, to meat mixture; work together until fluffy and light. A potato masher may be used, if desired.

Form mixture into small balls and brown in margarine. Add a little hot water and simmer for 15 to 20 minutes.

Serve with brown gravy made from drippings. Or you may prefer a richer gravy made with milk or cream as many Scandinavians do.

Lillian Peterson Drenckhahn

3/4 pound ground beef
1/4 pound lean ground pork
1/4 pound ground veal
2 eggs
1/2 cup milk
1/2 cup bread crumbs
2 teaspoons salt
pinch of ginger or nutmeg (optional)
1/4 teaspoon pepper
2 tablespoons minced onion, sauteed
margarine

MEAT BALLS IN TANGY SAUCE

3 slices dry bread
3/4 cup warm water
2 pounds ground beef chuck
1 egg
2 cloves garlic, finely chopped
1 medium onion, finely chopped
2 tablespoons Worcestershire sauce
1 teaspoon salt
1/2 teaspoon pepper
1/4 cup olive oil or salad oil
1 can (12-ounce) beer
1 package dried onion soup mix
1 cup or 1/2 pint thick sour cream

Soak the dry bread in water.

In a bowl, combine the meat, egg, garlic, onion, Worcestershire sauce, salt, pepper, and bread that was soaked in water. Blend well and form into about 30 balls.

In a frying pan, heat the oil and add meat balls. Cook over medium heat until well browned on all sides.

Add beer and soup mix and stir. Cover and simmer 10 minutes.

Add sour cream, mix, and heat just until well blended and heated through.

Serve with hot cooked rice or noodles.

Serves 6 to 8   *Helen Homen*

RICE AND BEEF PORCUPINES

1 pound ground beef
1/2 cup raw rice, well rinsed
3 tablespoons chopped onion
1/4 teaspoon poultry seasoning
1/4 teaspoon pepper
1 teaspoon salt
2 cans (8-ounce) tomato sauce and
     1 can water

Mix beef, rice, onion, and seasonings, and form into 10 to 12 small balls.

Brown lightly in an uncovered saucepan in 3 tablespoons oil.

Drain off excess fat and add tomato sauce and water. Cover tightly. Simmer for 45 to 60 minutes, or until rice is tender.

Margaret Gwartney

PRACHAS
Stuffed Cabbage Rolls

Russia

Clean and core cabbage and cook in boiling water until just flexible.

Meat Mixture:

Combine all ingredients to make meat mixture. Place a small amount of this mixture onto a leaf of cabbage and roll into a neat package. Secure with wooden toothpicks.

Sauté Sauce:

In a Dutch oven, sauté onion in butter; add salt and paprika. Place the pracha packages on top of the onions.

Tomato Sauce:

Combine the ingredients for the tomato sauce and pour on top of the prachas. Cover and bake at 300 degrees for about 1-1/2 hours, or until the meat is thoroughly cooked.

Note for dieters: After the prachas are done, it is a good idea to refrigerate, remove the fat at the top, and then re-heat.

Margaret Litman

1 head cabbage

Meat Mixture:

1 pound ground beef
1 tablespoon rice, uncooked
2 tablespoons sugar
1 tablespoon grated onion
1 tablespoon lemon juice
1 teaspoon salt
1/4 teaspoon paprika

Sauté Sauce:

1 small onion, sliced
2 tablespoons butter
1/2 teaspoon salt
1/4 teaspoon paprika

Tomato Sauce:

1 can (8-ounce) tomato sauce
1 can (10-ounce) tomato soup, undiluted
1/4 cup sugar
1/4 cup lemon juice

SWEET AND SOUR STUFFED CABBAGE

Hungary

Soak cabbage leaves in boiling water while preparing the meat mixture.

Combine meat, onion, rice, salt, and pepper. Drain cabbage leaves. Place a portion of meat in each cabbage leaf. Roll up and fasten with a toothpick, and then place into a deep kettle. Any remaining meat mixture can be shaped into balls and placed into the kettle with the cabbage rolls. Any remaining cabbage can be chopped and also placed into the kettle with the rolls and meatballs.

Combine the tomatoes, raisins, minced onion, vinegar, sugar, Karo syrup, and prunes, and pour into the deep kettle. Add water to cover. Bring to a boil, and cook at a slow boil for one hour.

Put a layer of gingersnaps over the tops of cabbage rolls. Reduce heat and simmer one hour longer.

Serves 6 to 8

Mimi Steindler

12 large cabbage leaves
boiling water
1 pound ground beef
1 small onion, grated
1/2 cup cooked rice
1/2 teaspoon salt
pepper, to taste
2 cups canned tomatoes
1/2 cup seedless raisins
1 onion, minced
2 tablespoons vinegar
2 tablespoons sugar
1/4 cup dark Karo syrup
1/2 cup pitted prunes (optional)
gingersnaps

KALDOMAR
Stuffed Cabbage Rolls

1 medium head cabbage, cleaned
   and cored
3 quarts water
4 teaspoons salt

Filling:

1 cup water
1/4 cup rice, rinsed and scalded
1 cup milk
1 pound ground beef
1 egg
1/3 cup milk or cream
2 teaspoons salt
1/4 teaspoon white pepper
2 tablespoons margarine
1 tablespoon brown sugar
2 cups water
toothpicks

Gravy:

Pan drippings
1-1/2 tablespoons flour
1/2 cup cream
salt and white pepper, to taste

Clean and core cabbage and boil in water and salt until leaves are easily separated. Drain.

In a separate pot, bring 1 cup of water to a boil. Add rice and simmer until water disappears. Add 1 cup milk and cook slowly until rice is tender (about 30 minutes), stirring occasionally.

Cool rice and mix with ground meat, egg, 1/3 cup milk or cream, salt and pepper.

Trim the leaf stem even with base of cabbage leaf; cut out thick center vein. Put 2 tablespoons of meat/rice mixture near stem end just below center of leaf. Fold stem end of leaf over to cover filling, then fold in both sides of leaf to enclose filling completely. Roll into a tight cylinder, pressing gently as you work to keep roll compact, and fasten with toothpick.

Heat margarine in skillet and brown rolls on all sides.

Mix brown sugar and 2 cups water and pour over rolls.

Bake in 325-degree oven for about 1-1/4 hours, basting occasionally.

Arrange the cooked cabbage rolls in a deep serving dish, seam side down, removing toothpicks. Remove drippings to saucepan and use to make gravy.

Pour gravy over cabbage rolls, and serve with boiled potatoes.

Gravy:

After you have poured the drippings into a saucepan, combine flour and cream and stir into drippings. Simmer 10 minutes on low heat, adding more milk or cream to desired thickness. Season and pour over rolls.

Lillian Peterson Drenckhahn

WILMINGTON BAKED STUFFED SANDWICH

Allow bread to thaw and rise. Roll very thin to size of cookie sheet. The sandwich should be the length of the sheet.

Brown ground beef in a skillet. Add green onions, olives, mushrooms, chopped cabbage, grated carrots, salt pepper, MSG, and garlic powder. Cook until vegetables are tender. Drain off fat.

Spread filling evenly, lengthwise, on middle third of dough; sprinkle with grated cheese. Fold over both sides of remaining dough to enclose, overlapping slightly. Fold ends under.

Place on a greased cookie sheet, seam side down.

Bake at 350 degrees for 25 to 30 minutes.

Serves 4 to 6   *Josephine Pittman*

1 loaf frozen bread (unbaked)
1 pound ground beef
1/4 cup chopped green onions
1 small can sliced olives
1 small jar sliced mushrooms
1 cup chopped cabbage
1/2 cup grated carrots
salt and pepper to taste
MSG to taste (optional)
garlic powder
1 cup grated cheddar cheese

SPIEDINI

Italy

Filling:

Fry hamburger. Add one clove garlic and season with salt and pepper. Remove with slotted spoon and place in medium bowl.

Sauté onion, carrot, and celery in the same pan as hamburger. Remove from pan and add to the bowl with hamburger.

Add plain bread crumbs, grated cheese, chopped parsley, the second clove of garlic, and tomatoes. Mix together.

Dip one side of steak in oil and then in bread crumb mix. Spread about 1 tablespoon of filling on meat and roll. Secure the rolled meat with steel pins or put on skewers. Then broil or barbeque about 15 minutes. Sprinkle with fresh lemon juice while cooking.

Note: This recipe can also be halved.

Serves 6 to 8   *Virginia Manzella*

Filling:

1 pound hamburger
2 cloves garlic, minced
salt and pepper
2 large onions, grated
2 large carrots, grated
2 large stalks celery, grated
1/2 cup fresh bread crumbs
1/2 cup grated cheese (1/2 Romano
     and 1/2 Parmesan)
1/2 cup tomatoes, canned
1/2 cup parsley, chopped

Bread Crumb Mix:

3 cups bread crumbs
3/4 cup grated cheese (1/2 Romano
     and 1/2 Parmesan)
1/2 cup chopped parsley
1/2 clove garlic, minced
salt and pepper

Veal:

2 pounds veal or top sirloin steak;
     have butcher slice into 3 x 3-inch
     pieces
1 cup oil
fresh lemon juice

ROAST OF VEAL

2 tablespoons olive oil or butter
5-1/2 to 6 pounds boneless veal roast
salt and pepper to taste
1/4 cup flour
1 medium onion, sliced
6 sprigs fresh parsley, cut coarsely
4 small cloves garlic, chopped
1/4 cup brandy or bourbon
1/2 cup white wine

Gravy:

3 tablespoons pan drippings
butter
salt and pepper
2 tablespoons flour
1-1/2 cups chicken broth, fresh or
    canned
water as needed
bouillon cube

Preheat oven to 425 degrees.

Place oil or butter in a shallow roasting pan in preheated oven. Salt and pepper veal and lightly dredge in flour. Place meat in heated roasting pan, fat side up. Bake for about 40 minutes, turning roast to brown evenly.

Scatter onions, parsley, and garlic over meat, and allow to brown, stirring when necessary.

Pour brandy and wine over meat, scraping bits of onion, etc., to prevent burning.

When liquor has been reduced, in about 15 to 20 minutes, remove meat from roasting pan and place on heat-proof platter. Pour half of pan juices over meat and reserve remainder for gravy. Cover roast with foil and return to oven.

Bake at 350 degrees for 45 to 60 minutes. Total baking time is about 2 hours.

Gravy:

In a sauce pan, degrease 3 tablespoons of pan juices. Add butter, if needed, and salt and pepper. Stir regularly over medium high heat. Add flour, stirring all the while. Add chicken broth and bouillon cube, using a whisk to prevent lumps. Lower flame to medium and continue cooking. Taste and adjust seasonings. Strain and pour into heated gravy boat.

Serves 8   *Dolores Lisica*

VEAL ITALIANO

Dip filets in egg and then in bread crumbs. Fry until golden brown and dry thoroughly on paper towels.

Prepare sauce.

Place cooked filets in a baking pan. Layer a small amount of sauce on top. Bake for 1/2 hour in a 350-degree oven.

Sauce:

Sauté onion in olive oil. Add tomatoes, wine, and basil, and cook for about 1/2 hour.

Serves 6 to 8   *Carmela Castognola*

3 to 4 pounds veal filets, sliced very
    thin
3 or 4 eggs, beaten
flavored bread crumbs

Sauce:

1 small onion, chopped
olive oil
1 can (29-ounce) whole tomatoes
1 cup sherry wine
1/2 cup chopped fresh basil

VEAL SCALLOPINI

In a skillet, sauté mushrooms in 5 tablespoons of hot butter until golden brown, or about 5 minutes.

Add onion and garlic. Sauté 5 minutes until onion is golden.

Add tomatoes, wine, salt, and tarragon, stirring until well blended. Reduce heat, stirring occasionally, and cook for 30 minutes.

Wipe veal with paper towels and sprinkle with salt and pepper. Heat remaining butter in another skillet. Add veal, a few pieces at a time, and cook until lightly browned on both sides, about 5 minutes. Remove the pieces of veal from the skillet as browned.

When all pieces have been browned, return all to skillet. Remove garlic from sauce and pour sauce over veal. Simmer, covered, for 5 minutes.

Sprinkle with Parmesan cheese and serve.

Serves 6   *Laura Divona*

8 tablespoons butter or margarine
3/4 pound fresh mushrooms, sliced
1 small onion, finely chopped
1 clove garlic, peeled, whole
3 cups coarsely chopped, peeled
    tomatoes, about 2 pounds
2/3 cup dry white wine
salt, to taste
1/4 teaspoon tarragon
12 thin slices of veal, about
    1-1/2 pounds
1/8 teaspoon pepper
grated Parmesan cheese

VEAL SCALLOPINI
With Artichokes and Peas

1/2 cup flour
1 teaspoon salt
1 teaspoon pepper
1-1/2 pounds veal, cut in 1 to 1-1/2
     inch strips
6 tablespoons butter or margarine
2 tablespoons salad oil
1 large onion, chopped
1/2 pound fresh mushrooms, sliced
1 or 2 cloves garlic, minced or
     mashed
1 cup dry white wine
1/2 to 1 cup regular strength chicken
     broth
1 tablespoon lemon juice
1/2 teaspoon whole thyme, crushed
1 cup sour cream
2 teaspoons flour
1 package (10-ounce) frozen peas,
     cooked per package directions
1 jar (6-ounce) artichoke hearts,
     drained

Mix 1/2 cup flour, salt, and pepper.

Pound veal pieces, then dip in the seasoned flour to coat both sides. Shake off extra flour.

In a frying pan heat 3 tablespoons butter and 2 tablespoons oil over medium-high heat. Without crowding meat in pan, brown each piece quickly on both sides. Set meat aside on a plate as it is browned.

Add remaining butter and sauté chopped onion, sliced mushrooms, and garlic over medium-low heat for about 5 minutes. Stir in wine, chicken broth, lemon juice, and crushed thyme. Put meat back in pan and simmer gently, covered, for 15 minutes or until meat is tender.

Blend the sour cream with 2 teaspoons flour, stir into the meat mixture until blended. (Can be cooled and refrigerated for later use at this point.)

Reheat slowly over low heat, stirring occasionally. If needed to thin gravy slightly, add a little more chicken broth.

Add peas, cooked according to package directions, and drained artichoke hearts to the gravy just so they are warmed. Serve.

Serves 4 to 6   *Nancy Hedges*

BARBECUED SPARE RIBS

6 to 8 pounds pork spare ribs or
     country-style ribs, cut into
     2-rib portions
2 to 3 lemons, sliced

Sauce:

1 cup catsup
2 cups water
1/4 cup Worcestershire sauce
1/4 cup vinegar
1 teaspoon salt
1 teaspoon chili powder
1 teaspoon celery seed
1/4 cup brown sugar
few drops Tabasco sauce

Place ribs, cut into 2-rib portions, in a baking pan, and put a slice of lemon on each portion.

Bake at 350 degrees for 45 minutes.

Mix sauce ingredients in a small pan and simmer for 1/2 hour.

Baste ribs with barbecue sauce several times, starting when ribs have been baking 45 minutes. Bake another 45 minutes, for a total baking time of 1-1/2 hours.

Margaret Spangler

ROULADE WITH HAM

On each scallop, place a piece of ham and pound thoroughly to press the two together.

Top the ham with a leaf of sage, or sprinkle with powdered sage, and roll the scallop up firmly. Tie it with string or fasten with toothpicks.

In a large skillet, heat butter and oil. Dust the rolls with flour and brown them in the hot butter and oil, rolling them around to be sure they are evenly browned.

Season with a little salt and pepper, and add the wine. Cover the skillet and cook gently for 8 to 10 minutes, turning the rolls once or twice during the cooking.

Cook noodles according to package instructions. Season with butter and cheese, if desired.

In the center of a hot platter, place a mound of cooked noodles, and arrange the rolls around the noodles.

Serves 4   *Helen Homen*

8 very thin scallops (veal or chicken)
8 thin slices of ham the same size
8 leaves of sage, or powdered sage
4 tablespoons butter
4 tablespoons oil
flour
salt and black pepper
1/3 cup white wine
cooked noodles (seasoned with butter
  and cheese, if desired)

BARBECUED COUNTRY-STYLE RIBS
(Top of Stove)

Cut ribs into serving-size pieces. Layer in deep pan or dutch oven.

Mix brown sugar, celery seed, and chili powder, and pat mixture onto ribs.

Pour undiluted soup over ribs. Cover and cook over very low heat at least 2 hours, or until ribs are tender.

Serves 4 to 6   *Nancy Hedges*

2 to 3 pounds country-style pork ribs
1 cup brown sugar, packed
1 tablespoon celery seed
1 tablespoon chili powder
1 can (10-ounce) tomato soup

ROAST SUCKLING PIG

1 suckling pig, 10 to 12 pounds (can be ordered from your butcher)
salt and pepper to taste
1 teaspoon thyme, or to taste
2 to 4 tablespoons olive oil

Preheat oven to 350 degrees.

Wipe pig with paper towels inside and out. Singe any stray body hair over a gas flame. Salt and pepper liberally. Rub on powdered thyme.

Heat olive oil in a large shallow roasting pan. Place pig in heated pan, turn regularly to brown evenly. Skin should be crisp and brown.

Roast for about 2 hours at 350 degrees.

Lower heat to 325 degrees and bake an additional half hour.

Serves 6 to 8   *Dolores Lisica*

SWEET AND SOUR PORK

1 pound lean pork, cut in 3/4 inch cubes
2 tablespoons soy sauce
1 egg white, lightly beaten
1 clove garlic, minced
1/4 cup cornstarch
cooking oil for deep frying
1 small onion, quartered
1 green or red bell pepper, cut into squares
1 large carrot, sliced into chunks
1 large can sliced pineapple, drained (reserve juice for sauce) and cut into chunks

Sweet and Sour Sauce:

1 tablespoon cornstarch
1/2 cup pineapple juice
2 tablespoons catsup
2 teaspoons soy sauce
1/2 cup brown sugar
1/3 cup vinegar

Marinate the pork chunks in a mixture of soy sauce, egg white, and garlic for 20 to 30 minutes.

Dredge marinated pork in cornstarch, coating the chunks completely. Deep fry in 2 inches of hot (375 degrees) oil for 5 minutes or until done. Drain on paper towels. Set aside.

Pour off all but 2 tablespoons of the oil. Quarter the onion, cut pepper into squares, and slice carrot into chunks. Stir fry for 2 minutes.

Add pineapple and sauce, stirring until hot.

Add meat and serve over rice.

Sweet and Sour Sauce:

Combine all ingredients in a medium saucepan. Bring to a boil, stirring frequently. Simmer until thickened and clear. Makes about 1 cup.

It is great for dipping fried won ton or egg rolls, too!

Beth Castagnola

EASY BAKED PORK CHOPS

Make sauce.

Place pork chops in a baking dish in a single layer. Place 1 to 2 tablespoons uncooked rice on top of each chop. Spoon sauce over, making sure all the rice is covered. Cover dish and bake 1/2 hour at 350 degrees.

Uncover and bake 15 to 20 minutes longer, depending on thickness of chops.

Sauce:

Chop onion and green pepper. Place in a saucepan. Add undrained crushed pineapple, sage, salt, pepper, and sherry. Simmer for 5 to 10 minutes.

Jacqueline P. Smith

4 to 6 pork chops, well-trimmed
uncooked white rice, 1 to 2
    tablespoons per person

Sauce:

2 tablespoons chopped onion
2 tablespoons chopped green pepper
1 can (8-ounce) crushed pineapple,
    undrained
1/2 teaspoon ground sage
salt and pepper
1/2 cup sherry, if desired

POLISH-STYLE PORK LOIN ROASTED IN BEER
Poland

Trim excess fat from the roast, leaving just a thin layer on the top.

Mix the flour, mustard, sage, and about 1 teaspoon of salt together on a large piece of wax paper. Roll the roast in the flour mixture until it is evenly coated. Put the roast into a deep covered roaster. Sprinkle with a bit more salt and pepper to taste. Pour the beer into the roaster (not directly on the roast). Cover and roast for 2 hours at 300 degrees, basting often.

Meanwhile, prepare the vegetables. Peel the onions and slice off the ends. Push the centers out of each onion and stuff with pitted prunes that have been soaked in warm water for an hour (one or two prunes per onion, depending on their size).

After the pork has roasted for 2 hours, add the vegetables to the pan and baste with the juices. Continue to cook uncovered for another 1-1/2 hours, basting often. Cook until the internal temperature of the pork reaches 160 to 165 degrees, it's brown and tender, and the vegetables are fork-soft.

Allow the roast to rest on a heated platter for about 10 minutes before carving. Using a slotted spoon, transfer the vegetables to a warm serving dish. Skim the fat off the pan juices and pass the juice at the table to accompany the meat and vegetables.

Jackie Olden
KNX Food Hour

1 pork loin roast (3 to 4 pounds)
2 tablespoons flour
1 tablespoon dry mustard
1 teaspoon sage
salt and pepper to taste
24 ounces beer
6 medium-sized yellow onions
12 soaked prunes, pitted
12 small carrots, peeled
3 medium-sized white rose potatoes
    with jackets, quartered

CORSICAN LAMB

8 ounces bacon, ground or finely
    chopped
9 large cloves garlic, peeled and
    ground or finely chopped
3 tablespoons finely chopped parsley
1 leg of lamb, 4 to 5 pounds
2 ounces olive oil
salt to taste
coarse, freshly ground pepper to taste
1 cup dry red wine

Combine bacon, garlic, and parsley to make a forcemeat (stuffing).

Remove knuckle from leg of lamb. With a sharp knife, make 3 or 4 deep stabs into the thick part of the meat. Spoon 2 to 3 teaspoons forcemeat into each incision and sew shut with string and a coarse needle.

Place lamb in a roasting pan or dutch oven without a rack. Pour olive oil over meat and sprinkle with salt and pepper.

Roast in a preheated oven at 400 degrees for 15 minutes.

Reduce heat to 350 degrees and roast 45 minutes longer, basting several times. Pour off all the fat from the pan and then pour the wine over the lamb. Roast 20 minutes longer, basting occasionally.

Let stand 15 minutes before slicing.

Buttered small shell pasta with Parmesan cheese is a nice accompaniment.

A very appropriate salad is watercress with a dressing made of 3 ounces olive oil, 1 ounce orange juice, 1/2 teaspoon mustard, salt, and pepper.

Serves 6 to 8   *Jackson Menze*

NAVARIN de MOUTON
Lamb Stew

France

1-1/2 pounds lean lamb (or leftover
    cooked lamb), cubed
1 large onion or 6 small onions,
    chopped
1 tablespoon butter
1 tablespoon flour
salt and pepper
1 clove garlic, minced
1 cup white wine
1 cup chicken broth
3 carrots, cubed
2 small turnips, cubed
2 potatoes, cubed

Brown the lamb with onions in butter.

Pour off the fat and sprinkle lamb with flour. Mix. Add salt, pepper, and minced garlic. Add wine and chicken broth. Simmer until meat is tender.

Cube carrots, turnips, and potatoes. Add to meat and simmer until vegetables are tender (about 1/2 hour).

Eloise Knoll

KAGIT KEBABI
Baked Lamb Packages

Turkey

Place butter and fat removed from lamb into a heavy saucepan and heat. Brown the lamb quickly in this fat. You may want to do it in two portions. Add the grated onion. Sauté five more minutes. Remove to a bowl.

Add a little more butter, if necessary, and sauté the boiling onions, potatoes, bell pepper, and carrots, until the potatoes and onions are golden. Add the herbs and stir well. Add the peas and meat and stir well.

Shape 4 large or 6 medium packages by dividing the mixture onto large squares of foil or parchment. Top mixture with additional butter. Bring the sides up and seal well. Use staples on parchment. Place packages on a cookie sheet and bake at 375 degrees for one hour and 45 minutes.

Cut the packages open with a sharp knife and serve. You eat right out of each package.

These are very good served with French or Turkish bread so that none of the juices are lost.

Serves 4 to 6   *Ruth Hamren*

1-1/2 pounds lamb, cubed, fat
    removed and saved
3 tablespoons butter
1 onion, grated
8 boiling onions, peeled
2 boiling potatoes, cut in large cubes
1 green bell pepper, sliced
2 medium carrots, scraped and sliced
1/4 teaspoon dried mint
1/2 teaspoon dried whole oregano
    leaves
1/2 teaspoon dried whole thyme
    leaves
1 teaspoon dill weed
1/4 cup parsley
1 cup peas, fresh or frozen
baking parchment or heavy duty
    aluminum foil
butter for topping

PATLICAN KEBABI
Lamb and Eggplant Stew

Turkey

Cut unpeeled eggplants into large cubes. Salt them and let stand for 20 minutes.

Rinse eggplant and pat dry. Sauté in hot butter and place in a pot or casserole.

If all the butter was absorbed by the eggplants, melt more and sauté meat quickly until brown. Add chopped onions and continue to sauté until onions are limp.

Pour onions and meat over eggplant. Add remaining ingredients. Cover and simmer over lowest heat (or in a 350-degree oven) for 30 to 45 minutes, or until meat is very tender. Add water, if necessary, during cooking.

Serve with bread or pilaf and a dollop of yogurt.

This is one of the most popular meat and vegetable combinations to be found in Turkey.

Ruth Hamren

2 medium eggplants
salt to taste
1/4 cup butter or margarine
1-1/2 pounds lamb cubes, cut from
    leg or shoulder
additional butter
1 large onion, chopped
1 can (16-ounce) stewed tomatoes
1/2 teaspoon salt
1/4 teaspoon cayenne
1/2 teaspoon whole thyme
1/2 teaspoon rosemary

SWEDISH LEG OF LAMB

5 to 5-1/2 pounds leg of lamb
1 tablespoon salt
1 teaspoon dry mustard
dash garlic powder
1 onion, sliced
1 cup strong coffee
2 teaspoons sugar
2 tablespoons light cream
1/4 cup brandy
1/2 cup water
2 tablespoons flour
3/4 cup light cream
2 tablespoons currant jelly
hot cooked rice

Heat oven to 350 degrees.

Wipe lamb with a damp cloth. Rub meat with salt, mustard, and garlic powder. Place in a shallow roasting pan; cover with onion slices.

Roast, uncovered, for 2-1/2 to 3 hours.

Halfway through cooking time, baste with a mixture of coffee, sugar, 2 tablespoons light cream, brandy, and water. Turn meat and baste other side. Finish roasting.

Remove lamb to a hot platter.

In the roasting pan, skim off fat. Stir in flour, 3/4 cup cream, and currant jelly. Cook, stirring constantly, until bubbly. Pour into heated gravy bowl and serve on the side.

Serve with rice.

Serves 8   *Jacqueline P. Smith*

On Boiling Meat

"All kinds of meat are best put over the fire in cold water in the proportion of a quart to every pound of meat. The fibres are thus gradually dilated, and the meat more tender. The fire should be moderate, and the water should heat gradually."

—*The Young Housekeeper's Friend*, 1845

~Poultry~

POULTRY

ALMOND CHICKEN WITH BUTTON MUSHROOMS

Marinade:

Mix all ingredients of marinade and set aside.

Sauce:

In a small saucepan, combine all sauce ingredients. Bring to a boil, stirring frequently. Lower heat and simmer until thickened and clear. Set aside.

Almond Chicken:

Debone chicken breast and dice into 1/2-inch chunks. Mix chicken with marinade. Let stand for 30 minutes.

Pinch ends off Chinese snow peas and set aside.

Slice water chestnuts and bamboo shoots, and set aside.

Heat 2 tablespoons oil in wok. Add chicken and stir fry until it is no longer pink. Push to the side.

Add snow peas, water chestnuts, bamboo shoots, and button mushrooms. Stir fry for 1 minute.

Add sauce. Cook and stir for 30 seconds or longer.

Turn onto a serving platter. Top with toasted almonds.

Rose Marie Castagnola

1 whole chicken breast, deboned, diced into 1/2-inch chunks
1/4 pound Chinese snow peas (pea pods)
4 water chestnuts, sliced
1/4 cup sliced bamboo shoots
2 tablespoons oil
1/2 cup button mushrooms
1/4 cup halved toasted almonds

Marinade:

1 egg white
1/4 teaspoon salt
1/8 teaspoon white pepper
1 tablespoon oil
1 teaspoon cornstarch

Sauce:

1 teaspoon cornstarch
1/2 teaspoon sugar
1/2 teaspoon salt
2 tablespoons sherry
1 tablespoon oyster sauce
1 clove garlic, minced
1 teaspoon ginger root, grated or minced
1/4 cup chicken stock

ARROZ CON POLLO
Chicken and Rice

Mexico

In a dutch oven, brown chicken in oil.

Add chopped onion and minced garlic, and fry a few minutes longer.

Add tomato sauce, saffron, curry powder, chicken broth, salt, and pepper. Cover and cook for 20 minutes.

Add rice; stir well; cover and simmer for 15 minutes.

Add peas and mushrooms. Cook 15 minutes longer.

Serves 4 to 6   *Thomaline Aguallo Buchan*

3/4 cup olive oil
1 cut-up frying chicken (or 1 package thighs and 1 package legs)
1 small onion, chopped
1 clove garlic, minced
1/2 cup tomato sauce
1/8 teaspoon powdered saffron (optional)
1/2 teaspoon curry powder
2-1/2 cups chicken broth
salt and pepper, to taste
1 cup uncooked rice
3/4 cup frozen peas
1/4 cup sliced fresh mushrooms

PILEČE RIŽOT
Chiken with Rice

Yugoslavia

2 slices bacon, minced
1/4 cup olive oil
1/2 cup + 2 tablespoons flour
3 pounds chicken, cut in serving
    pieces, breast deboned and cut
    in cubes
2 large onions, chopped
1 cup mushrooms, sliced
2 tablespoons minced parsley
4 cloves garlic, pressed
1/2 cup white wine
3 tomatoes, peeled and chopped
1 can (8-ounce) tomato sauce
1 can chicken broth
2 or more soup cans water
1-1/2 cups converted rice, rinsed
grated Parmesan cheese (optional)

Seasonings:

1-1/2 teaspoons salt, or to taste
1 teaspoon MSG (optional)
1/2 teaspoon allspice
1/2 teaspoon white pepper
1/4 teaspoon black pepper

Mince bacon. Place bacon and oil in a large Dutch oven.

Dredge chicken pieces lightly in 1/2 cup flour. Place in hot oil and bacon in Dutch oven and brown over medium heat.

Add chopped onions and seasonings, stirring often. Add mushrooms, parsley, and pressed garlic.

Sprinkle 2 tablespoons flour over chicken mixture and stir until flour is absorbed. Pour wine over all and cook on high heat until wine is reduced. Stir constantly to prevent sticking.

Add peeled and chopped fresh tomatoes and tomato sauce. Stir and cook over medium heat for 5 minutes.

In a separate saucepan, heat broth and water. Pour half of broth and water over chicken mixture, reserving remaining half. Cook for 15 to 20 minutes over medium low heat.

Add rice, stirring to combine evenly and adding broth as needed. The pot may be covered. Cook for 25 to 30 minutes, stirring regularly. Sprinkle with Parmesan cheese before serving, if desired.

Serves 4 to 6   *Dolores Lisica*

BAKED BREAST OF CHICKEN

6 chicken breast halves (8 ounces
    each), boned and skinned
garlic salt, to taste
1/2 cup butter, melted
1 teaspoon paprika
3 tablespoons lemon juice
1 cup sour cream, room temperature
1/4 cup sherry
2 cans (4-ounce) mushrooms stems
    and pieces
generous dash of cayenne pepper

Preheat oven to 375 degrees.

Sprinkle chicken with garlic salt.

Mix together butter, paprika, and lemon juice. Brush meat with butter mixture. Place in shallow baking pan. Bake under foil tent until tender, about 30 minutes, brushing occasionally with remaining butter mixture.

In a bowl, blend together sour cream, sherry, mushrooms, and cayenne pepper. Pour mixture over chicken for last 15 minutes of baking.

Jean Miner

BREAST OF CHICKEN PAPRIKASH IN CHAMPAGNE

Halve, bone, and skin the chicken breasts. Sprinkle with paprika, salt, and pepper.

Place in a flameproof casserole with shallots, butter, and champagne.

Poach in a 350-degree oven, covered, for 10 minutes.

Remove chicken from oven and transfer to serving plate. Keep warm.

Reduce the cooking liquid by 2/3. Add heavy cream and reduce until thickened. Strain. Pour sauce over breasts and serve immediately.

Serves 6 *Bobbie Miller*

3 chicken breasts, halved, boned and skinned
3 tablespoons paprika
salt and pepper, to taste
2 tablespoons chopped shallots
1/4 cup butter
1 pint champagne
1-1/2 pints heavy cream

CHEDDAR-CHICKEN CASSEROLE

Cook rice according to package instructions.

Cut cheese into 8 equal sticks.

Cut chicken breasts in half. Pound to flatten each to 1/4 inch thickness. Roll each piece around a stick of cheese. Dip in beaten egg, then in bread crumbs. Brown in margarine; set aside.

Dissolve bouillon cube in boiling water.

Cook onion and green pepper in margarine until tender. Add flour, salt, pepper, and bouillon. Cook until thickened. Add rice and mushrooms. Pour into shallow casserole. Top with chicken.

Bake at 400 degrees for 20 minutes.

Serves 8 *Lucy DiMeglio*

2 cups cooked white rice
1 package (10-ounce) Cracker Barrel Brand sharp cheddar cheese
4 chicken breasts, boned, skinned
2 eggs, beaten
3/4 cup dry bread crumbs
1/3 cup margarine
1 chicken bouillon cube
1 cup boiling water
1/2 chopped onion
1/2 cup chopped green pepper
2 tablespoons flour
1 teaspoon salt
1/4 teaspoon pepper
1 can (3-ounce) sliced mushrooms, drained

CHICKEN BREASTS CLARISSE

8 chicken breasts
lemon juice
garlic powder
1 can condensed cream of chicken
    soup
2/3 can dry sherry (use empty
    soup can)
1 can (8-ounce) mushrooms and liquid

Place chicken breasts in a flat baking dish. Rub with lemon juice and sprinkle with garlic powder. Bake at 450 degrees for 15 minutes.

Combine soup, sherry, and mushrooms with liquid. Reduce oven to 325 degrees. Pour soup mixture over chicken and continue to bake an additional 45 to 60 minutes, or until brown.

If dinner is delayed, this dish holds very well. The soup, sherry, and mushrooms with liquid can be doubled so that there is more sauce to put over a side dish of rice, if desired.

Serves 6 to 8   *Nancy Hedges*

CHICKEN CACCIATORE MUNIO

1/2 onion
handful fresh parsley
1 clove garlic
1 small hot chili pepper
1 frying chicken, cut up
oil
1 can (8-ounce) tomato sauce
1/2 cup dry white wine
8 ounces water
salt and pepper to taste

Chop finely together the onion, parsley, garlic, and chili pepper. Set aside.

In a 9- or 10-inch frying pan, brown chicken, onion, and herbs in oil.

Add tomato sauce, wine, and water to cover chicken. Cover. Simmer slowly for 1 hour. Add salt and pepper to taste.

Serves 4   *Sue Munio*

CHICKEN CACCIATORE SPENCE

1 cut up roasting chicken or
    8 to 10 chicken thighs
3/4 cup flour
salt to taste
2 medium onions, chopped
1/2 cup vegetable oil
1 cup canned tomatoes
2 tablespoons tomato paste
1/2 teaspoon thyme
1/2 teaspoon parsley
1/2 teaspoon basil
1/2 cup white wine
4 ounces mushrooms

Shake chicken in a bag with flour and salt.

Brown chicken and onions in oil in an electric frying pan at 340 degrees.

Add balance of ingredients. Cover and cook until tender at 200 degrees. Adjust liquid during cooking period.

Betty Spence

CHICKEN FRICASSEE WITH MEATBALLS

Sauce:

Combine onion, catsup, and water in a covered pan on low heat. Add chicken and tomato sauce. Cook 1/2 hour.

Meatballs:

Combine meatball ingredients and shape into walnut-size balls. Add to chicken sauce and cook for 1 hour.

Selma Streicher

Sauce:

1 onion, diced
1 tablespoon catsup
few drops water
chicken giblets, necks, wings from 3 chickens, cut up
1 can (8-ounce) tomato sauce

Meatball Mixture:

1 tablespoon cornflake crumbs
1-1/2 pounds chopped ground beef
1 grated onion
1 teaspoon seasoned salt

CHICKEN DIVAN

Cook chicken in water, covered, no salt, for 1 hour if not boned—1/2 hour if boned. Reserve broth if desired for white sauce.

Make white sauce (or use 4 or 5 cans Aunt Penny's white sauce). Add nutmeg, mayonnaise, whipped cream, sherry, and Worcestershire sauce. Cook 15 minutes.

Cook broccoli in uncovered pan, no salt. Drain well. Arrange in a large flat casserole. Salt and pepper. Spread chicken over top. Salt and pepper. Add sauce and cover with Parmesan cheese.

Bake, uncovered, at 350 degrees until brown and bubbly, about 45 minutes.

White Sauce

Melt butter in saucepan. Add flour, stirring until well blended (3 to 4 minutes). Stir in milk. Add salt and white pepper to taste.

Serves 6 to 8   *Dorothy Sumich*

8 boned chicken breasts (halves)
water to cover
5 cups white sauce (medium)
1 teaspoon nutmeg
1/2 cup mayonnaise
1/2 cup cream, whipped
3 tablespoons sherry
1 teaspoon Worcestershire sauce
1 large bunch broccoli (or 2 packages frozen spears)
salt and pepper to taste
1 cup Parmesan cheese, grated

White Sauce

10 tablespoons butter (1-1/4 sticks)
7-1/2 to 10 tablespoons flour
5 cups milk, or 2-1/2 cups each milk and chicken stock
salt and white pepper to taste

CHICKEN EASY

4 boneless chicken breasts
1/4 cup flour
2 tablespoons oil
2 tablespoons butter
1 lemon
1/2 cup or more white wine
chopped parsley

Skin chicken breasts; wash and dry; dredge in flour.

Fry chicken in oil and butter on one side until white. Turn pieces and squeeze 1/2 lemon over chicken on cooked side. Cook other side, then squeeze other half of lemon over that side.

Add wine. Sprinkle with chopped parsley. Cook until done and sauce is reduced.

Carole Haagenson

CHICKEN KORMA
(Curry)

India

1/2 cup yogurt
3/4 cup sour cream
1 teaspoon paprika
1/2 teaspoon salt
1 small roasting chicken
1 brown onion, thinly sliced
oil
1 teaspoon tumeric
1 teaspoon cumin powder
5 cloves garlic, minced, or 1 teaspoon
    garlic powder
1 tablespoon grated fresh green ginger
    or 1 teaspoon powdered ginger
few coriander leaves
few cilantro leaves
2 teaspoons poppy seeds, ground
2 teaspoons sesame seeds, ground
2 cardamom seeds, slit

In a large bowl, make a marinade: mix yogurt, sour cream, paprika, and salt, and set aside.

Skin and wipe chicken, and cut into 12 pieces. Make small incisions all over with a sharp knife or fork and place in marinade. Marinate for 1 hour or more.

Fry onion in oil until dark brown. Add remaining ingredients. Cook 10 to 15 minutes over medium heat.

Add chicken and marinade. Add a little water and cook until the chicken is done and the sauce becomes a little thick.

Yoriko Mahdi

CHICKEN IN PHYLLO

Halve and bone chicken breasts. Place in a sauté pan, together with chicken stock and chablis. Add minced celery stalks, minced carrots, and minced onion, parsley, salt, and pepper. Cover and cook over medium heat at slow simmer until chicken is tender, about 15 minutes. Remove chicken; set aside to cool.

Reduce stock to about 2 cups. Purée vegetables and stock in blender or food processor. Pour purée into top half of double boiler and keep hot.

In a 1-cup saucepan, make a roux: melt 3 tablespoons butter, blend in flour and cook over medium heat for 2 minutes, stirring constantly. Add roux to heated puree, whisking until smooth. Place top half of double boiler on direct heat and bring contents to a slow boil, stirring over medium heat about 2 minutes or until sauce has thickened. Return pan to double boiler and keep sauce very warm.

Preheat oven to 350 degrees. Place each chicken breast at one end of a phyllo sheet, crosswise to length of phyllo. Top each breast with 1 teaspoon sauce. Fold sides of phyllo inward to partially cover chicken. Roll chicken in phyllo the entire length of sheet. Brush tops with remaining butter and place on greased baking sheet. Bake for about 15 minutes or until phyllo is nicely browned. Then brush with melted butter and bake for an additional 15 minutes. Serve with warm sauce.

If desired, after wrapping chicken in phyllo and brushing generously with butter, you may refrigerate or freeze this dish. Freeze sauce separately. Bake directly from freezer using above instructions, adding 15 to 20 minutes to the baking time.

Jean Miner

4 whole chicken breasts, halved
    and boned
4 cups chicken stock
1 cup chablis
2 celery stalks, minced
2 carrots, minced
1 onion, minced
6 sprigs parsley, minced
salt and freshly ground pepper to taste
3/4 stick butter
3 tablespoons flour
8 sheets phyllo dough (may be
    purchased ready-made)

CHICKEN-PORK ADOBO

Philippines

2 pounds pork, cut into 1" cubes
2 cloves garlic
2 pounds chicken, cut into serving
 pieces
butter
6 to 8 cups water
1/2 cup soy sauce
1/2 cup vinegar
2 tablespoons brown sugar
1 teaspoon salt
2 teaspoons peppercorns

Cut pork into 1-inch cubes. In a large saucepan, lightly brown the pork and garlic.

In a separate pan, sauté chicken in a little butter. Then add to pork.

Add water, soy sauce, vinegar, sugar, salt, and peppercorns. Simmer on low heat until meat is tender, about 2 hours.

Serve with steaming hot rice.

Note: This recipe can be made using only pork or only chicken.

Eloise Knoll

CHICKEN MARSALA WITH CAPELLINI

2 tablespoons olive oil
2 tablespoons butter
1/2 cup flour
1 whole chicken breast, deboned and
 cut into 1-inch chunks
1 package chicken wings (10),
 tips removed
salt and pepper, to taste
2 onions, sliced thin
4 green onions, sliced thin,
 white portion
1 cup sliced mushrooms, fresh or
 canned
4 cloves garlic, pressed
8 sprigs parsley, minced
1/4 cup pine nuts (optional)
1/4 teaspoon rosemary
1/4 teaspoon oregano
1/8 teaspoon allspice
1 tablespoon grated Parmesan cheese
1 tablespoon flour
3/4 cup Marsala wine
2 cups chicken broth
3/4 to 1 pound Capellini pasta

In a large cast iron skillet, heat oil and butter on medium high heat. Lightly dredge wings and chunks of chicken breast in flour and brown, adding wings first, then breast chunks. Sprinkle lightly with salt and pepper.

When chicken is golden brown, add onions, green onions, mushrooms, garlic, parsley, and pine nuts. Stir constantly, turning chicken wings to brown evenly.

Sprinkle rosemary, oregano, allspice, and 1 tablespoon each of flour and grated Parmesan cheese over chicken and stir to combine evenly. Pour wine over mixture, stirring constantly. When wine is reduced, add chicken broth and stir to combine. Lower heat to a simmer. Cook for 20 to 30 minutes. Taste and adjust seasonings. Add water if necessary.

Cook pasta in boiling salted water for 2 to 3 minutes. Drain and rinse.

Arrange pasta on heated serving platter. Arrange wings and pour chicken sauce over pasta evenly. Sprinkle with additional Parmesan cheese, if desired.

Serves 6 to 8   *Dolores Lisica*

CHICKEN WITH BABY CORN

Cut chicken into bite-sized pieces; place in medium-sized bowl. Add cornstarch, sherry, salt, pepper, oyster sauce, and sesame oil. Toss together; combine well. Set aside and marinate for 30 minutes or more.

Pour 2 inches of boiling water into a small saucepan. Add baby corn and sliced bamboo shoots. Cook for 1 minute. Drain and set aside.

Heat 3 teaspoons oil in a wok or heavy skillet. Add marinated chicken and ginger; stir fry for about 2 minutes. Add baby corn and bamboo shoots. Dissolve cornstarch in chicken broth and add to chicken mixture. Bring to a boil, reduce heat, cover, and simmer for 5 minutes.

Serve with steamed rice.

Serves 4   Ling Y. Hsieh

2-1/2 cups boneless chicken (raw)
1-1/2 tablespoons cornstarch
1 tablespoon sherry or dry
    white wine
1/4 teaspoon salt
1/4 teaspoon white pepper
2 tablespoons oyster sauce or
    1-1/2 tablespoons soy sauce
1 tablespoon sesame oil
boiling water
1 cup baby corn
1/2 cup sliced bamboo shoots or
    Chinese straw mushrooms
3 teaspoons salad oil
3 to 4 slices fresh ginger
1 teaspoon cornstarch
1/2 cup chicken broth
steamed rice

CHICKEN WITH VEGETABLES CHINESE STYLE

Bone and skin chicken. Cut into 2-1/2 x 1/2 inch strips.

Mix ginger, salt, and paprika and toss with chicken strips.

Heat oil in skillet. Add chicken pieces and sauté about 5 minutes over moderate heat, stirring frequently. Push chicken to one side of skillet.

Add sliced celery, green pepper strips, and chopped onion and stir fry about 5 minutes.

Add undrained tomatoes, rosé, and soy sauce. Heat to simmering. Turn heat low, cover and cook 5 minutes.

Blend cornstarch with cold water, and stir into mixture. Cook, stirring constantly, until sauce thickens slightly.

Serve at once over bean sprouts or rice.

Serves 4   Helen Homen

4 large half-breasts of chicken, boned
    and skinned
1 teaspoon powdered ginger
salt to taste
3/4 teaspoon paprika
2 tablespoons oil
1-1/2 cups celery, diagonally sliced
1/2 cup green pepper strips
1/2 cup onion, coarsely chopped
1 can (14-1/2 ounces) tomatoes
1/2 cup rosé wine
2 tablespoons soy sauce
1 tablespoon cornstarch
1 tablespoon cold water

HONEY-VINEGAR CHICKEN

1 can (8-ounce) crushed pineapple
1/4 cup wine vinegar
1/4 cup honey
1 teaspoon Worcestershire sauce
1 teaspoon salt
1 teaspoon pepper
1/4 teaspoon ground ginger
1 broiling chicken, cut in halves or
   in serving pieces

Blend all marinade ingredients well. Pour over chicken and marinate 4 to 5 hours in refrigerator, turning occasionally.

Broil chicken, brushing frequently with marinade.

Josephine Pittman

KAYAKU GO-HAN
Chicken Rice

Japan

2 cups short grain rice
2 cups water
2 pieces dry mushroom, cut in strips
   (soaked 15 minutes in warm
   water)
strips of hard-boiled egg for
   decoration
1-1/2 uncooked chicken breasts, cut
   in thin strips
3/4 cup carrots, cut in small strips
3/4 cup radish (daikon), cut in thin
   strips
2 abage (processed bean product), cut
   in strips
cooking oil
1 tablespoon rice wine
2 tablespoons soy sauce
1 tablespoon sugar
3 tablespoons water
2/3 teaspoon salt

Wash rice well and soak in 2 cups water for 30 minutes. Drain and set aside.

Place dried mushroom in a small bowl with warm water. Soak for 15 minutes.

Hard-boil egg which is to be used for decoration.

Cut chicken breasts, carrots, radish, soaked mushrooms, and abage in strips.

In a small pan, heat oil. Sauté chicken lightly and quickly on high heat. Add all other ingredients, except egg and rice, and cook quickly.

In large heavy skillet, combine rice with cooked ingredients. Bring to a boil over high heat. Stir. Reduce heat and cook about 15 minutes.

Turn heat off and let steam 15 minutes longer.

Decorate with strips of hard-boiled egg.

Yoriko Mahdi

PARMESAN BAKED CHICKEN

3 pounds chicken, cut up
1/4 cup prepared mustard
1/2 teaspoon tarragon leaves,
   crushed
1/4 cup grated Parmesan cheese
1 tablespoon chopped parsley

Coat chicken pieces evenly with mustard.

Place pieces in a 10 x 12-inch baking dish and sprinkle with tarragon, cheese, and parsley.

Bake at 350 degrees until crisp and tender, about 40 to 60 minutes.

Doris Berg

JESSIE'S CHICKEN AND NOODLES

Chicken:

Put chicken in a large pan. Cover with water. If desired, add one or more of the optional vegetables and seasonings to the water. Boil until chicken is tender. Remove cooked meat from bones. Set meat aside. Reserve broth to use in cooking noodles.

Noodles:

Mix flour and salt; add beaten eggs. (Note: If you want noodles to have more color, add a few drops of yellow food coloring to eggs). Mix well. Knead dough a few times. Roll to desired thickness on a well-floured board. Sprinkle with flour and roll as for a jelly roll. Cut in desired width. Unroll cut noodles and let dry for about 20 minutes. Drop in boiling broth (add more water, if necessary).

When noodles are almost done, add chicken to noodles. Thicken broth with cornstarch and water if you like, and cook until done.

This is nice to serve with a green salad and hot rolls, with a sherbet for dessert.

My recipe is a typical midwestern dish—originally not fancy or spicy, just good wholesome food. My hometown is Des Moines, Iowa, where Mom and Dad still live in the home where I spent my childhood. Mom is nearly 81 years old and is still making her chicken and noodles and "fish-eye" cookies (see Cookies and Candy section for recipe) for Dad. She does quilting and crocheting and cans many things that Dad raises in their garden.

Serves 6   Fran Henderson

Chicken:

1 frying chicken, disjointed
optional vegetables and seasonings:
  chopped onion
  garlic
  chopped carrots
  celery
  bay leaf
cornstarch (optional)

Noodles:

1 cup flour
1 tsp salt
2 eggs, beaten
reserved broth

On Poultry

"Young fowls have a tender skin, smooth legs, and the breast bone yields to the pressure of the finger. The best are those that have yellow legs. The feet and legs of old fowls look as if they have seen hard service in the world."

—*The Young Housekeeper's Friend*, 1845

COUNTRY FRIED CHICKEN

1 chicken for frying, cut up
1 teaspoon paprika
1/2 teaspoon Accent (optional)
1/2 teaspoon pepper
1/2 teaspoon garlic powder
1/2 teaspoon salt
1/2 teaspoon curry powder
1 cup buttermilk
1/2 cup flour
1/2 cup pancake mix
cooking oil

Rinse and dry chicken. Mix paprika, Accent, pepper, garlic powder, salt, and curry powder, and season chicken. Let stand for 4 hours.

Pour buttermilk over chicken. Soak for about 5 minutes. Then pour off liquid.

Mix flour and pancake mix. Dredge chicken in flour mix and brown in covered skillet for 20 to 30 minutes.

Uncover the last 10 minutes of frying to recrisp skin.

Josephine Pittman

ORANGY BARBEQUE CHICKEN
(National Chicken Cooking Contest Winner)

1 broiler-fryer chicken, cut up
1 cup catsup
6 whole cloves
1 medium onion, chopped
1 clove garlic, finely chopped
2 tablespoons butter
2 tablespoons steak sauce
2 tablespoons Worcestershire sauce
1 tablespoon oil
1 tablespoon vinegar
1-1/2 tablespoons prepared mustard
1/2 teaspoon hot pepper sauce
1/4 teaspoon salt
1/4 teaspoon pepper
juice from 1 large orange
peel of 1/2 orange, chopped

On a rack in a large shallow pan, place chicken, skin side up, in a single layer. Bake, uncovered, at 350 degrees for 40 minutes.

Turn chicken. Bake 40 minutes or until fork can be inserted in chicken with ease.

To make sauce, mix together remaining ingredients. Cook, stirring until boiling. Cover and simmer 40 minutes.

Turn chicken to skin side up, cover with sauce (reserving some sauce to serve on side with meal), and bake uncovered for 15 minutes.

Serves 4   *Nancy Kaliterna*

ROAST DUCK

1 duck (4 to 4-1/2 pounds), fresh
    or defrosted
salt
pepper
1 jar good orange marmalade
1/2 cup rosé wine

Season duck with salt and pepper.

Coat with marmalade and wine.

Wrap in aluminum foil and roast 2-1/2 hours at 350 degrees.

Uncover, baste, and roast an additional 1/2 hour.

Serves 2   *Jacqueline P. Smith*

GAME HENS WITH FLAMING CHERRY SAUCE

If frozen, thaw hens as directed on the package. Set giblets aside for other uses. Rinse well and pat dry. Sprinkle cavities with seasoned salt and pepper. Place hens breast sides up, slightly apart, in a roasting pan. Combine butter with seasoned salt, ginger, and paprika. Brush over hens. Bake hens, uncovered, in a 350-degree oven until leg joints move easily, about 1 hour. During the last half hour, baste birds several times with pan drippings.

When hens are roasted, discard excess fat from pan juices and stir juices into the cherry sauce. Arrange hens on a serving plate and garnish with orange wedges. Keep warm.

To flame birds, warm brandy in a small container. Ignite and pour, flaming, into the sauce. While still flaming, spoon sauce over birds.

Cherry Sauce:

Drain cherries, reserving 1/3 cup of the syrup.

In a pan, combine the 1/3 cup syrup with 2/3 cup water, bouillon cube, onion, cloves and cinnamon. Bring to boil, stirring. Reduce heat and simmer for 10 minutes.

Strain, discard cloves and onion. Return sauce to pan.

Blend 1 tablespoon cornstarch and 1 tablespoon water until smooth. Add to sauce and cook, stirring until boiling and sauce thickens. Stir in the cherries, lemon peel, and lemon juice. Add salt and pepper to taste and lower heat until ready to serve.

Serves 2 to 4   *Jean Miner*

2 Rock Cornish game hens (20 to 24 ounces each), fresh or frozen
seasoned salt and pepper
2 tablespoons butter or margarine, melted
1/2 teaspoon seasoned salt
1/2 teaspoon ground ginger
1/2 teaspoon paprika
cherry sauce
orange wedges
2 tablespoons brandy (optional)

Cherry Sauce:

1 can (8-ounce) pitted dark sweet cherries
2/3 cup water
1 chicken bouillon cube
1 small onion, cut in wedges
8 whole cloves
1/4 teaspoon ground cinnamon
1 tablespoon cornstarch
1 tablespoon water
1/4 teaspoon grated lemon peel
1 tablespoon lemon juice
salt and pepper, to taste

PORT WINE GAME HENS

6 Rock Cornish game hens
4 to 4-1/2 cups wild rice stuffing (or
    stuffing of your choice)
2 tablespoons butter
1/2 cup currant jelly
2 tablespoons lemon juice
2 teaspoons mace
salt
1/4 cup port wine

Stuff each hen and rub with butter.

In a small saucepan, combine currant jelly, lemon juice, mace, salt, and wine. Bring to a boil and simmer for 3 to 5 minutes.

Roast hens, uncovered, at 350 degrees for 1-1/2 to 1-3/4 hours, basting with sauce.

Serves 6   *Jacqueline P. Smith*

DIETER'S TURKEY SAUSAGE

1 pound ground turkey
1/2 teaspoon thyme
1 teaspoon sage
1/2 teaspoon anise seeds
1/8 teaspoon pepper

Add thyme, sage, anise seeds, and pepper to turkey and mix well. Refrigerate overnight for maximum flavor.

Form into patties and brown in a skillet. Cook to desired doneness.

Yield: 6 patties   *Doris Berg*

~Fish and Seafood~

FISH/SEAFOOD

BAKED FISH

In 2 tablespoons oil, sauté onion until golden.

Add tomatoes, garlic, paprika, salt, lemon juice, and rest of oil. Simmer 20 minutes.

Place fish in a baking dish and cover with sauce. Bake at 350 degrees for 30 minutes.

Garnish with parsley and lemon slices before serving.

This is a low cholesterol dish.

Serves 4   *Betty Di Masi*

4 tablespoons oil
2 medium onions, sliced
1 can (2 pounds) tomatoes
1 clove garlic
1/2 teaspoon paprika
1 teaspoon salt
juice of 1/2 lemon
2 pounds fish (striped bass, red
     snapper, carp, mackerel)
parsley & lemon slices

BAKED FISH AU GRATIN

Place fillets in a greased, 8-inch square baking pan. Sprinkle with salt and pepper and bake at 400 degrees for 8 minutes.

In a mixing bowl, combine yogurt, onion soup mix, and lemon juice.

Remove fish from oven. Drain off liquid and turn fillets. Spread yogurt mixture on fillets and sprinkle with cornflake crumbs, Parmesan cheese, and parsley. Bake 10 to 15 minutes longer, or until fish flakes easily with a fork.

Serves 4   *Lillian Peterson Drenckhahn*

1 pound sole fillets
1/4 teaspoon salt
1/8 teaspoon black pepper
1/2 cup plain yogurt
1 tablespoon dry onion soup mix
1 tablespoon lemon juice
1/4 cup cornflake crumbs
2 tablespoons grated Parmesan
     cheese
1 tablespoon chopped parsley

BAKED FISH SUPREME

Arrange fillets in buttered casserole dish. Sprinkle with olive oil and lemon juice.

In a bowl, mix bread crumbs, minced garlic, chopped parsley, and grated Parmesan cheese; add melted butter. Pat this mixture onto fillets.

Bake at 350 degrees for 45 minutes.

Serves 6 to 8   *Carmela Castagnola*

6 large sea bass fillets, cut thickly
1 to 2 tablespoons olive oil
juice of 1 lemon
1 cup bread crumbs
minced garlic
chopped parsley
1/4 cup Parmesan cheese, grated
1/4 pound butter, melted

BAKED FISH WITH SPINACH

Greece

3 pounds rockfish (or any other fish)
3 medium tomatoes, sliced
     1/4-inch thick
1 lemon, thinly sliced
2 cloves garlic, thinly sliced
1/4 cup olive oil
salt and pepper
1/4 cup water
1 pound spinach, washed and drained
minced parsley

Wash and clean fish; place in a small baking pan or aluminum foil. Place tomatoes slices, lemon slices, and garlic slices onto fish. Add olive oil, salt, and pepper. Cover with enough water to keep the fish moist.

Bake at 350 degrees for 30 minutes to 1 hour.

Cover fish with spinach and bake for an additional 30 minutes. Be sure to baste often and add additional water, when needed.

Garnish with parsley and serve.

Mrs. C. J. Petrofanis

BAKED HADDOCK

1-1/2 pounds haddock fillet
1 cup hot milk
1 can frozen cream of shrimp soup,
     thawed
3/4 cup cheddar cheese, shredded
3 tablespoons cooking sherry
1/4 cup cheddar cheese, grated
paprika

Bake fish in hot milk at 350 degrees for 1/2 hour. Drain and reserve liquid.

Heat soup, 3/4 cup milk drained from fish, shredded cheese, and sherry on low heat for 5 to 10 minutes. Pour over fish.

Sprinkle grated cheese and paprika over fish and put under broiler or in oven until slightly brown and bubbling.

Betty Di Masi

BAKED SALMON IN CREAM

2 to 4 salmon steaks (1/2 pound
     each)
6 teaspoons lemon juice
1 cup heavy cream
3 to 4 tablespoons minced onion

Place salmon steaks in a flat, buttered baking dish. Sprinkle with lemon juice. Mix cream and onion and pour onto salmon.

Bake, uncovered, at 400 degrees for about 25 minutes, or until fish flakes.

Spoon the thick cream sauce over the steaks before serving.

Serves 3 to 4   *Nancy Hedges*

BAKED SALMON LOAF

Preheat oven to 350 degrees.

Place salmon in a large bowl; flake with fork. Remove bones and skin if desired. Add all remaining ingredients and mix well.

Turn into a greased 9 x 5 x 3-inch loaf pan. Bake for 40 to 50 minutes, or until done.

Variation: If you prefer salmon cakes, mix the ingredients together, form into cakes, and fry in hot oil until brown on both sides.

Serves 4   *Helen Homen*

1 can (1-pound) salmon
3/4 cup fresh bread crumbs
1 egg, slightly beaten
3/4 cup milk
2 tablespoons minced onion
1/2 teaspoon salt
1/8 teaspoon pepper
2 tablespoons melted butter or
    margarine
3 tablespoons lemon juice
2 tablespoons snipped parsley or
    parsley flakes

BARBECUED SWORDFISH

Wipe swordfish steaks with paper towel to dry the surface. Salt and pepper and set aside.

In a small bowl, combine all the ingredients for the basting sauce.

When barbeque coals turn white, place grill on barbeque to heat. Grill must be hot to prevent fish from sticking.

Brush basting sauce on both sides of steaks before placing on grill. Grill for about 8 to 10 minutes on one side. When brown, turn steak and continue grilling for an additional 8 to 10 minutes. Baste regularly.

Remove from grill and pour remaining basting sauce over steaks.

Serve immediately.

Variations: Fresh salmon, sea bass, and shark steaks may be prepared using the same method. Spanish mackerel may be used, but skin should be scored to allow heat to penetrate. Grilling time will be longer.

Serves 6   *Chris Lisica*

6 swordfish steaks, 1-1/4 inch thick
salt and pepper

Basting Sauce:

3 cloves garlic, pressed
2 tablespoons fresh parsley,
    finely minced
1/4 teaspoon Tabasco
6 tablespoons olive oil
juice from 1/2 lemon

BOILED FISH

2 large onions, chopped
1/3 cup olive or salad oil
4 stalks celery, cut into 2-inch lengths
1 potato, cut into 6 pieces
salt and pepper, to taste
2 quarts water
3 to 5 pounds sea bass or rock cod,
    cut into chunks (do not fillet)
4 cloves garlic, chopped
handful of fresh parsley, chopped
2 tablespoons olive oil (optional)
1 cup converted rice (optional)

Sauté onions in oil until golden.

Add celery, potatoes, salt, and pepper. Sauté for an additional 3 or 4 minutes.

Add 2 quarts of water. Bring to a boil, and continue boiling for 20 to 30 minutes.

Put fish chunks into broth. Add garlic and parsley that have been chopped together. Add more water so that fish is covered. Bring to a boil and cook 20 minutes on low heat. Do not stir. Shake pan to prevent burning or sticking to pan.

When the fish is done, the meat will fall away from the bone when gently touched with a fork. Don't overcook.

For a side dish, strain the fish broth and heat. In a separate pan, heat 2 tablespoons olive oil. Add 1 cup of rice and stir. Add broth to rice gradually as rice cooks.

Serves 4 to 6   *Chris Lisica*

BROILED TROUT

4 trout, cleaned
salt and pepper
8 teaspoons Dijon mustard
cooking oil
1/4 cup butter
1 tablespoon minced parsley
juice of 1 lemon

Sprinkle trout with salt and pepper and spread both sides of each fish with a thin layer of Dijon mustard, using about 2 teaspoons per fish.

Arrange trout on a greased broiler rack and broil about 3 inches from heat for 15 minutes, turning once and brushing with oil frequently throughout cooking time.

While fish are broiling, make d'hotel butter: cream the butter and mix in minced parsley and lemon juice.

Arrange fish on warm serving platter and spread with the savory butter. Garnish with lemon wedges and serve with cucumber salad, if desired.

Helen Homen

CIGO'S CIOPPINO

In a large Dutch oven or saucepan, sauté onions, parsley, and garlic in oil until onions are tender.

Add oregano and basil, and season to taste with salt and pepper. Cook and stir a few minutes to blend flavors.

Stir in vinegar and wine. Simmer 5 minutes to blend flavors.

Drain and chop tomatoes, reserving liquid. Stir in tomatoes. Simmer 5 minutes; then add tomato liquid. Simmer 15 minutes.

Add fish, crab meat, squid, scallops, shrimp, and clams. Simmer 10 to 15 minutes until clams open and fish and shellfish are tender, but not dry.

Serves 6 to 8   *Cigo's Restaurant*

2 onions, chopped
1 bunch parsley, washed and chopped
    (discard stems)
6 cloves garlic, minced
1/4 cup oil
1 tablespoon oregano
1 tablespoon basil
salt
white pepper
1/2 cup red wine vinegar
1 cup chablis
2 cans (1 pound each) tomatoes
1 pound fresh fish, any type, cut
    into pieces
1 pound crab meat
2 cleaned squid, cut into strips
1 pound scallops
1 pound large shrimp
1 dozen clams

MAC McKEE'S CIOPPINO

Sauté half the garlic in 2 tablespoons oil until lightly brown. Add half the wine.

In a separate skillet, heat 1/2 cup oil. Dredge cod, snapper, sculpin, scallops and squid in flour; fry a few at a time until golden on all sides. Remove fish, and set aside.

Add remaining oil to skillet used to fry fish, together with remaining garlic, clams, mussels, oysters, crab legs, and fried squid. Simmer 10 minutes.

Add remaining wine and minced clams. Simmer over high heat 2 minutes.

Add clam juice, tomatoes, chopped parsley, MSG and saffron, and season to taste with salt and pepper. Simmer 15 minutes.

Add remaining fried fish. Simmer 10 minutes longer.

Add tomato paste to thicken sauce. Simmer 5 minutes.

Serves 6 to 8   *Mac McKee*

4 to 5 cloves garlic, crushed
1 cup olive oil
1-1/2 cups dry white wine
1/2 pound rock cod fillet, cut in
    chunks
1/2 pound red snapper fillet, cut in
    chunks
1/2 pound sculpin fillet, cut in chunks
1 pound scallops
3/4 pound squid, cleaned and cut
    into pieces
flour
10 each of clams, mussels, oysters
3 small cracked king crab legs
1 can (6-1/2 ounces) minced clams
3 bottles (8 ounces each) clam juice
3 cups fresh tomatoes, peeled
    and crushed
1/2 teaspoon chopped parsley
dash MSG
salt and pepper
dash powdered saffron
1 to 2 teaspoons tomato paste

TRUTANICH CIOPPINO

2 onions, chopped
1/2 bell pepper, chopped
6 cloves garlic, minced
1/4 cup olive oil
9 ounces tomato paste
4 cups water (enough to cover fish)
1/4 cup vinegar
1 teaspoon salt
1 teaspoon sugar
1 4-pound rock cod fish fillet
2 large lobster tails
2 large king crab legs
1 pound shrimp
1/2 bunch parsley, chopped

In a small frying pan, sauté onions, bell pepper and garlic in oil.

In a large sauce pan, mix tomato paste with water. Heat and add vinegar, salt, and sugar. Add onion mixture and boil for 10 minutes.

Add seafood and simmer 10 minutes. *Do not stir fish.* To blend, tilt pot (with good lid) to one side. Cover, remove from heat and let stand 10 minutes. To serve, sprinkle with fresh parsley.

Nick Trutanich

CRAB MEAT SOUFFLÉ

2 cans (7-ounce) crab meat
2 cups light cream
3 cups soft bread crumbs
2 cups mayonnaise
4 hard boiled eggs, chopped
salt and pepper, to taste
1 tablespoon grated onion (optional)
1/2 to 3/4 cup buttered bread crumbs

In a bowl, clean and flake crab meat.

In a separate bowl, pour cream over bread crumbs to absorb moisture. Add crab meat, mayonnaise, and chopped hard-boiled eggs, and season to taste with salt and pepper. Add 1 tablespoon grated onion, if desired. Mix well and place in a 1-1/2 quart buttered baking dish.

Top with buttered bread crumbs and refrigerate for at least 1 hour.

Bake at 375 degrees for 1 hour.

Serves 6 to 8   *Betty McKinney*

CURRIED HALIBUT

2 large onions, sliced
3 tablespoons butter
curry powder
pepper
4 halibut steaks
1 clove garlic, sliced thin
finely chopped chives

Sauté onions in butter until golden in color.

Mix curry powder and pepper well, and rub into steaks.

Add steaks, garlic, and chives to onions, and simmer, covered, on low heat, until tender.

Remove fish to a platter. Pour pan juices over steaks and serve.

Serves 4   *Betty Di Masi*

FISH FILLETS SOUFFLÉ

Sauté onions in butter or oil.

In a casserole, place spinach soufflé and cover with onions. Place fish fillets onto spinach soufflé, and pour vermouth over. Cover with sour cream, and sprinkle with Parmesan and paprika.

Cover and bake at 350 degrees for 40 to 45 minutes, or until fish flakes.

Betty Di Masi

1/4 to 1/2 cup onions, thinly sliced
butter or oil
2 packages Stouffer's spinach soufflé, thawed
3 to 5 flounder fillets
1/4 cup dry vermouth
1 carton (16-ounce) sour cream
Parmesan cheese
dash paprika

OCTOPUS SALAD

Wash octopus in cold salted water. Have 3 quarts of water boiling briskly. Holding octopus by the head, dip body twice in the boiling water, and then drop it into the boiling water. Allow water to reach a rolling boil; lower heat to a simmer and cover. Simmer for 30 minutes *without lifting the lid*.

Remove from heat, still not lifting the lid, and allow to stand for another 30 minutes in the *covered* pot.

Remove octopus from pot, cool and slice in 1/2-inch or larger pieces. Season with salt and pepper and place in a large bowl.

Add chopped red onions, green onions, garlic, olive oil, and vinegar. Toss to mix thoroughly.

Chill and serve.

Serves 4 to 6

Chris Lisica

3 pounds octopus
3 quarts boiling salted water
salt and pepper to taste
1 small red Bermuda onion, chopped fine
4 green onions, thinly sliced
1 small clove pressed garlic (optional)
2 to 3 tablespoons olive oil
1 to 2 teaspoons red wine vinegar

OVEN FRIED SQUID

5 pounds squid
1-1/2 cups bread crumbs
3 cloves garlic, finely chopped
3 tablespoons parsley, finely chopped
1/4 cup grated Parmesan cheese
1-1/4 teaspoons salt
1/2 teaspoon pepper
olive oil (for dipping)

Cut the head of each squid above the eyes. Slit body and remove cartilage and viscera. Rinse well and drain on paper toweling.

Combine bread crumbs, garlic, parsley, cheese, salt, and pepper in a paper bag.

Dip each squid in oil; drop a few pieces of squid in the bag and shake, coating all surfaces.

Roll each piece jelly-roll style, and insert a toothpick to hold in place.

Place on a lightly oiled cookie sheet and bake at 375 degrees for 15 minutes.

Excellent served as an hors d'oeuvre.

John Cigliano

PARKER'S POACHED CATFISH

2 pounds catfish fillets, fresh or frozen
2 cups boiling water
1/4 cup lemon juice
1 small onion, thinly sliced
1 teaspoon salt
3 peppercorns
2 sprigs parsley
1 bay leaf
paprika

Egg Sauce:

1/4 cup butter or margarine
2 tablespoons flour
3/4 teaspoon dry mustard
1/2 teaspoon salt
dash pepper
1-1/4 cups milk
2 hard-cooked eggs, chopped
1 teaspoon chopped parsley

Thaw fish, if frozen. Remove skin and bones. Cut fish into 6 portions.

Place fish in a well greased 10-inch skillet. Add boiling water, lemon juice, onion, salt, peppercorns, parsley, and bay leaf. Cover and simmer 5 to 10 minutes, or until fish flakes easily.

Carefully remove fish to hot platter. Pour egg sauce over fish and sprinkle with paprika.

Egg Sauce:

To make egg sauce, melt butter and stir in flour, mustard, salt, and pepper. Add milk gradually, and cook and stir until thick and smooth. Add hard-cooked eggs and chopped parsley. Heat. Makes 1-1/2 cups sauce.

Serves 6   *Betty Di Masi*

PESCADO EN SALSA VERDE
Fish in Green Sauce

Salsa Verde:

Remove husks from tomatillos. Place in 1/2 inch water in a saucepan; bring to a boil. Cover and simmer 10 minutes, or until tomatillos are tender. Drain and cool.

In a blender or food processor, grind tomatillos, green onions, garlic, parsley, and the green chile until puréed.

Heat 2 teaspoons oil in a saucepan. Add tomatillo green sauce and salt to taste. Bring to a boil. Then simmer gently for 15 minutes. Keep hot.

Fish:

Rub fish with lime juice and salt. Let stand 10 minutes. Brush with oil and put on a sheet of oiled parchment placed on a baking sheet. Bake at 400 degrees for 12 to 15 minutes.

Serve at once, topped with green sauce.

Serves 4   *Betty Di Masi*

Salsa Verde:

1 pound tomatillos
3 green onions, including tops
1 clove garlic
1 tablespoon parsley
1 fresh or canned long green chile
2 teaspoons oil
salt

Fish:

2-1/2 pounds whole red snapper
lime juice
salt
oil
parchment paper

POACHED COD WITH LEMON VEGETABLES

Allow cod to stand at room temperature 20 minutes, unwrapped.

Cut each semi-frozen block of fish into 3 sections. Season with salt and pepper to taste. Wrap tightly in foil. Place package in boiling water. Cook for 25 minutes, turning package once. Unwrap and drain. Cooked fish will flake easily when tested with fork.

While fish is cooking, slice zucchini and carrots into julienne strips and cook in butter and chicken broth until crisp tender, about 3 minutes.

Combine lemon juice and cornstarch and stir into hot liquid. Cook over medium heat, stirring constantly, until thick and smooth. Stir in nutmeg and salt to taste.

To serve, arrange poached fish on top of vegetables in lemon sauce. Place sliced lemon on top of fish and sprinkle with green onion.

Serves 6   *Betty Di Masi*

2 pounds frozen cod fillets
salt and pepper, to taste
4 large zucchini
8 large carrots, peeled
6 tablespoons butter or margarine
3 cups chicken broth
1/2 cup lemon juice
3 tablespoons cornstarch
1/2 teaspoon nutmeg
lemon slices
1/2 cup sliced green onion

POACHED FISH HUNTER'S STYLE

1 onion, chopped
1/4 cup chopped celery
1/2 cup sliced mushrooms
2 tablespoons oil
1 can (15 ounce) tomato sauce
1/2 teaspoon salt
1/8 teaspoon pepper
1/2 cup dry white wine or clam broth
2 tablespoons minced parsley
4 to 6 fish fillets, about 5 ounces each

Chop onion and celery; slice mushrooms. Cook in oil until onion is tender but not browned.

Add tomato sauce, salt, pepper, wine, and parsley. Bring to a boil, reduce heat, and simmer 20 minutes. Add water if sauce becomes too thick.

While sauce is cooking, roll fish fillets jellyroll-fashion and fasten with toothpicks. Arrange fish roll 1 layer deep in sauce. Cover and simmer 15 to 20 minutes or until fish flakes easily with a fork.

Serves 4 to 6   *Betty Di Masi*

POACHED FISH WITH DILL SAUCE

2 salmon or other fish steaks,
    1 inch thick
1 teaspoon salt
4 peppercorns
juice of 1/2 lemon
1 bay leaf
1/4 cup dry white wine
water

Mustard Dill Sauce:

2 tablespoons butter or margarine
1 tablespoon chopped green onion
2 tablespoons flour
1 cup light cream
1 tablespoon prepared mustard
1/8 teaspoon dried dill weed
1/2 teaspoon salt
dash white pepper
2 tablespoons chopped pimiento
1 tablespoon lemon juice

Place fish in a skillet and sprinkle with salt, peppercorns, lemon juice, bay leaf, and wine. Add enough water to cover fish. Cover and simmer over low heat until salmon turns pink throughout, 10 to 15 minutes.

Drain salmon and place on heated platter and top with mustard dill sauce.

Mustard Dill Sauce:

To prepare sauce, melt butter in a small saucepan. Add chopped green onion and cook gently just until softened.

Stir in flour. Blend in cream, mustard, dill, salt, and pepper. Cook and stir over low heat until mixture thickens. Do not boil.

Add chopped pimiento and lemon juice.

Serve over fish. Makes about 1/2 cup.

Serves 2   *Betty Di Masi*

POACHED FISH WITH TOMATO

Sprinkle fish with salt and pepper.

Melt 1 tablespoon butter in a 10-inch skillet and add green onion, shallots, and garlic. Place fish over onion mixture. Arrange tomato slices on fish and sprinkle with parsley. Pour wine around fish.

Cut a circle of wax paper to fit skillet. Tear a small hole in center and place on fish. Bring to a boil, cover and cook over low heat about 10 minutes, or until fish flakes easily with a fork.

Remove cover, paper, and garlic. Pour cream around fish.

Blend remaining butter with flour and stir into cream. Move skillet in circular motion to combine and thicken sauce.

Spoon some of the sauce over fish. Garnish with chopped parsley, if desired. Serve from skillet.

Serves 4 to 6   *Betty Di Masi*

1-1/2 pounds fish fillets
salt
pepper
2 tablespoons butter or margarine
1/4 cup minced green onion
2 shallots, minced
1 clove garlic, whole
2 tomatoes, thickly sliced
1 tablespoon minced parsley
1/4 cup dry white wine or vermouth
1/4 cup light cream
1 teaspoon flour

POACHED SHARK REMOULADE

Place shark fillets in a deep baking pan. Top with onion slices, if desired. Add water until pan is half full.

Bake at 400 degrees for 45 minutes.

Pour off water. Serve with remoulade sauce.

Remoulade Sauce:

To prepare sauce, mix lemon juice, vinegar, mustard, horseradish, parsley, paprika, and cayenne pepper. Beat in oil. Add chopped celery, chopped green onions, and minced capers.

Makes about 2-1/2 cups.

Serves 4   *Betty Di Masi*

4 shark fillets, about 6 ounces each
sliced onion (optional)
water

Remoulade Sauce:

2 tablespoons lemon juice
2 tablespoons tarragon vinegar
2 tablespoons prepared mustard
2 tablespoons horseradish
1 tablespoon parsley
1 teaspoon paprika
1/4 teaspoon cayenne pepper
1 cup oil
1/4 cup finely chopped celery
1/4 cup finely chopped green onion
1 tablespoon minced capers

SALMON CRÊPES

Crêpe Batter:

3 eggs
1-1/2 cups milk
2 tablespoons butter or margarine,
    melted
1-1/2 cups all purpose flour
1/2 teaspoon salt

Salmon Filling:

1 can (1-pound) salmon, drained
    and flaked
1 can (3 ounce) chopped mushrooms,
    drained
3 hard-cooked eggs, chopped
1 teaspoon grated onion
1 cup dairy sour cream
pepper, to taste
1/4 teaspoon salt

Cheddar Sauce:

1/2 stick butter or margarine
1/4 cup flour
1/4 teaspoon salt
dash pepper
2-1/2 cups milk
1 teaspoon Worcestershire sauce
1/2 pound or 2 cups cheddar cheese,
    shredded

To make crêpe batter, beat eggs and add milk.

Pour into a separate bowl the melted butter; add flour and salt. Beat with rotary or electric beater until smooth (should be consistency of heavy cream; if too thick, add more milk), then let stand one hour.

Heat a 7- or 8-inch skillet and brush with butter. Pour about 1/4 cup batter into skillet and rotate so batter covers bottom evenly. Brown on one side, turn and brown on other. Continue until all batter is used.

In a separate bowl, mix the ingredients for salmon filling. Put 2 tablespoons of the mixture onto each crêpe, roll up and place in well buttered shallow baking dish.

Make sauce; pour over crêpes (crêpes can be frozen at this point, if desired). Bake in hot oven, about 400 degrees, 15 to 20 minutes, or until hot and bubbly.

Cheddar Sauce:

To make cheddar sauce, melt butter in saucepan. Blend in flour, salt, and pepper. Cook, stirring constantly, just until bubbly.

Stir in milk, continue cooking and stirring until sauce thickens and bubbles 1 minute.

Stir in Worcestershire sauce and shredded cheese until cheese is melted.

Makes 2-1/2 cups.

Yield: 15 crêpes   *Betty Di Masi*

SALMON CROQUETTES

1 can (15-1/2 ounce) salmon
3 eggs
1 cup cracker crumbs
2 tablespoons flour
1/4 cup minced or chopped onion
salt and pepper to taste
shortening or cooking oil

Debone salmon and mash.

Beat eggs and add to salmon. Add cracker crumbs, flour, onion, salt, and pepper, and mix well. Shape into 8 oblong pieces.

Fry in skillet which is 3/4 full of shortening or cooking oil.

Variations: Tuna, crab, or chicken may be substituted for salmon.

Yield: 8 croquettes   *Josephine Pittman*

SAUCY SALMON

Sauté celery in margarine until tender.

Add soup, milk, and salmon. Heat about 5 minutes.

Add lemon juice and sliced olives. Serve over rice.

Margaret Gwartney

3 tablespoons butter or margarine
2 or 3 stalks celery, sliced
1 can cream of celery soup
1/2 cup milk
1 large can salmon
2 tablespoons lemon juice
1/3 cup green stuffed olives, sliced

SEA STEW

Fish Broth:

Place all ingredients in a large pot, with water to cover. Simmer for about an hour. Strain. Use broth as a base for the stew.

Sea Stew:

Prepare all seafood for use in the stew. Refrigerate the portion you will use in the stew. Use bones and bits of fish you cut off to make the Fish Broth.

When the Fish Broth is ready, place onions, green pepper, and celery in hot olive oil in a large pot, and sauté until the onions are soft and translucent.

Add garlic and flour. Add fish broth to cover vegetables. Add tomatoes, chili powder, marjoram, sugar, salt, pepper, and MSG. Bring to a boil, then turn heat down and simmer for about 20 minutes to combine flavors.

Add wine.

Season seafood and fish with salt and pepper. Add to broth and vegetable mixture which has been brought to a boil. Turn heat down to a simmer. Add saffron and cook for about 10 minutes or until fish pieces are flaky and shrimp is pink.

Serve piping hot with rice. Delicious with sourdough garlic bread.

Mrs. Gene Kaplan

Fish Broth:

Fish bones, heads, tails, and any bits
left after cutting fish up for stew
1 onion, in 8 pieces
1 stalk celery, including leaves
4 sprigs parsley
water to cover
salt and pepper to taste
MSG (optional)

Sea Stew:

1 pound cleaned shrimp (optional)
1 pound scallops (optional)
1 to 1-1/2 pounds halibut, sea bass,
red snapper, cut in bite-size
pieces (add 1 or 2 pounds if
shrimp and scallops are omitted)
2 tablespoons olive oil
2 onions, chopped
1 green pepper, chopped
2 stalks chopped celery (include tops)
1 clove garlic, pressed
1-1/2 tablespoons flour
1 can (2-1/2 pounds) whole tomatoes
1 teaspoon powdered chili
1/2 teaspoon marjoram
1 teaspoon sugar
salt and pepper, to taste
MSG (optional)
1/2 cup dry white wine
1/4 teaspoon saffron

SEAFOOD LUNCHEON DISH

1 can frozen shrimp soup, thawed
2/3 cup milk
1/4 cup grated cheddar cheese
1/2 cup mayonnaise
2 cups fine noodles, crushed lightly
1 can (4-1/2 ounces) shrimp
1 can (6-1/2 ounces) crab meat
1 can (5 ounces) sliced water
    chestnuts, drained
1 can French fried onion rings,
    crushed

Mix soup, milk, grated cheese, and mayonnaise. Fold in uncooked noodles, shrimp, crab meat, and water chestnuts.

Pour into greased 2-quart casserole. Bake covered at 325 degrees for 20 minutes.

Un-cover and bake 10 minutes.

Sprinkle with onion rings and bake an additional 10 minutes or until noodles are tender.

Serves 6   *Ruth Shannon*

TORTAS DE CAMARON CON CHILE
Shrimp Patties with Chili Sauce

Mexico

5 medium potatoes
1/4 cup evaporated milk
2 tablespoons flour
2 eggs, beaten
salt and pepper to taste
1 package (4 ounces) dried,
    powdered shrimp
1 bunch green onions, chopped
    (garnish)

Sauce:

1 tablespoon flour
1-1/2 cups cold water
1/4 cup corn oil
1 clove garlic, chopped
1 package (2 ounces) chili powder

This is a traditional lenten dish served in our family.

Boil potatoes until tender; peel and mash.

Add milk, flour, beaten eggs, salt, and pepper. Stir and whip until smooth.

Add shrimp and mix until firm enough to be formed into small patties.

Fry in oil until brown.

Make sauce.

Dip patties into sauce and arrange on platter; pour remaining sauce over them and garnish with chopped green onions.

Sauce:

Place flour in a saucepan, and add cold water a little at a time, while stirring, to make a smooth paste.

Add corn oil, chopped garlic, and chili powder. Mix until smooth, and bring to a simmer. Simmer 15 minutes or until smooth and medium thick.

Delia Gonzalez

SHRIMP AND CRAB MEAT AU GRATIN

Melt butter and add salt, garlic, and MSG. Stir in flour until smooth. Gradually stir in hot milk. Stir in 1/2 cup Parmesan cheese until blended. Add shellfish and cheddar cheese. Bring to a boil and turn off heat.

Mix remaining Parmesan cheese with paprika and sprinkle half the mixture evenly on the bottom of buttered individual dishes or 1 large au gratin dish. Stir shellfish mixture well. Then turn into dish or dishes. Sprinkle with remaining Parmesan cheese/paprika mixture.

Bake at 450 degrees for 8 minutes until cheese melts.

Note: May be frozen or refrigerated before baking.

Serves 4 to 6   *Dolores Lisica*

1/4 cup butter or margarine
1 teaspoon salt
1/2 teaspoon pressed garlic
1/2 teaspoon MSG (optional)
1/2 cup flour
3 cups hot milk
1 cup grated Parmesan cheese
10 ounces crab meat, shelled
10 ounces raw shrimp, shelled and
    deveined
1/2 cup grated cheddar cheese
1/2 teaspoon paprika

SHRIMP CASSEROLE

Cook shrimp for 5 minutes in boiling, salted water. Drain.

Put shrimp in 2-quart casserole (reserving 8 shrimp for topping). Sprinkle with lemon juice and salad oil.

Cook rice as directed on package.

Sauté green pepper and onion 5 minutes.

Reserve 1/4 cup almonds. Add remaining almonds and all the rest of the ingredients (excluding shrimp for topping) to shrimp in casserole. Toss well. Bake uncovered 35 minutes at 350 degrees.

Top with 8 shrimp and 1/4 cup slivered almonds. Bake 20 minutes longer.

Serves 8   *Jacqueline P. Smith*

2-1/2 pounds large raw shrimp
1 tablespoon lemon juice
3 tablespoons salad oil
3/4 cup raw regular rice
2 tablespoons butter or oleo
1/4 cup minced onion
1/4 cup minced green pepper
3/4 cup slivered almonds
1/2 cup sherry
1 teaspoon salt
1/8 teaspoon pepper
1/8 teaspoon mace
dash red pepper
1 can tomato soup
1 cup heavy cream

SHRIMP STROGANOFF

2 pounds shrimp, shelled and
    deveined
6 tablespoons butter
1-1/2 cups sliced mushrooms
4 tablespoons minced onion
1 clove garlic, minced or puréed
3 tablespoons flour
1 cup consommé or 1/4 cup dry white
    wine and 3/4 cup water
1 teaspoon prepared light mustard
1 cup sour cream
2 tablespoons chopped dill
salt and pepper, to taste
brown rice

Shell and devein shrimp.

Melt 3 tablespoons butter in a large skillet. Add shrimp and sauté 3 to 5 minutes, until shrimp are tender. Remove from skillet and keep warm.

Melt remaining butter in same skillet. Add sliced mushrooms and sauté for 2 minutes, turning frequently.

Add minced onion and garlic and sauté until tender, but not brown, stirring occasionally.

Add flour, consommé or wine/water and mustard. Cook until thickened, stirring constantly.

Remove from heat and blend in sour cream and chopped dill.

Return to heat, but do not boil. Add salt and pepper. Return shrimp to skillet and heat through.

Serve over a bed of brown rice.

Serves 4 to 6   *Lucy DiMeglio*

SKIMPY SHRIMP

6 slices buttered bread
1 small can small shrimp
1/2 pound shredded cheddar cheese
dry mustard
3 eggs
1 cup milk
1/2 teaspoon salt
1/4 teaspoon pepper
dash cayenne pepper

Cut bread into cubes. Arrange half in a 1-1/2 quart baking dish. Spread with half of shrimp and half of cheese. Sprinkle with mustard.

Add remaining bread, shrimp, and cheese.

Beat eggs; add milk, salt, pepper, and cayenne pepper. Mix well and pour over the bread/shrimp/cheese in the baking dish.

Bake at 325 degrees for 40 minutes.

Ruth Shannon

SOLE WITH CHIVES

Butter a baking dish large enough to hold the fish side by side. Then add 1 cup fish stock.

Clarify the butter, then pour the warm butter into a deep plate. Roll the fish in it, one at a time; dredge one side in bread crumbs, and lay crumb side up in prepared baking pan. Dribble the remaining butter over the fish and bake at 325 degrees for about 15 minutes. Remove fish from pan and keep warm.

Over a moderately high heat, add vermouth and wine, the remaining fish stock, and shallots to the baking pan. Boil down until the liquid has almost entirely evaporated.

Add créme fraîche and stir in tomato paste. Bring the sauce to a boil and cook, stirring constantly, until thickened.

Add a squeeze of lemon and taste for seasoning. Add salt and pepper to taste. Pass the sauce through a fine sieve (optional), return it to the stove and keep over low heat. At the last moment, stir in 1 tablespoon butter.

Distribute the sauce evenly onto four large heated plates. Sprinkle liberally with chives and rest the sole on top.

Créme Fraîche:

Add buttermilk or sour cream to heavy cream. Place the mixture in a jar, shake it, and let it stand at room temperature, uncovered, for one or more days until it is thick.

Cover and refrigerate. It will keep for several weeks.

Serves 4   *Bobbie Miller*

2 cups fish stock (may be purchased
        in bouillon cube form)
16 tablespoons butter, clarified
8 pieces of fillet of sole
4 cups dry bread crumbs
6 tablespoons dry vermouth
1 cup dry white wine
2 shallots, finely chopped
2 cups créme fraîche (purchase or
        make at home)
2 teaspoons tomato paste
1 lemon
salt and pepper
1 tablespoon butter
3 tablespoons chopped chives

Créme Fraîche:

2 teaspoons buttermilk, or
        2 teaspoons sour cream
2 cups heavy cream

SQUID PATTIES

5 pounds squid
1 onion, chopped
3 eggs
2 cups bread crumbs
parsley, finely chopped
garlic, finely chopped
salt and pepper, to taste

Slice squid from head to tail and remove all viscera. Remove slippery membrane on outer skin. Wash thoroughly.

Boil squid for 3 minutes. Drain in colander until almost dry. Grind in meat grinder (medium size grind).

Mix all ingredients together and form into patties.

Fry in oil until brown.

Carmine Mineghino

TUNA PACÍFICO

1-1/3 cups rice, cooked
1/4 cup oil
1 cup chopped onion
1 cup chopped celery
1/2 clove garlic, minced
1 tablespoon flour
1 tablespoon salt
1 teaspoon chili powder
1-1/2 cups water
2 cups canned tomatoes
2 cups tuna fish, flaked

Cook rice according to package instructions.

Heat oil in a large skillet. Add onion, celery, garlic, and cooked rice. Sauté until onion is tender, stirring occasionally.

Add flour, salt, and chili powder and mix well. Add water and tomatoes and stir until thoroughly mixed. Bring quickly to a boil, cover tightly and simmer 10 minutes.

Add tuna and heat 1 minute longer.

Serves 6   *Betty Di Masi*

On Fish

"Purchase those which have just been caught. Of this you can judge by their being hard under the pressure of the finger. Fish lose their best flavor soon, and a few hours make a wide difference in the taste of some sorts."

—*The Young Housekeeper's Friend,* 1845

~Casseroles~

CASSEROLES/ONE-DISH MEALS

CASSEROLE ITALIANO

Cut zucchini into 1/4-inch slices and cook in a small amount of water until barely tender; drain.

Melt butter in heavy skillet. Add onion and garlic and cook and stir until onion is tender but not browned. Add meat and cook, stirring occasionally, until meat begins to brown.

Stir in rice and basil. Spread half the zucchini slices in a greased casserole. Top with meat mixture, then cottage cheese and remaining zucchini.

Combine soup and water and pour over mixture. Sprinkle with cheese.

Bake at 350 degrees for 35 to 40 minutes.

Emmy Ruud;

1-1/2 pounds zucchini
2 tablespoons butter
1 cup minced onion
bit of garlic, minced
1 pound ground beef
1 cup instant rice
1 teaspoon basil
1 pint creamed cottage cheese
1 can (10-1/2 ounce) tomato soup
2/3 cups water
1 cup shredded sharp cheese

CREAM CHEESE CASSEROLE

Brown meat. Add salt, pepper, garlic powder, and tomato sauce. Let simmer about 10 minutes.

Cook noodles according to package directions.

Butter a 2-quart casserole; alternate meat sauce and noodles in dish, ending with sauce.

Beat sour cream with cream cheese until smooth. Add onions and dab over top of casserole. Sprinkle grated cheese over the top.

Bake 30 minutes at 350 degrees.

Serves 6   *Ida Tandy*

1-1/2 pounds ground meat
salt, pepper, and garlic powder
    to taste
2 cans (8 ounces each) tomato sauce
    (or 1 can tomato
 sauce and 1 can tomato soup)
8 ounces noodles
1/2 pint sour cream
3 ounces cream cheese
6 green onions, chopped
1 cup cheddar cheese, grated

CHILI ENCHILADAS

1 tablespoon shortening or oil
1/2 large onion, chopped
1/2 pound ground beef
1 can (15-1/2 ounce) chili without
    beans
1/4 teaspoon salt and dash pepper
1/4 teaspoon crushed red pepper
    seeds (optional)
1/2 cup sour cream
1 package flour tortillas (or see recipe
    for Speedy Tortillas, below)
butter, melted
1/2 pound grated cheddar cheese

Speedy Tortillas

1 cup Bisquick
1/4 cup water
cornmeal

Heat oven to 350 degrees.

Sauté 2 tablespoons onion and ground beef in a little melted shortening or oil. Add the chili, salt, pepper, and pepper seeds. Cover and simmer for 10 minutes.

Remove from heat and add sour cream.

Brush tortillas on both sides with melted butter. Place 1 or 2 tablespoons chili mixture, 1 teaspoon onion, 1 teaspoon grated cheese in center of each tortilla. Roll up and place in 2 rows in a 13 x 9 x 2-inch baking dish. Spoon remaining chili mixture over the rolled tortillas, being careful to cover each tortilla. Sprinkle remaining onion and cheese over top.

Bake uncovered 15 minutes or until cheese melts.

Speedy Tortillas

Mix Bisquick and water. Knead about one minute on board lightly dusted with cornmeal. Shape into 8 balls. Flatten each ball into a 5-inch circle.

Bake on ungreased griddle until slightly browned on both sides. Keep soft between towels.

Serves 4   *Helen Homen*

EASY MEXICAN MACARONI CASSEROLE

1-1/2 cups uncooked elbow macaroni
1-1/2 pounds ground beef
2 tablespoons dried, minced onion
    (or 1 fresh onion, minced)
1 can (7-ounce) green chile salsa
2 cups grated sharp cheddar cheese
salt and pepper, to taste
1 can (10-ounce) Snap-E-Tom
    tomato cocktail
2 large tomatoes, sliced

Cook elbow macaroni, following package instructions, until almost tender. Drain.

Brown beef until crumbly. Drain excess fat.

Combine macaroni, meat, onion, salsa, 1 cup of grated cheese, salt, and pepper, spoon into a greased 1-1/2 quart shallow casserole. Pour Snap-E-Tom over mixture. Top with tomato slices and sprinkle with remaining grated cheese.

Bake in a pre-heated oven (350 degrees) for 30 to 35 minutes, or until bubbly.

Allow to stand for 5 minutes before serving.

Serves 6   *Cecily Mardesich*

TORTILLA CHIP CASSEROLE

Brown meat in skillet and drain. Add onion, olives, and tomato sauce, and season to taste.

In a bowl, mix cottage cheese, sour cream and green chile peppers.

Butter a 13 x 9-inch baking dish and fill with a layer of crushed tortilla chips, a layer of meat, one of the sour cream mixture, and one of jack cheese. Repeat layers, then sprinkle extra olives on top.

Bake uncovered at 350 degrees for 45 minutes.

Vicki Boutté

1-1/2 pounds ground meat
1/4 to 1/2 cup chopped onion
1 small can chopped olives
2 cans (8 ounce) tomato sauce
salt and pepper to taste
1/2 pint cottage cheese
1/2 pint sour cream
1 can diced green chiles (large or small, depending on spiciness desired)
1 bag (8 ounces) tortilla chips
1 pound shredded jack cheese

TEXAS HASH

Heat shortening. Add onion, green pepper and celery. Cook until tender, but not browned.

Push vegetables to side of skillet. Add meat and cook until it loses its pink color, stirring occasionally to keep crumbly.

Drain off excess fat and mix meat and vegetables. Cover and simmer over very low heat for 3 minutes.

Add tomatoes, chili powder, salt, and pepper and simmer additional 20 minutes.

Meanwhile, cook spaghetti according to package directions until just tender (do not overcook).

Combine spaghetti and meat sauce and turn into a 2-quart casserole. Chill until ready to bake, if desired.

Top with cheese and bake at 350 degrees 25 to 30 minutes, or until bubbling hot.

Serves 6 to 8

Pat Trutanich

3 tablespoons shortening
1 medium onion, chopped
1 small green pepper, chopped
2 or 3 stalks celery, chopped
1 pound ground beef
1 can (1 pound) tomatoes
1 teaspoon chili powder
1 teaspoon salt
1/2 teaspoon pepper
8 ounces spaghetti
1 cup coarsely shredded cheddar cheese

LAYERED ZUCCHINI CASSEROLE

1 pound hamburger
3 small zucchini, sliced and boiled
    3 minutes
1 can (7-ounce) diced Ortega chile
    peppers
1-1/2 cups cooked rice
1/2 pound grated jack cheese
2 large tomatoes, sliced
1/2 cup chopped onion
1/2 cup chopped green pepper
2 cups sour cream
1/2 teaspoon oregano
1/2 teaspoon garlic powder

Brown hamburger and drain off excess fat. Divide into 3 portions.

Slice the zucchini and boil for just 3 minutes.

Divide the zucchini, chile peppers, cooked rice, grated jack cheese, and tomatoes into thirds.

Combine the onion, green pepper, sour cream, oregano, and garlic powder, blend well and divide into thirds.

In a casserole, layer ingredients: 1/3 hamburger, 1/3 chile peppers, 1/3 rice, 1/3 zucchini, 1/3 sliced tomatoes, 1/3 sour cream mixture, and 1/3 cheese. Continue layering until all ingredients are used, ending with cheese.

Bake, covered, at 350 degrees for 45 minutes. Uncover and bake for an additional 15 minutes.

Serves 4   *Helen Homen*

DIXIE CASSEROLE

Medium White Sauce

3 tablespoons butter or margarine
3 tablespoons flour
2 cups milk
1/2 teaspoon salt
few grains pepper

Dixie Casserole

6 hard cooked eggs, sliced
1/2 pound sliced cooked ham
1-1/2 cups cooked or canned whole
    kernel corn
2 cups medium white sauce
1 cup soft bread crumbs
butter or margarine

Medium White Sauce

Melt butter. Blend in flour. Add milk gradually, season to taste.

Cook and stir for 5 minutes, or until thick.

Dixie Casserole

Hard-boil eggs. Peel and slice.

Place half of eggs and ham in a casserole. Add half of corn, then cover with half of white sauce. Layer with remaining eggs, ham, corn and sauce. Top with crumbs. Dot with butter.

Bake at 400 degrees for 15 minutes.

Claire Grainger

BAKED PORK CHOPS AND VEGETABLES CASSEROLE

Sprinkle pork chops with salt, pepper, and paprika. Brown in hot oil. Remove from pan and drain. Using the same skillet (with pork chop drippings poured out), over low heat, blend undiluted soup, sour cream and parsley until smooth. Add frozen potatoes and stir until all are coated with mixture. Then stir in drained green beans until they are coated. Stir the mixture gently so that both the potatoes and green beans keep their shapes. Place this mixture in the bottom of a shallow, ungreased casserole. Cover with the pork chops.

Place aluminum foil over the top and bake 45 minutes at 400 degrees, until sauce is bubbly and potatoes are hot and tender.

Serves 4 to 6   *Nancy Hedges*

4 to 6 pork chops (about 1 pound)
salt and pepper, to taste
paprika
2 teaspoons salad oil
1 can (10-1/2 ounce) cream of
    mushroom soup, undiluted
1 cup dairy sour cream
2 tablespoons parsley flakes
4 cups frozen hash brown potatoes
1 can (16 ounce) cut green beans,
    drained

PORK CHOP NOODLE CASSEROLE

Brown pork chops on one side. Turn and season with mustard.

Cook noodles according to directions on package.

Put noodles in 1-quart casserole. Top with chops, browned side next to noodles.

Pour soup, water, and onion into skillet. Stir and heat and then pour over chops in casserole. Cover.

Bake at 350 degrees for 1/2 hour. Uncover and bake another 1/2 hour to brown chops, or until chops are tender.

Serves 4   *Nancy Hedges*

4 pork chops, cut 1/2 inch thick
1 teaspoon prepared mustard
2 cups hot cooked noodles
1 can (10-1/2 ounce) cream of
    chicken soup
1 cup water
1 tablespoon chopped onion

129

SAUSAGE BRUNCH CASSEROLE

1 pound ground seasoned sausage
5 eggs
1 can (13-ounce) evaporated milk
1-1/2 slices bread, cubed
2 cups cheddar cheese, grated

Fry sausage until browned, then drain thoroughly on paper towels.

In a bowl, beat eggs and evaporated milk slightly. Add sausage, cubed bread, and cheddar cheese.

Pour into a buttered 9 x 9-inch casserole and cover with foil. May be prepared early and refrigerated.

In a 350-degree oven, bake uncovered for 45 minutes, or until firm.

Serves 6   *Nancy Hedges*

SCALLOPED HAM, POTATOES AND CARROTS

1 thin center slice uncooked ham
     (about 3/4 pound)
2-1/4 teaspoons flour
1 can condensed cream of mushroom
     soup, undiluted
1 cup milk
3 cups thinly sliced, pared potatoes
1 cup thinly sliced, pared carrots
1/4 cup minced onion
3/4 teaspoon salt
1/4 teaspoon pepper

Preheat oven to 375 degrees.

In a skillet, brown ham lightly on both sides. Remove. Cut into serving pieces.

Stir flour into drippings left in skillet. Add soup, and slowly stir in milk. Heat, stirring; bring to a boil.

Slice potatoes and carrots, and mince onions.

In 2-quart casserole, arrange layers of ham, potatoes, carrots, and onions, until all are used; sprinkle vegetables with combined salt and pepper.

Pour soup mixture over ham and vegetables.

Bake, covered, 1 hour.

Uncover and bake an additional 15 minutes, or until potatoes and carrots are tender.

Serves 3 to 4   *Helen Homen*

TAMALE PIE

Crust:

In a saucepan, over medium heat, combine cold water, salt, chili powder and corn meal. Cook until thickened (about 15 minutes). Stir frequently.

Line the sides and bottom of a buttered 2-quart casserole with 2/3 of the cornmeal mixture.

Filling:

Melt shortening in a skillet. Brown meat.

Chop green pepper, onion, and celery. Add to meat. Add olives, tomatoes, corn, garlic, chili powder, and salt. Simmer about 20 minutes.

Place filling in casserole on top of crust lining. Top with remaining crust, then sprinkle with cheese.

Bake in moderate 350-degree oven for about 45 minutes.

Serves 8   *Helen Homen*

Corn Meal Crust:

5 cups cold water
2 teaspoons salt
1 teaspoon chili powder
1-1/2 cups yellow corn meal

Filling:

2 tablespoons shortening
1 pound ground beef
1 cup chopped green pepper
1 cup chopped onion
1/2 cup chopped celery
1 cup sliced ripe olives
2 cups tomatoes
1 cup (8-3/4 ounces) cream-style corn
1 clove crushed garlic
1 tablespoon chili powder
2 teaspoons salt
1 cup grated cheese

TUNA PAPRIKASH

Cook noodles as directed on package, then drain.

In a large bowl, combine soup, mushrooms, sour cream, paprika, and lemon juice. Stir in tuna, onions and noodles.

Turn into a greased casserole. If desired, top with crumbs and butter.

Bake at 350 degrees for 35 to 40 minutes.

Emmy Ruud

1 package (8 ounces) noodles
1 can cream of mushroom soup, undiluted
1 can (3-ounce) mushrooms, undrained
2 cups sour cream
2 tablespoons paprika
1 tablespoon lemon juice
2 cans (7 ounces each) tuna
1 can (16-ounce) whole onions, drained

CHARISMATIC CHICKEN

1 package (9-ounce) artichoke hearts
3 tablespoons butter
2 cups fresh mushrooms, sliced
2 cups cooked chicken, cubed
1 envelope chicken gravy mix
1/8 teaspoon dried marjoram,
    crushed
4 ounces Swiss cheese, cubed
1 tablespoon dry sherry
1/2 cup soft bread crumbs

Cook artichoke hearts as directed and drain.

Slice mushrooms, and sauté in 2 tablespoons butter until tender.

Combine artichokes, mushrooms, and cooked and cubed chicken in a 1-1/2 quart casserole.

Prepare gravy as directed. Remove from heat. Add marjoram and cheese. Stir until cheese is melted. Add sherry; mix, then pour over chicken in casserole.

Combine remaining butter with bread crumbs and sprinkle over chicken.

Bake, uncovered, in a 375-degree oven for 30 minutes or until heated through.

Garnish with snipped parsley.

Serves 6   Nancy Hedges

CHICKEN AND ARTICHOKE CASSEROLE

1 broiler-fryer chicken (3-1/2 pounds),
    cut up
salt, pepper and paprika
4 tablespoons, or more, butter
1 can (14 ounces) artichoke hearts,
    drained and halved
1/4 pound mushrooms, sliced
2 tablespoons flour
3 tablespoons dry sherry
2/3 cup regular-strength chicken
    broth
1/4 teaspoon dry rosemary

Rinse chicken pieces; pat dry. Lightly sprinkle each piece with salt, pepper, and paprika. Set aside.

Melt the butter in a wide frying pan over medium heat; add chicken a few pieces at a time and cook until browned on all sides. Transfer to a shallow 3-quart casserole and tuck artichokes in between; set aside.

Drain off all but 3 tablespoons of the drippings from frying pan. Add the mushrooms and cook until golden. Stir flour into mushrooms and cook 1 minute. Add sherry, broth, and rosemary. Cook, stirring, until sauce thickens. Pour evenly over chicken and artichokes.

Cover and bake in a 375 degree oven for 40 minutes, or until thigh meat is no longer pink near bone when cut.

Serve with brown rice or pilaf.

Serves 4 to 6   Lucy DiMeglio

CHICKEN CACCIATORE CASSEROLE

Place chicken pieces in a shallow casserole. Sprinkle with salt, pepper, and garlic powder.

Cut green pepper in strips. Slice onion. Arrange both on top of chicken in casserole. Pour tomatoes over all.

Bake at 350 degrees for one hour, or until done.

Carole Haagenson

1 chicken, cut up
salt and pepper
garlic powder
1 green pepper, cut in strips
1 onion, sliced
1 large can (29 ounces) tomatoes

CHICKEN DIVAN CASSEROLE

Simmer chicken breasts in salted water for 45 minutes. Remove from water, drain, remove bones, and cut into large cubes.

Cook broccoli as directed and cut into large pieces.

Butter a 9 x 13-inch baking pan. Line pan with broccoli. Layer chicken over broccoli.

In a bowl, combine soup, lemon juice, and mayonnaise. Stir. Pour sauce over chicken. Add grated cheese on top.

Melt butter and mix with bread crumbs; sprinkle on top of casserole.

Bake at 350 degrees for 30 minutes.

Serve with salad and buttered rolls.

Serves 6 *Giovanna Mannino*

6 chicken breasts
3 packages (10-ounce) frozen
    broccoli spears
2 cans (10-ounce) cream of chicken
    soup
1 teaspoon lemon juice
1 cup mayonnaise
2 cups cheddar cheese, grated
2 tablespoons butter or margarine,
    melted
1/2 cup bread crumbs

CHICKEN ENCHILADAS

3 cups cooked cut-up chicken
1 chopped onion, chopped finely
1 cup chopped black olives
1 cup grated cheese
2 tablespoons butter or oil
1 can enchilada sauce
1 dozen flour tortillas
lettuce, shredded
sour cream

Cook chicken. Cut up into small pieces. Set aside.

Chop onions and olives, and grate cheese.

In a large skillet, sauté onions in butter or oil until transparent. Add chicken, grated cheese, and olives, and mix well.

In a saucepan, heat together enchilada sauce and 1/2 can of water.

Dip each tortilla in sauce, fill with chicken mixture, roll, and secure with a toothpick. Place in a buttered casserole, seam side down. Pour enough sauce over top of each roll to moisten.

Bake about 20 minutes at 300 degrees.

Serve with extra sauce, shredded lettuce, and sour cream.

Serves 4 to 6   *Helen Homen*

CHICKEN PARADISE

1 cup cooked chicken, diced
1/2 cup diced celery
1/4 cup diced onion
1/2 cup cashews
1 can golden mushroom soup
1/4 cup of broth (or water)
dash white pepper
1 can (3-ounce) of chow mein noodles

Cook chicken; dice. Set aside.

Dice celery and onion. Set aside.

Combine chicken, celery, onion, mushroom soup, broth (or water), half of the noodles, nuts (reserving some for use as a garnish), and white pepper. Mix well and put into a well greased casserole. Sprinkle the rest of the nuts on top.

Bake uncovered at 325 degrees for 30 minutes.

Serve immediately, using remainder of chow mein noodles as a side dish.

Serves 6   *J. Rothwell*

MEXICAN CHICKEN CASSEROLE

Salt chicken and wrap in foil. Bake one hour at 400 degrees. Save broth. When cool, bone and cut meat into bite-sized pieces.

Cut tortillas into strips 1 to 1-1/2 inches wide.

Mix soups, onions, milk, and salsa.

Place 1 or 2 tablespoons of the juice from the chicken in the bottom of a 2-quart baking dish. Then layer, starting with tortillas, then chicken, soup/salsa mixture, and grated cheese. Top with remaining cheese. Let stand in the refrigerator for 24 hours to allow the flavors to blend.

Bake at 300 degrees for 1 to 1-1/2 hours.

Serves 8   *Lupe Hulett*

4 whole chicken breasts
salt
1 dozen corn tortillas
1 can cream of chicken soup
1 can cream of mushroom soup
1 onion, chopped finely
1 cup milk
2 cans Ortega green chile salsa
1 pound cheddar cheese, grated

CHICKEN AND SOUR CREAM ENCHILADAS

Place chicken breasts in a large skillet; cover with cold water. Add salt to taste. Simmer for 30 to 40 minutes. Remove from skillet. Drain, cool, and dice into bite-sized pieces. Reserve any broth remaining in skillet for other uses.

Using same skillet, combine soup, diced chicken, sour cream, and half of the grated cheese and green chiles, and heat.

Dip each tortilla in hot fat. Remove to plate. Spoon 2 to 3 tablespoons of the cream mixture onto it, and roll up. Place, seam side down, in a buttered oblong pan or oven-proof baking dish. Enchiladas should fit snugly in the pan so they will keep their shape.

Pour remaining mixture over top of enchiladas. Sprinkle generously with remaining cheese.

Bake 25 to 30 minutes at 325 degrees.

Lucy DiMeglio

4 or 5 chicken breasts, cooked
    and diced
3 cans cream of chicken soup
1 pint sour cream
4 cups grated sharp cheddar cheese
1 can (4-ounce) diced Ortega chiles
15 corn tortillas
1/2 cup vegetable oil

SOUTHERN BAKED CHICKEN AND RICE

1 cup rice, uncooked
6 chicken breasts
salt and pepper to taste
Adolph's seasoned tenderizer
    (optional)
1 can cream of mushroom soup
1 can onion soup
1/2 can water

Place uncooked rice in bottom of roaster. Place chicken breasts on top of rice. Season with salt, pepper, and Adolph's.

Mix soups and water together and pour over chicken and rice.

Bake, covered, at 350 degrees for 1 to 1-1/2 hours.

Remove cover and cook 1/2 hour longer. You may have to add a small amount of water near the end of cooking time.

Serves 6   *Rosemarie Powers*

SHIPWRECK

2 potatoes, sliced
1 large onion, sliced
1 cup celery, sliced
1/2 pound hamburger
1/2 cup rice, uncooked
1 can red kidney beans
1 can tomato soup, undiluted

Layer the potatoes, onion, celery, hamburger, rice, and kidney beans into a buttered 2-quart casserole.

Pour soup over the ingredients.

Bake at 350 degrees for 1 to 1-1/2 hours.

Ruth Shannon

CHILE EGG BAKE

12 eggs
1/2 cup all-purpose flour
1 teaspoon baking powder
1 pound Monterey jack cheese,
    shredded
1 pint creamed small curd cottage
    cheese
1/2 cup melted butter or oleo
1 cup diced mild green chiles

Beat eggs until lemon in color; add rest of ingredients, mixing well. Add chiles last.

Pour into a 9 x 13-inch baking dish which has been generously buttered.

Bake at 350 degrees until center is firm and top is brown, about 45 minutes.

May be made the evening before serving (mixing only). However, add chiles just before baking the next morning.

Serves 12   *Nancy Hedges*

CHILE RELLENO CASSEROLE GILHOOLEY

Slice cheeses rather thick. Chop chiles.

Put half of chiles on bottom of 9 x 13-inch baking dish. Add cheddar slices, then remaining chiles, following with jack cheese slices.

Separate the eggs. To the yolks, add flour and evaporated milk. Blend well.

Beat whites and blend with yolk mixture. Pour over the casserole and let stand for an hour.

Bake at 325 degrees for 25 minutes.

Remove from oven and spread with salsa picante. Return to oven and bake for about 20 minutes more. Let stand awhile before serving.

Lydia Ramos Gilhooley

1 pound cheddar cheese
1 pound jack cheese
1 large can (7 ounces) of chiles
4 eggs, separated
1 tablespoon flour
1 large can evaporated milk
salsa picante, mild, medium, or hot,
    as preferred

CHILE RELLENO CASSEROLE MANNINO

Grease an 8 x 11-inch pan.

Slice chiles and place a layer of them on bottom of pan. Then layer the jack cheese, another layer of sliced chiles, and the cheddar cheese.

Combine eggs, milk, flour, baking powder, and garlic powder, and beat or blend. Pour over top of casserole.

Bake at 350 degrees for 30 minutes.

To make a sauce, combine tomato and picante sauces with oregano and simmer 15 minutes.

Serves 4 to 6   *Giovanna Mannino*

1 can (7 ounce) whole Ortega chiles,
    rinsed and drained
4 ounces grated cheddar cheese
4 ounces grated jack cheese
6 eggs, beaten
3/4 cup milk
1 tablespoon flour
1 teaspoon baking powder
1/2 teaspoon garlic powder
1 can (8-ounce) tomato sauce
1/4 cup picante sauce (salsa)
1 teaspoon oregano

COTTAGE CHEESE BRUNCH DELIGHT

1 pound jack cheese, shredded
1 cup milk
1 cup flour
1 pint cottage cheese
6 eggs, lightly beaten
1/2 cup butter, melted

Shred the jack cheese into a bowl. Add the milk, flour, cottage cheese, lightly beaten eggs, and half the melted butter.

Spread remaining half of melted butter into a 12 x 7-inch baking dish.

Pour cheese mixture into dish and bake at 375 degrees for 40 minutes or until golden and set.

Serves 12 to 15   *Nancy Hedges*

MONTEREY OVEN BRUNCH

8 slices bacon
4 green onions, thinly sliced
8 eggs
1 cup milk
2 cups shredded Monterey jack cheese

Fry bacon until brown, drain, and crumble.

Slice onions and sauté in a small amount of bacon drippings until limp.

Beat eggs with milk; stir in bacon, onions and 1-1/2 cups cheese.

Pour into greased 2-quart baking dish.

Bake, uncovered, in 350-degree oven for 35 to 40 minutes, or until mixture is set and top lightly browned.

When almost done, sprinkle with remaining cheese and return to oven until cheese melts. Serve immediately.

Serves 4 to 6   *Nancy Hedges*

RANCHERO SOUFFLÉ

Sauce:

Pour tomatoes into a pan and mash with a fork. Chop onions and add to tomatoes. Add tomato paste, diced green chiles, oregano, and cayenne pepper. Bring to a boil.

Soufflé:

Grease a 9 x 13-inch baking dish. Arrange a layer of sliced bread on bottom. Spread with half each of the sauce, cheese, and bacon. Repeat the layers.

Beat eggs, and add milk and mustard. Pour over casserole. Cover and chill 8 to 24 hours.

Bake, uncovered, in 350-degree oven until hot and puffed in center, about 55 minutes.

Let stand 20 minutes, then cut into squares.

Serves 8 to 10   *Clara Love*

Sauce:

1 can (15-ounce) tomatoes, mashed
1 large onion, chopped
1 can tomato paste
1 can diced green chiles
1 teaspoon dry oregano
1/8 teaspoon cayenne pepper

Soufflé:

3/4 pound loaf sour dough bread
1 pound sharp cheddar cheese, shredded
1 pound bacon, crisply cooked & crumbled
6 eggs
3 cups milk
2 teaspoons dry mustard

BLINTZ CASSEROLE

Melt half of the stick margarine in a 10 x 12-inch casserole. Roll the blintzes in the margarine to coat them; then arrange in the casserole. Beat the eggs. Mix in the rest of the ingredients. Pour over blintzes.

Bake 1 hour at 350 degrees.

Serves 8   *Selma Streicher*

1/4 pound margarine
12 blintzes (may use frozen)
4 eggs
1 large carton sour cream
1/4 cup sugar
1 tablespoon orange juice or
    1 teaspoon vanilla

SEAFOOD CASSEROLE

1 can (6-1/2 ounces) crab meat
1 can (4-1/2 ounces) shrimp
3/4 cup mayonnaise
3/4 canned milk
1 to 1-1/2 cups soft bread crumbs
   (no crusts)
1 grated onion
garlic to taste
1/2 cup cracker crumbs
1/4 cup melted butter or margarine

Combine ingredients (except cracker crumbs and butter). Mix well and place in a shallow casserole.

Then combine cracker crumbs and butter; spread over mixture in casserole.

Bake at 350 degrees for 20 minutes.

Cut into squares to serve.

Variation: May also be baked in a pie plate and cut into wedges.

Serves 4 to 6   *Ida Tandy*

~Vegetables~

VEGETABLES

ARTICHOKES DALMATIAN STYLE

Rinse artichokes with cold water and cut off stems. Using a sharp knife or scissors, cut off sharp tips and remove tougher outer leaves. Gently spread apart leaves to leave space for stuffing.

Combine bread crumbs, onion, garlic, cheese, salt, pepper, and peas; toss to blend thoroughly.

Heat broth and water in a medium size saucepan. Liquid should reach to about 3/4 of the artichokes. Stuff artichokes with bread crumb mixture and place upright in broth to cook. Pour 1 tablespoon oil over each artichoke. Bring to a boil and lower heat. Simmer, covered, for 1 hour or until leaves come off easily. Do not stir; shake pan to prevent sticking.

Serves 4   *Dolores Lisica*

4 artichokes
1/2 cup fresh bread crumbs
1/2 small onion, minced
2 cloves garlic, pressed
2 tablespoons grated Parmesan cheese
salt and pepper to taste
1 cup fresh or frozen green peas
1 can chicken broth
2 soup cans water
4 tablespoons olive oil or more (optional)

ASPARAGUS

"Wash it, trim off the white ends, and tie it up in bunches with a twine or a strip of old cotton. Throw them into boiling water with salt in it. Boil twenty-five minutes or half an hour. Have ready two or three slices of toasted bread, dip them in the water and lay them in the dish. Spread them with butter and lay the bunches of asparagus upon the toast. Cut the strings with a scissors and draw them out without breaking the stalks; lay thin shavings of butter over the asparagus, and send it to the table."

Copied from *The Young Housekeeper's Friend*, written in 1845.

Margretta Marshall

NEW ENGLAND BAKED BEANS

1 pound white beans (such as
     Great Northerns)
1/2 teaspoon baking soda
1 pound salt pork, slashed
1 cup white sugar
2 tablespoons molasses
salt
1 large onion, sliced

Place beans in pan and cover with enough water to leave beans covered with two inches of water. Soak overnight.

In the morning, boil in the same water for 10 minutes and drain.

Add warm tap water to cover beans again and bring to a second boil. When the water boils, add baking soda. Boil gently for about 20 minutes. Drain and wash well.

Add fresh water to cover, bring to a boil for a few minutes; remove from heat.

Add salt pork, pushed down into beans, sugar, molasses and salt. Mix up and add enough water to make very juicy. Slice one onion and place on top of the beans.

Transfer the beans to a shallow baking dish and bake, uncovered, 8 hours at 350 degrees, adding water as necessary to keep them from getting too dry.

Variations: Cook beans for 8 hours in a slow cooker, and then bake two hours in oven at 350 degrees; or cook beans 1 hour in a pressure cooker and 2 hours in oven at 350 degrees.

Jacqueline P. Smith

OLD FASHIONED BAKED BEANS

1 pound navy or pea beans
5 cups water
2 teaspoons dry mustard
1/4 teaspoon pepper
1 tablespoon salt
3 onions, quartered
1/4 cup brown sugar
1/4 cup molasses
2 tablespoons sweet pickle juice or
     2 tablespoons vinegar with a
     speck of cinnamon and cloves
1/4 pound bacon or salt pork
pepper

Pick over beans, discarding bad looking ones; wash. Cover with 3 cups water. Soak 8 hours or overnight.

Add 2 cups water, mustard, pepper, salt, quartered onions, brown sugar, molasses, and sweet pickle juice (or vinegar/cinnamon/cloves). Boil, covered, about 1 hour, or until skins of beans begin to wrinkle.

Preheat oven to 250 degrees. Cut bacon into 1/2-inch pieces. Place in a 2-quart bean pot. Cover with hot beans and their liquid. Generously sprinkle with pepper. Bake, covered, 6 to 8 hours or until tender.

When beans are two-thirds baked, add about 3/4 cup water, or enough to just cover.

Uncover last 1/2 hour of baking.

Serves 4 to 6   *Helen Homen*

THIS OLD HOUSE CHILI BEANS

A restaurant called "This Old House" in San Luis Obispo serves this bean dish.

Sauté onion in butter until tender.

Stir in brown sugar until well mixed.

In a large saucepan, combine rest of ingredients and mix well. Stir in onion mixture until well mixed. Cover and simmer over low heat until meat is cooked, about 30 to 35 minutes.

Refrigerate overnight to blend flavors.

Reheat to serve.

Serves 8   Lillian Peterson Drenckhahn

1 small onion, diced
2 tablespoons butter or margarine
1/2 cup brown sugar, packed
2 cans (1 pound 13 ounces each) pinto beans
1 cup catsup
1/4 pound ground beef
1/4 pound bacon, chopped
1-1/2 teaspoons chili powder
1-1/2 teaspoons garlic powder
1-1/2 teaspoons onion powder
1 teaspoon hot pepper sauce

GREEN BEANS, SQUASH AND POTATOES

Cook green beans about 10 minutes.

Cut potatoes lengthwise into 4 or 5 slices. Cut zucchini into chunks. Add to green beans and cook until tender.

When cooked, drain and place back into cooking pan. Add salt, pepper, and olive oil. Mix gently, heat for 2 or 3 minutes, and serve.

Serves 6   Minnie Cvitanich

2 pounds green beans
2 medium potatoes, cut lengthwise in 4 or 5 slices
3 zucchini squash, cut in chunks
salt and pepper, to taste
2 to 4 tablespoons pure olive oil

GREEN BEANS WITH POTATOES

Wash green beans; remove tips and strings.

Peel potatoes and slice lengthwise into 4 pieces each. Place in salted in a saucepan in boiling water and cook 8 to 10 minutes.

Add beans and cook together until beans are tender, but firm; about 15 minutes.

Drain, add pressed garlic, salt and pepper, and olive oil. Gently mash some of the potatoes with a wooden spoon and stir to combine.

Return to heat and warm through for about 2 minutes.

Serves 4   Jermina Ursich

1-1/2 pounds green beans
2 medium potatoes
2 cloves garlic, pressed
salt and pepper, to taste
3 to 5 tablespoons olive oil

ETLI TAZE FASULYE
Green Beans with Meat

Turkey

1 large onion, chopped
4 tablespoons butter or margarine
2 pounds fresh green beans
1 pound lamb cubes, cut from leg
    or shoulder
1 can (8 ounce) tomato sauce
1 can (16-ounce) stewed tomatoes
1 cup water
1 teaspoon salt
1/4 teaspoon cayenne pepper

In a stew pot, sauté chopped onion in butter for 10 to 15 minutes.

String beans and cut lengthwise. Cube lamb, removing as much fat as possible. Add beans and lamb to pot and sauté until meat absorbs its own juice and beans turn yellow.

Add remaining ingredients. Cover and simmer 1 to 1-1/2 hours or until meat is quite tender. You may add more water, if necessary. If you prefer, simmer the meat in a 350-degree oven.

Ruth Hamren

WHITE BEANS
a la Athens Hilton

Greece

1-1/2 cup large white dry beans
1 medium onion, chopped
1/4 cup olive oil
1 clove garlic, finely minced
2 tablespoons tomato paste
2 cups cold water
salt and pepper to taste
chopped parsley

Cover the beans with water and soak overnight.

Drain the beans.

In a large saucepan, sauté the onion in the olive oil until it is tender but not brown.

Add the garlic, tomato paste, and drained beans to onion mixture and cover with 2 cups of cold water. Simmer, uncovered, for 1 hour, or until beans are tender.

Season with salt and pepper, and sprinkle with parsley.

Serves 6   *Mrs. C.J. Petrofanis*

LIMA BEAN-SOUR CREAM CASSEROLE

Cover lima beans with water and soak overnight.

In the morning, drain and put in 2-quart saucepan. Cover with fresh water and bring to a boil; simmer until tender not mushy (45 minutes to 1 hour).

Drain, and rinse in hot water. Pour beans into 1-1/2 quart casserole.

Mix together brown sugar, flour, salt, molasses, and sour cream. Add to beans; mix gently.

Bake at 350 degrees for 1 hour.

Serves 8   *Mildred Davis*

1 pound dried tiny lima beans
water to cover
3/4 cup brown sugar
2 teaspoons flour
1 tablespoon salt
1 tablespoon molasses
1 cup sour cream

TASTY CHILI BEANS

Cook ham hock separately until tender, changing water once or twice. Cut off meat and skin from hock and dice both into bite-sized pieces. Set aside.

In a deep pot, braise ground beef; pour off grease. Sprinkle with cumin, salt, and pepper to taste. Add beans and ham hock meat and skin pieces.

Place tomatoes in a blender 2 or 3 at a time and chop. *Do Not Purée.* Add chopped tomatoes and reserved juice to bean/meat mixture. Bring to a simmer.

Add diced onion, oregano, garlic powder, salsa, and more cumin to taste. Simmer for an hour without stirring too much, so as not to break the beans up.

Serve with cornbread and salad.

Megan Flynn Johnson

1 ham hock (unsmoked)
1 pound ground beef
cumin
salt and pepper to taste
2 cans (8 ounces each) pinto beans
1 can (12-ounce) tomatoes, drained;
    liquid reserved
1 onion, diced
oregano
garlic powder
1 bottle La Victoria "Ranchera"
    Chili Salsa

CORN PUDDING

In a bowl, beat eggs. Add melted butter, sugar, salt, flour, and milk; mix well. Add corn and stir well.

Pour into a greased 1-1/2 quart casserole.

Bake at 350 degrees for 30 minutes, or until firm.

Serves 6   *Anne Terry*

3 eggs
1 tablespoon melted butter or
    margarine
1 tablespoon sugar
dash salt
1 tablespoon flour
1 cup milk
1 cup whole kernel or cream-style
    corn

BROCCOLI AND CORN CASSEROLE

2 packages chopped frozen broccoli
1/4 pound butter
2 cans (16-ounce) cream style corn
2 slices day old bread, cubed
4 eggs
bread crumbs

Cook broccoli until tender, then drain.

Place in a large mixing bowl with 3/4 stick of butter. Add corn, cubed bread, and eggs. Mix well. Pour mixture into a buttered casserole.

Brown bread crumbs in remaining butter and sprinkle on top of broccoli and corn mixture.

Bake at 350 degrees for 45 minutes: covered for 30 minutes, uncovered for last 15 minutes.

Zella Splittgerber

CORN AND BROCCOLI DISH

1 package (10-ounce) frozen chopped broccoli (nice size bunch of fresh broccoli, steamed and cut into small pieces can be used)
1 can (16-ounce) creamed corn
2 eggs, beaten
3/4 cup saltine crackers, crumbled
1/2 cup melted margarine
1 tablespoon minced onion, dried or fresh
salt and pepper
grated cheese (any kind)

Steam broccoli. Drain and cut into small pieces.

Combine broccoli, creamed corn, and beaten eggs. Stir well.

Add most of crumbled crackers and melted margarine (reserve some of each for topping) and stir.

Add minced onion, salt, and pepper. Mix well.

Pour into a greased 1-1/2 quart casserole or baking pan. Sprinkle with remaining crackers and margarine, and top with grated cheese.

Bake in 350-degree oven for 30 to 35 minutes, or until top is light brown and mixture is firm.

Serve hot.

Note: Can be prepared ahead of time and refrigerated. Add about 5 more minutes cooking time.

Anne Terry

WALNUT BROCCOLI

Cook broccoli until just tender. Drain and place in a shallow, greased 9 x 13-inch baking dish.

In a saucepan, melt 1/2 cup butter. Blend in flour and chicken bouillon. Simmer, stirring, for 3 to 4 minutes.

Blend in milk. Cook, stirring, until thickened. Pour over broccoli.

Heat water and 6 tablespoons butter together and pour over stuffing mix. Stir in nuts. Top broccoli with this mixture.

Bake in a pre-heated oven at 400 degrees for 20 minutes or until thoroughly heated and stuffing begins to brown.

Note: Can be refrigerated unbaked overnight and baked the next day for a slightly longer period of time.

Serves 8 to 10   *Nancy Hedges*

3 packages (10-1/2 ounce) frozen,
    chopped broccoli
1/2 cup butter
1/4 cup all-purpose flour
2 teaspoons instant chicken bouillon
2 cups milk
2/3 cup water
6 tablespoons butter
2/3 of a 7-ounce package fine bread
    stuffing mix
2/3 cup chopped walnuts

CARROT CASSEROLE

Prepare stuffing as directed on package and set aside.

Slice carrots and place in a saucepan with a little bit of water. Cook until barely tender on top of stove, or 6 to 7 minutes in a microwave oven. Drain.

In a large saucepan, melt 2 tablespoons butter; add chopped onion and celery and cook until tender, but not browned.

Add soup and shredded cheese (less 1/8 cup of cheese reserved for top) and stir until cheese is melted; add carrots and mix. Season to taste.

Pour into 2-quart casserole. Cover carrots evenly with stuffing mixture. Sprinkle remaining cheese on top.

Bake at 350 degrees for 25 minutes.

Variation: 1 can (10- or 13-ounce) of albacore tuna can be substituted for cheese; should be added to casserole along with carrots.

Serves 6   *Betty Spence*

3 cups (1 package) Stove Top
    stuffing mix
4 cups sliced carrots
2 tablespoons butter or margarine
1 cup chopped onion
1 cup celery, chopped
1 can (10-3/4 ounces) celery soup
3/4 cup shredded cheddar cheese
salt and pepper to taste
oregano, thyme and parsley, if desired

MARILYN'S COMPANY CARROTS

2 pounds carrots
1/2 cup mayonnaise
1 tablespoon horseradish
1 tablespoon minced onion
1 tablespoon parsley flakes
salt and pepper to taste
1/2 cup buttered bread crumbs

Cook carrots in salted water until tender but crisp. Reserve 1/4 cup liquid from cooked carrots. Cut carrots into strips.

Combine liquid with mayonnaise, horseradish, minced onion, and parsley flakes. Season to taste. Pour sauce over carrot strips in casserole and top with bread crumbs.

Bake at 350 degrees for 20 minutes.

Betty McKinney

MUSHROOM CASSEROLE

1 pound mushrooms
4 tablespoons butter or margarine
8 slices white or wheat bread,
    buttered
1/2 cup chopped onions
1/2 cup chopped celery
1/2 cup chopped green pepper
1/2 cup mayonnaise
1/4 teaspoon pepper
2 eggs, slightly beaten
1-1/2 cups milk
1 can cream of mushroom soup
1/2 cup shredded cheddar cheese

Slice mushrooms and sauté in about 4 tablespoons butter, until most of liquid is absorbed.

Chop onions, celery, and green pepper, and add to mushrooms. Mix. Add mayonnaise and pepper, and mix well.

Butter bread slices. Cut 3 slices into 1-inch squares and place in bottom of a greased 2-1/2 quart casserole.

Turn 1/2 of the mushroom mixture into the casserole.

Cut 3 more bread slices into squares and place on top of mushroom mixture. Top with remaining mushroom mixture.

Beat the eggs slightly. Add milk and cream of mushroom soup. Mix well, then pour into casserole.

Refrigerate at least one hour, or overnight.

Dice remaining 2 slices of buttered bread and place on top of casserole.

Bake, uncovered, at 350 degrees for 40 to 50 minutes. Remove from oven and sprinkle cheese over top. Bake 10 minutes longer.

Serves 8   *Zella Splittgerber*

POTATO CHEESE CASSEROLE

Preheat oven to 450 degrees.

Slice potatoes and place in a buttered 2-quart baking dish. Pour melted butter over the top. Season with salt and pepper.

Bake 20 to 30 minutes or until tender.

Remove from oven and sprinkle with cheese. Bake additional 5 minutes or until cheese is melted.

Bernice Cunningham

6 medium or 3 very large potatoes, sliced
1/4 cup butter, melted
1/2 teaspoon regular or seasoned salt
1/8 teaspoon white pepper
1 cup grated Swiss cheese
3 tablespoon freshly grated Parmesan cheese

COLCANNON

Ireland

Place unpeeled potatoes in a large saucepan with enough water to barely cover. Bring to a boil, reduce heat, and simmer 35 to 40 minutes or until potatoes are soft.

Add cabbage 15 to 20 minutes before potatoes are done. Drain, peel potatoes and mash with half of the butter. Add salt, pepper, and chopped onion, mixing well.

Chop cabbage coarsely and add to potato mixture, mixing lightly but thoroughly.

Place mixture in greased baking pan and bake at 350 degrees for 7 to 10 minutes or until heated through.

Make a well in center of each serving and pour in some of the remaining melted butter.

Serves 6

Betty Di Masi

6 potatoes
1 small head cabbage
1/2 cup butter, melted
1-1/2 teaspoons salt
1/2 teaspoon pepper
1 onion, chopped

ITALIAN POTATO PIE

Italy

bread crumbs
6 large potatoes
1/4 pound butter
4 eggs
1/4 cup milk
1/4 cup grated Parmesan cheese
1/2 cup salami, diced
1/2 pound Mozzarella, diced
salt and pepper to taste
2 to 3 teaspoons butter (to dot on finished pie)

Grease pie pan; sprinkle with bread crumbs.

Preheat oven to 350 degrees.

Boil potatoes; rice or mash while hot and melt butter over hot potatoes. Add eggs, milk, and grated Parmesan cheese until blended. Mix in diced salami and Mozzarella. Season to taste with salt and pepper.

Pour filling into prepared pie pan. Sprinkle top with bread crumbs and dot with butter.

Bake at 350 degrees until brown.

This is a recipe my grandmother brought with her from Ischia, Italy.

Giovanna Mannino

CARROT AND POTATO SAUTÉ

2 carrots
2 medium potatoes
1-1/2 tablespoons olive oil or butter
1 small onion, chopped finely
salt and pepper to taste

Boil together whole carrots and potatoes. Remove when tender and mash lightly with a potato masher. Leave some small lumps.

Sauté finely chopped onion in oil or butter until soft and golden. Add salt and pepper. Add potatoes and carrots, and stir lightly to blend. Cook for about 1 minute longer.

Serve with boiled chicken or beef.

Serves 2 to 4   *Dolores Lisica*

SCALLOPED POTATOES—QUICK AND EASY

Using a large cast iron skillet, melt butter on medium heat. Add sliced onions and sauté until soft and golden, not browned.

Peel potatoes, then slice into 1/4-inch slices.

Sprinkle flour on onions and stir until well mixed. Add milk; stir and bring to a simmer. Add potatoes, salt, pepper, and white pepper to taste, and a dash of nutmeg. Add water. Bring to a boil, then lower heat to medium. Stir often. You may cover skillet at this point. Cook for about 30 minutes.

Grated cheddar cheese may be added last 5 minutes of cooking time.

Serves 4   *Dolores Lisica*

1-1/2 tablespoons butter
1/2 medium onion, sliced
3 medium potatoes
1 tablespoon flour
1 cup milk
salt, pepper, white pepper
dash of nutmeg
1 cup water, or more as needed
1/2 cup grated cheddar cheese
    (optional)

SWEET POTATO CASSEROLE

Mix sweet potatoes, eggs, 1 cup sugar, margarine, salt, and vanilla with a mixer; add cream until 'sloppy."

Pour into a buttered 9-inch square pan or a 1-1/2 quart casserole.

Combine flour, margarine, and 1/2 cup brown sugar; mix with a fork. Add chopped pecans; mix. Sprinkle evenly over top of casserole.

Bake, uncovered, for 35 minutes at 350 degrees.

Rosemarie Powers

3 cups cooked sweet potatoes
3 eggs
1 cup sugar
1/2 stick soft margarine
1/2 teaspoon salt
1 teaspoon vanilla
1/2 to 3/4 cup cream
2 tablespoons flour
1/4 stick margarine
1/2 cup brown sugar
1/2 cup chopped pecans

DALMATIAN SAUERKRAUT

2 large cans sauerkraut
2 slices bacon, diced
1 tablespoon olive oil
2 pounds fresh spare ribs
1 large onion, chopped fine
3 cloves garlic, minced
2 tablespoons fresh parsley, minced
3 tablespoons tomato sauce
1 apple, peeled and grated
1/4 teaspoon salt
1/4 teaspoon pepper
2 cups chicken broth

Rinse sauerkraut in cold water. Drain and set aside.

Place diced bacon and olive oil in a large skillet and heat. Add spareribs; cook until browned, about 10 minutes.

Add chopped onion, minced garlic, and minced parsley; brown with the ribs about 5 minutes, stirring often.

Add sauerkraut and cook 15 minutes, stirring frequently.

Add tomato sauce, grated apple, salt, pepper, and chicken broth. Mix well, cover, and cook over a low flame for about 1-1/2 hours, or until spareribs are tender and liquid absorbed. Stir frequently.

Serves 6 to 8   *Mary Lou Nizetich*

SLAV SAUERKRAUT

2 cans (27 ounces each) sauerkraut
2 small onions, chopped
3 cloves of garlic, chopped
4 slices bacon, chopped
2 teaspoons flaked parsley or
     4 to 5 sprigs of fresh parsley
dash of pepper
1/8 teaspoon each nutmeg,
     cinnamon, and allspice
1 can consommé
1 chicken bouillon cube

Lightly rinse sauerkraut; drain and set aside.

Chop onions, garlic, bacon, and fresh parsley. Brown in a large skillet. Add sauerkraut, pepper, nutmeg, cinnamon, and allspice. Mix and continue browning for about 10 to 15 minutes.

Add consommé and bouillon cube, and simmer for about 1 hour or more.

Minnie Cvitanich

STEWED TOMATOES

"Scald them in order to remove the skins. Cut them up and put them into a saucepan, with a little salt, a bit of butter, and some fine crumbs of bread or pounded cracker. Let them stew gently an hour; if you like them sweet, add sugar ten minutes before serving."

Copied from *The Young Housekeeper's Friend*, written in 1845.

Margretta Marshall

CARMELA'S VEGETABLE AND CHEESE PIE

Sauté garlic in butter and olive oil. Discard garlic.

Stir in chopped green onions, grated zucchini, and grated carrots. Cook, stirring, until most of liquid is absorbed. Set aside.

In a large bowl, beat eggs. Add cheeses. Beat until well blended. Mix in zucchini mixture. Season to taste.

Line a buttered 13 x 9-inch baking dish with 6 to 8 sheets of filo, brushing each with melted butter. Top with zucchini mixture. Cover with remaining sheets of filo, brushing each sheet with melted butter. Cut into squares with sharp knife before baking.

Bake at 350 degrees for 45 to 55 minutes.

Note: Can be frozen before baking.

Carmela Castagnola

2 cloves garlic
butter
olive oil
1/2 cup finely chopped green onions
3 cups grated zucchini
3 cups grated carrots
5 eggs
1 pound ricotta cheese
1 cup shredded jack cheese
1/2 cup grated Parmesan cheese
1 package filo dough

SPINACH FRITTERS

Cook spinach according to package directions; drain and set aside to cool.

Beat eggs and milk together; add bread crumbs, grated cheese, chopped parsley, minced garlic, salt, and pepper. Then add spinach. Make small patties and brown in oil.

Virginia Manzella

2 packages (10-ounce) frozen chopped spinach
3 eggs
1/2 cup milk
1/2 cup bread crumbs
1/2 cup grated cheese (Romano & Parmesan)
1 teaspoon chopped parsley
1/2 clove garlic, minced
salt and pepper to taste

SPINACH PIE

Cook spinach according to package directions; drain, squeeze out moisture, and set aside.

Cook bacon; drain on paper towel, crumble, and set aside.

Mix ingredients in order and put in pie crust.

Bake at 350 degrees for one hour.

Kathy Rogers

1 package frozen spinach
6 strips bacon, crumbled
12 ounces Swiss cheese, grated
2 tablespoons flour, to toss with cheese
1 cup milk or cream
3 eggs, beaten
1/2 teaspoon salt
dash of pepper
dash of nutmeg
1 unbaked 9-inch pie crust

SPINACH PUDDING

1 package (10-ounce) frozen chopped
    spinach
3/4 cup milk
1 tablespoon butter or margarine
2 eggs, lightly beaten
3/4 cup shredded Swiss cheese
1/2 teaspoon salt
pepper
1 tablespoon finely chopped onion
1 can (2-ounce) mushrooms, drained
nutmeg

Cook spinach according to package directions and drain well.

Heat milk and butter until milk is hot and butter has melted; remove from heat and stir in spinach and remaining ingredients, except nutmeg. Blend well. Turn into buttered 1-quart casserole. Sprinkle top with a dash of nutmeg and place dish in a pan of hot water.

Bake at 325 degrees 50 minutes to 1 hour or until knife inserted near center comes out clean.

Eloise Knoll

SPINACH AND RICE CASSEROLE

3 cups cooked rice
3 cups chopped spinach
1 onion, finely chopped
4 tablespoon butter
2 cups grated jack cheese

Cook rice according to instructions on package. Place a layer of half the rice in bottom of a well buttered 2-quart baking dish.

Cook chopped spinach according to package instructions; drain.

Chop onion finely. Sauté in 1 tablespoon butter. Add spinach, mix well, and layer half of the mixture over rice in casserole. Sprinkle with 1/2 of grated cheese.

Repeat layers and dot with butter.

Bake at 350 degrees for 20 minutes.

Betty Peterson

On Vegetables

"After being well washed, they should be laid in water, excepting corn and peas, which should be husked and shelled with clean hands, and not washed, as some of the sweetness is thereby extracted."

—*The Young Housekeeper's Friend*, 1845

SPINACH SOUFFLÉ

Cook chopped spinach per package instructions. Drain.

In a large bowl, beat eggs; add spinach, butter, flour, salt, and pepper and blend. Add cubed cheese and cottage cheese. Mix well.

Bake in an 8 x 10-inch casserole at 350 degrees for 35 to 40 minutes or until golden brown.

Top with 2 mashed hard-cooked eggs, if desired.

Nancy Hedges

1 package frozen chopped spinach, cooked and drained
3 eggs
1/4 cup butter
4 tablespoons flour
salt and pepper to taste
1/4 pound American cheese, cubed
1/4 pound brick cheese, cubed
1 pound carton cottage cheese
2 hard-cooked eggs, if desired

SPINACH STRATA

If fresh spinach, cook and drain. If frozen spinach, thaw; then squeeze moisture out.

Cover bottom of greased, shallow 2-quart baking dish with half of the slices of bread.

In a medium size saucepan, sauté chopped onion in margarine and remove from pan. In same pan, add spinach, dill weed, salt, and pepper and sauté slightly.

Spread onion/spinach mixture over bread layer. Cover with one cup of shredded cheese. Add second layer of bread slices.

Beat eggs; mix in milk. Pour over casserole and chill at least one hour or overnight.

Sprinkle with remaining cheese and bake, covered, at 375 degrees for 45 minutes.

Cool, still covered, ten minutes before cutting in squares. Aluminum foil does well for cover. Cooling ten minutes still covered makes it easy to "peel off".

Serves 6

Mary Carpenter

3/4 cup cooked fresh spinach or 2 packages (10-ounce) frozen chopped spinach
1/2 loaf day-old French bread or any other bread, sliced thinly
1 cup chopped onion
2 tablespoons margarine
1 teaspoon dill weed
1 teaspoon salt
dash of pepper
6 ounces or 1-1/2 cups Swiss cheese, shredded
3 eggs, beaten
2-1/2 cups milk

RICE JARDIN

1-1/4 cups cooked rice
3/4 cup onions, chopped
1 cup zucchini, thinly sliced
1 tablespoon safflower oil
1/2 cup whole kernel corn, drained
1/3 cup tomatoes, chopped
1/2 cup celery, chopped
1/4 teaspoon salt
1/4 teaspoon oregano
1/4 teaspoon parsley and/or basil
1 piece green chile (1 x 2-inch),
    chopped

Cook rice according to package instructions.

In a large skillet, sauté chopped onions and thinly sliced zucchini in oil until tender. Add corn, chopped tomatoes, chopped celery, cooked rice, salt, oregano, parsley, and basil. Cover and simmer 15 minutes. To add a bit of zip, chop up a 1 x 2-inch piece of green chile and add before simmering.

Serves 2   Betty Spence

CRANBERRY SQUASH

4 cups mashed cooked acorn squash
1-1/2 cups halved raw cranberries
4 tablespoons melted butter or
    margarine
2 eggs
1/2 cup sugar
salt and pepper to taste
brown sugar
nutmeg
chopped pecans (optional)

Cook squash; mash. Halve raw cranberries. Melt butter.

In a large bowl, beat squash with eggs and 3 tablespoons melted butter; stir in cranberries and sugar. Add salt and pepper to taste. Spoon into greased casserole. Drizzle top with remaining melted butter, touch of brown sugar and nutmeg. Chopped pecans can also be added, if desired.

Bake uncovered in 400-degree oven for 30 minutes.

Betty Di Masi

SQUASH CASSEROLE

4 cups squash (yellow & zucchini)
1 pepper, chopped
1 onion, chopped
1-1/2 cups Pepperidge Farm stuffing
    mix, or bread crumbs plus 1
    teaspoon poultry seasoning or
    ground sage.
1/2 stick margarine, melted
1 can cream of mushroom soup

Slice squash. Chop pepper and onion and add to squash. Mix well. Add 1 cup of stuffing mix and toss to combine. Melt margarine and pour over mixture. Toss. Pour in undiluted mushroom soup and mix well.

Pour into a greased 10 x 12-inch baking dish. Sprinkle with remaining stuffing mix.

Bake at 350 degrees for 45 minutes.

Delia Du Ross

ZUCCHINI AND BACON

Wash and drain zucchini. Steam in boiling water for 3 minutes. Drain and place in Dutch oven. Add tomatoes with half the juice removed.

Fry bacon until crisp. Drain on paper towel, then crumble and set aside.

Remove all but 3 tablespoons bacon fat from frying pan, then sauté onions, bell pepper, celery, and garlic, in bacon fat; add to zucchini and tomatoes, with bay leaves and other seasonings. Simmer for about 5 minutes until vegetables are crisp and tender. Stir in bacon and serve.

Josephine Pittman

6 medium zucchini, sliced
1 large can (29-ounce) tomatoes
1 pound bacon
2 medium onions, chopped
1 bell pepper, chopped
3 stalks celery, diagonally sliced into
   1/4-inch pieces
1 clove garlic, mashed
3 tablespoons bacon fat
3 bay leaves
1 teaspoon oregano
1 teaspoon thyme
1 teaspoon chili powder
1 tablespoon sugar
salt and pepper to taste

ZUCCHINI CASSEROLE

Cut zucchini into 1-inch slices. Parboil in salted water about 10 minutes. Drain and place in a single layer in a buttered 9 x 11- or 11 x 13-inch pan.

Brown onion in butter and stir in flour. Add wine and soup and mix well. Pour over zucchini. Sprinkle with grated cheese.

Bake at 350 degrees for 30 to 40 minutes.

Serves 6 to 8   *Jacqueline P. Smith*

4 to 5 medium zucchini, sliced 1 inch
   slices
1 large onion, chopped
2 tablespoons butter
2 tablespoons flour
1/2 cup white wine or sherry
1 can cream of mushroom soup
1/2 cup grated American cheese

ZUCCHINI MELANGE

Melt butter in skillet. Add sliced zucchini, sliced mushrooms, and quartered tomatoes. Sprinkle with garlic salt. Cook gently over medium heat until zucchini reaches desired doneness.

Top with cheese. Cover pan and cook over low heat until cheese melts, or about 3 minutes.

Remove cover, stir, and serve.

Margaret Spangler

4 tablespoons margarine or butter
6 medium zucchini, sliced
1/2 pound mushrooms, sliced
2 to 3 tomatoes, quartered
garlic salt
2 slices Swiss cheese

159

ZUCCHINI PANCAKES

1-1/2 cups grated zucchini
1/2 cup whole wheat flour
1/4 cup wheat germ or bran
3 tablespoons onion, finely chopped
1/4 to 1/2 cup Parmesan cheese
1/4 teaspoon oregano
1/4 teaspoon basil
1/4 teaspoon celery salt
2 tablespoons mayonnaise
2 eggs
1 tablespoon safflower oil or butter

Grate zucchini, press dry between paper towels, and set aside to add last to batter.

In a large bowl, mix flour and wheat germ (or bran). Chop onion finely; add to flour and mix. Mix in cheese. Add oregano, basil, and celery salt, and mix. Add mayonnaise and mix well. Beat eggs lightly and mix in. Add zucchini and mix well.

In a medium size skillet, heat oil or butter. Spoon 2 tablespoons of the batter onto skillet; flatten batter. Cook over medium heat (260 degrees) until bown on both sides, about 5 minutes per side.

Betty Spence

ZUCCHINI PUDDING

4 large zucchini, coarsely grated
1 onion, grated
1 cup (heaping) cornflakes
4 eggs
1 cup milk
salt and pepper to taste
pinch of poultry seasoning (optional)
2 tablespoons oil

Grate zucchini and onion into a large bowl. Add cornflakes and mix. Lightly beat eggs and mix in. Add milk, salt, pepper, and poultry seasonings and mix well.

Heat 2 tablespoons oil in a 2-1/2 quart casserole for 15 minutes. Pour mixture into casserole.

Bake at 350 degrees for 40 minutes.

Serves 4 to 6   *Ethel Bazell*

Breads

BREAD

SIRNICA
Easter Sweet Bread

In a large pot, crumble yeast in lukewarm milk until completely dissolved. Add 1 cup flour, salt, 2 teaspoons sugar, orange rind and juice, and lemon rind. Mix, cover, then set aside.

Using large bowl with electric mixer, cream butter and salad oil; add 1 cup sugar, 4 eggs (one at a time), and egg yolks. Add vanilla, orange extract, rum or whiskey. Gradually add 2 cups of flour and beat well.

Add egg mixture to yeast mixture; gradually knead in 4 cups flour. Place dough on floured pastry cloth or board, knead until elastic and no longer sticky. Add up to 1 additional cup of flour if needed.

Place dough in greased pan or bowl, cover lightly and place in a warm place. Let rise until double in size, approx. 1-1/2 hours.

Punch down and shape dough into 5 equal rolls; then place them next to each other in a large buttered angel food cake pan. (You may choose to use round pans or to form into a loaf.) Cover lightly with clean towel and let rise until double.

Bake at 325 degrees for 50 to 60 minutes. Bread should be medium golden brown. May be glazed with beaten egg white and sprinkled with sugar when almost completely baked, or drizzled with an orange icing when removed from baking pan.

Orange Icing:

Mix together until smooth. Spoon onto warm bread.

This is a highly prized recipe given to me by Mrs. Maria Dorotich many years ago. I have not tampered too much with perfection.

Dolores Lisica

2 cakes yeast
1 cup lukewarm milk
1 cup flour
1/2 teaspoon salt
2 teaspoons sugar
1 small orange, rind and juice
1 small lemon, rind only
1/4 pound butter, at room
    temperature
1 tablespoon salad oil
1 cup sugar
4 eggs
2 egg yolks
2 tablespoons vanilla
2 tablespoons orange extract
2 tablespoons rum or whiskey
6 to 7 cups flour

Orange Icing:

1/4 cube (1 ounce) butter
1 cup powdered sugar
1/2 large orange, pulp and juice

DILL BREAD

1 packet dry yeast
1/4 cup warm water
1 cup creamy cottage cheese, at
    room temperature
2 tablespoons sugar
1 tablespoon instant dry onion
1 tablespoon soft butter
2 teaspoons dill seed
1 teaspoon salt
1/4 teaspoon soda
1 egg, unbeaten
2 to 2-1/2 cups sifted flour

In a small bowl, soften yeast in water.

In a large bowl, combine cottage cheese, sugar, dry onion, butter, dill seed, salt, soda, egg, and yeast. Mix well.

Gradually add flour to form a stiff dough. Beat after each addition. Cover and let rise in warm place until doubled in size, about 1 hour.

Punch dough down. Place in a greased 2-quart casserole. Cover with a clean towel and let rise about 35 minutes.

Bake at 350 degrees for 40 to 50 minutes, until golden brown. Brush top with butter and sprinkle lightly with salt.

G. Ryan

PAEHINHOS DE QUEIJO
Cheese Rolls

Portugal

1 package dry yeast
1 cup warm milk
2 tablespoons sugar
2 teaspoons salt
1/4 pound butter
3 eggs, slightly beaten
3/4 cup light beer
7 to 8 cups all-purpose flour
2 cups grated Muenster or Swiss
    cheese

In a large bowl, sprinkle yeast on warm milk and stir until dissolved. While stirring, add sugar, salt, butter, and eggs. Let stand 10 minutes.

Add beer and 3 cups flour. Stir until bubbles appear, then add cheese. Let rise until double in bulk.

Add 3 more cups of flour. Knead well. Add extra flour if needed. Let rise again until double in bulk.

Divide dough into 2 portions. Roll out one portion to 3/8 inch thick. Butter lightly and cut into triangles. Roll each triangle into a crescent shape (roll from wide end toward point, then bend ends toward each other to end up in a crescent shape). Place on greased cookie sheet. Cover with clean towel and let rise again about 30 to 40 minutes, or until dough springs back when lightly pressed with a finger.

Repeat with second portion of dough.

Bake at 375 degrees for about 20 minutes.

Jean Miner

PANDESAL
Dinner Rolls

In a small bowl, soften yeast in about 1/2 cup lukewarm water.

Sift 6 cups flour into a large bowl.

In a small bowl, dissolve salt and sugar in 1-1/2 cups water; while stirring, add gradually to flour. Add yeast, then shortening and mix thoroughly.

Turn out onto lightly floured board. Knead until smooth. Place in a greased bowl and let rise 2 hours.

Brush oil on top of the dough. Punch and fold the edges toward the center and turn over, the smooth side up. Cover with damp cloth. Let stand for 1 hour.

Divide the dough into four equal portions. Place one portion on a lightly floured board and pat with hands into a rectangular shape about 1/2 inch high. Lengthwise, roll tightly into a 1-1/2 inch diameter log. Sprinkle with bread crumbs and let stand for 30 minutes. Repeat for other 3 portions of dough.

With a knife, cut each log into 1-inch pieces. Arrange, touching, on greased baking sheets, with cut side up, and let rise for about 1 hour and 15 minutes.

Bake at 400 degrees for about 15 minutes.

Yield: 3 dozen   *Eloise Knoll*

1-1/2 teaspoons dry yeast
2 cups water
6 cups sifted bread flour
3 teaspoons salt
1/4 cup sugar
1/4 cup shortening
bread crumbs

FINNISH BISCUITS

1 cup lukewarm water
1 cup and 2 teaspoons sugar
2 packages yeast
4 cups milk
1/4 pound margarine
dash salt
11 cups flour
1 teaspoon cardamom
2 eggs

Mix lukewarm water, 2 teaspoons sugar, and yeast, and let stand for 10 minutes.

Scald 4 cups milk and add margarine. Allow margarine to melt and then cool mixture. Stir in 1 cup sugar and dash salt. Stir in 4 cups flour and cardamom, eggs, and yeast mixture. Mix well.

Gradually add 7 cups flour and knead lightly. Let stand to rise until double in size (about 1 to 1-1/2 hours).

To make braided loaves: Divide dough into two equal parts. Put one part on a lightly floured board. Roll into rectangular shape about 14 inches long and 8 inches wide. Cut lengthwise into 3 equal parts. Place lengths about one inch apart on greased cookie sheet. Braid loosely, beginning at the middle and working toward each end in turn. Seal ends well (tuck under and pinch). Repeat for second loaf. Cover with a clean towel and let rise for about 1 to 1-1/2 hours).

Bake at 375 degrees for 20 to 25 minutes.

If you wish, you may brush with sugar and water mixture after baking.

Veni Hill

GERMAN POTATO PANCAKES

1/2 package dry yeast
1 cup warm milk
2 cups flour
1 teaspoon sugar
5 large potatoes
parsley
1 egg
pinch of salt

In a large bowl, place milk. Sprinkle yeast over milk and stir to combine. While stirring, add flour, sugar, and salt. Mix well and let rise 20 tp 30 minutes.

Grate the potatoes and let sit for about 15 minutes, then pour off liquid. Add to yeast mixture, stirring lightly.

Form into pancakes and fry on hot griddle.

Serve with applesauce for Sunday brunch.

Eloise Knoll

CDQ SWEET ROLLS *(Can Do Quick)*

Using an electric mixer, dissolve yeast in water in the large mixing bowl.

Add buttermilk, eggs, 2-1/2 cups flour, butter, sugar, baking powder and salt. Blend 30 seconds on low speed, scraping sides and bottom of bowl. Beat 2 minutes on medium speed. Stir in remaining flour. Dough should be sticky.

Take out of bowl and knead on lightly floured board for at least 5 minutes. Place in a large greased bowl, let rise in warm place until doubled in size, about 1 hour.

Shape as desired. My favorite method is to take a large handful of dough, roll into a pie-shaped round, brush generously with melted butter. Cut into wedges, roll each slice like a jelly roll, place on a greased cookie sheet with point under and let rise until double in size.

A variation is to spread orange marmalade on top of the butter. Let rise until double.

Bake in a 375 degree oven for 15 minutes.

Maria Dorotich

2 packages dry yeast
1/2 cup lukewarm water
1-1/4 cups buttermilk
2 eggs
5-1/2 cups flour, more or less
1/2 cup soft butter
1/2 cup sugar
2 teaspoons baking powder
2 teaspoons salt
orange marmalade (optional)

MAKE-YOUR-OWN BISCUIT MIX

Measure all ingredients into one bowl. Mix with fingers.

Store in a tightly covered container in a cool place.

This mix can be substituted for Bisquick in any recipe.

Yield: 13 cups   *Eloise Knoll*

9 cups flour
4-1/2 tablespoons baking powder
1 tablespoon salt
1/4 cup sugar
1-1/2 cup shortening

HOMEMADE BISCUITS

2 cups homemade biscuit mix
2/3 cup milk

Add milk to biscuit mix and mix until moistened.

Spoon or cut into shapes and place in greased pan with sides of biscuits touching. Bake at 400 degrees for 10 minutes.

Eloise Knoll

GRAMMIE'S BISCUITS

2 cups flour
4 tablespoons shortening
1/2 teaspoon salt
3 teaspoons baking powder
3/4 cup milk

Mix flour, shortening, salt and baking powder by hand until it is a sandy consistency. Add 3/4 cup milk and stir just to moisten.

Roll out gently and cut with shot glass (or any biscuit cutter) dipped in flour.

Place in greased pan with sides touching.

Bake at 400 degrees for 8 to 10 minutes.

Eloise Knoll

GRANDMA'S BANANA BREAD

1/3 cup margarine
1/2 cup sugar
2 egg whites
1-1/2 cups unsifted flour
1 teaspoon baking powder
1/2 teaspoon baking soda
1/2 teaspoon salt
1 cup mashed ripe bananas
1/2 cup chopped walnuts

Cream margarine with sugar. Add egg whites and beat well.

In a separate bowl, blend flour with baking powder, baking soda and salt. Add to creamed mixture alternately with mashed bananas, then stir in nuts.

Turn into a greased 8-1/2 x 4-1/2 x 2-1/2 inch loaf pan. Bake at 350 degrees for about 55 minutes, or until done. Remove from pan and cool.

Tastes great spread with cream cheese.

Karen Brickner

CRANBERRY NUT BREAD

Preheat oven to 350 degrees.

Chop cranberries. Grate orange rind and mix with cranberries. Set aside.

In a large bowl, combine butter, sugar, orange juice and beaten eggs. Stir until blended. Add cranberries/orange rind mixture. Blend.

In a separate large bowl, sift together flour, salt, baking powder, and baking soda. Add nuts and stir through flour until well coated.

Stir dry ingredients into liquid ingredients until thoroughly moistened.

Pour batter into 2 well buttered 8-1/2 x 4-1/2 x 2-1/2 inch loaf pans. Let stand 20 minutes before baking.

Bake at 350 degrees for about 1 hour, or until nicely brown. Test with wooden toothpick.

Lucy DiMeglio

3/4 cup fresh chopped cranberries
2 tablespoons grated orange rind
1/2 cup melted butter
1-1/2 cups white or brown sugar
1-1/3 cups orange juice
2 large eggs, beaten
5 cups flour
1 teaspoon salt
1 tablespoon baking powder
1 teaspoon baking soda
2 cups chopped nuts

MEXICAN CORN BREAD

Grate cheddar cheese and set aside.

In a large bowl, mix together creamed corn, cornmeal, cottage cheese, cheddar cheese, chiles and baking powder.

Melt butter and mix in slowly.

Beat egg whites until stiff and fluffy. Slowly add yolks, one at a time, beating until foamy. Then add egg mixture to corn mixture.

Spoon into greased 9 x 13-inch baking dish.

Bake 45 minutes at 350 degrees. Bread is done when the top is dry and almost cracked.

Carmen Bonilla and Delia Du Ross

1 pound extra sharp cheddar cheese, grated
1 can (17-ounce) can white creamed corn (yellow can be used)
1 cup white cornmeal
1 carton (8-ounce) cottage cheese
1 can (7-ounce) can green chiles, chopped
1 teaspoon baking powder
1/4 pound butter
3 eggs, separated

PEANUT BUTTER BREAD

2 cups sifted flour
2 teaspoons baking powder
1 teaspoon salt
1 teaspoon baking soda
1-3/4 cup sugar
3 eggs
1 cup milk
1-3/4 cup peanut butter
1/4 cup cooking oil

In a large bowl, sift flour, baking powder, salt, baking soda, and sugar together.

In another bowl, beat eggs; beat in milk, peanut butter, and oil with egg beater. Then add gradually to dry ingredients, while beating with a spoon.

Pour into a greased and floured 5 x 9 inch loaf pan.

Bake 1 hour at 350 degrees.

Josephine Pittman

PUMPKIN BREAD

4 eggs
3 cups sugar
1-1/2 teaspoons salt
1 teaspoon cinnamon
1 teaspoon nutmeg
3-1/2 cups flour
2 teaspoons baking soda
2/3 cup cool water
2 cups pumpkin
1 cup oil
nuts, raisins, or chocolate chips
    (optional)

In a large bowl, beat the eggs. While stirring, gradually add the sugar; the salt, cinnamon, and nutmeg; flour and baking soda; cool water; pumpkin; and oil. Add nuts, raisins, or chocolate chips if desired. Mix thoroughly.

Oil two 5 x 9 inch loaf pans and spoon mixture into pans.

Bake at 350 degrees for 1 hour.

Cool in pans for 1 hour and remove to rack.

Vicki Boutté

SOUTHERN SPOON BREAD

1 cup corn meal
2 cups milk
1 teaspoon salt
1 teaspoon baking powder
2 tablespoons melted shortening
1 cup milk
3 well beaten egg yolks
3 stiff-beaten egg whites

Preheat oven to 325 degrees.

Cook corn meal in 2 cups of milk until consistency of mush. Remove from heat.

While stirring, add salt, baking powder, shortening, and 1 cup milk.

Add beaten egg yolks. Then fold in stiffly beaten egg whites.

Bake in greased 2-quart casserole in oven for 1 hour.

Top servings with butter.

Serves 6   *Mildred Niehoff*

SOUTHERN PUMPKIN BREAD

Soak raisins in hot water until plumped up. Drain. Chop walnuts.

In a large bowl, beat eggs, then add sugar and beat until smooth. Add oil, pumpkin, and water and mix well.

In another large bowl, sift flour together with soda, nutmeg, and salt. Add chopped walnuts and mix to cover walnuts. Add to pumpkin mixture. Stir in raisins. Beat by hand about 200 times.

Grease and flour four 1-pound coffee cans (or a tube pan or loaf pans) and fill half full.

Bake at 350 degrees for one hour or until done (it will start to draw away from sides of pan and be firm to the touch).

Turn cans upside down to remove and cool when taken from oven. When cool, wrap in plastic wrap.

Anonymous

3/4 cup light seedless raisins
3/4 cup dark seedless raisins
1 cup chopped walnuts
4 eggs
3 cups sugar
1 cup oil
2 cups plain pumpkin
2/3 cup water
3-1/3 cups flour, sifted
2 teaspoons soda
1 teaspoon nutmeg
1 teaspoon salt

SCONES

Very traditionally English. Scones are halved and eaten with butter, jam and thick whipped cream. Serve with tea. In a large bowl, mix flour, baking powder, salt, and sugar.

Rub margarine in with fingers. Add milk gradually mixing it in quickly with a knife. Make soft dough.

Roll lightly on a floured board. Make ping-pong ball size dough balls. Flatten to 1/2 inch thick. Brush tops with milk. Place on greased cookie sheet.

Bake at 400 degrees until golden brown, about 15 to 20 minutes.

Jackie Morrison

2 cups flour
4 teaspoons baking powder
1/2 teaspoon salt
2 tablespoons sugar
4 tablespoons margarine
buttermilk to mix (approximately 1 cup)

PAUL REVERE ROLLS

1 loaf thin-sliced bread
1 egg
1/2 cup milk
1/4 pound butter, melted
Parmesan cheese, grated (enough
    to coat each roll)

With rolling pin, flatten each slice of bread to make it thinner.

Mix together egg and milk. Dip 1 slice of bread into egg mixture and place between two un-dipped slices. Continue until all bread is used.

Cut into strips or desired shapes. Dip into melted butter and roll in Parmesan cheese. Arrange on greased cookie sheets. Bake at 400 degrees for 8 to 10 minutes.

Note: May be frozen on cookie sheets before baking. When frozen, remove from cookie sheets and store in baggies in freezer.

G. Ryan

ZUCCHINI BREAD

5 eggs, beaten
1-1/8 cups oil
2-1/4 cups sugar
1-1/2 teaspoons grated lemon peel
3/4 teaspoon orange extract
1/2 teaspoon vanilla
3 cups grated zucchini
3-3/4 cups flour
1-1/4 teaspoons salt
3/4 teaspoon cinnamon
1/2 teaspoon ginger
1-1/2 teaspoons baking soda
3 teaspoons baking powder
3/4 cup chopped nuts

In a large bowl, beat eggs. Gradually add oil and sugar. Beat well. Add lemon peel, orange extract, vanilla, and zucchini. Beat well.

In another bowl, combine flour, salt, cinnamon, ginger, baking soda, and baking powder. Gradually stir flour mixture into egg mixture. Add nuts and mix well.

Pour into 2 greased and floured 9 x 5 inch loaf pans. Bake at 350 degrees for 1 hour.

Cool in pans on wire rack until bread separates from pan.

John Gault

BRAN MUFFINS

3/4 cup whole wheat flour
1/3 cup bran
2 teaspoons baking powder
1/2 teaspoon baking soda
1 tablespoon sugar
2 tablespoons vegetable oil
1 egg
1/2 cup low fat milk
1/4 cup raisins

Mix flour, bran, baking powder, baking soda, and sugar in a bowl. Add oil, egg, milk, and raisins. Stir just to combine ingredients.

Spoon into lightly oiled muffin tins. Bake in 400 degree oven 15 to 20 minutes.

Yield: 6 muffins

Doris Berg

APPLE-BUTTERMILK PANCAKES

Sift the whole wheat flour and baking soda. Add egg yolks, shredded apple and buttermilk. Stir.

In a separate bowl, beat egg whites to soft peaks and fold into flour mixture.

Drop batter by spoonfuls onto oiled, heated griddle or frying pan. Turn once when golden brown or bubbles appear.

Serve with butter and syrup.

Serves 3 to 4   *Thelma E. Mathers*

1-1/2 cups whole wheat flour
1 teaspoon baking soda
2 eggs, separated
1 apple, shredded
1-1/2 cups (approximately) buttermilk

PLATTAR
Swedish Pancakes

Sweden

Sift flour into bowl; add sugar and salt. Then add eggs and milk gradually, stirring until well blended. Let stand for 2 hours.

Heat a well-oiled pancake pan (or ordinary skillet). The batter should be very thin; fry until nicely browned.

Serve immediately.

Lillian Peterson Drenckhahn

1 cup flour
2 tablespoons sugar
1/4 teaspoon salt
3 eggs
3 cups milk

SWEDISH PANCAKES

Measure the flour, salt, sugar, and nutmeg into a bowl.

Stir in milk, melted butter, orange peel, and beaten eggs.

Pour a thin layer into a hot, buttered frying pan and brown quickly on both sides.

If desired, serve with sour cream and canned lingonberries or plums.

Margaret Litman

3/4 cup flour
1 teaspoon salt
1 tablespoon sugar
1/2 teaspoon nutmeg
1-3/4 cup milk
2 tablespoons melted butter
1 teaspoon grated orange peel
4 eggs, beaten

LATKES
Potato Pancakes

4 large potatoes
1 onion
2 eggs
1/3 cup flour
1 teaspoon baking powder
salt and pepper, to taste
oil

Cut potatoes to fit feed tube of food processor. Grate, using very light pressure. Place potatoes in a colander and rinse under cold water to remove starch.

Grate onion in processor, leaving onion in bowl. Insert steel blade in processor. Add grated potatoes, eggs, flour, and baking powder. Process for a few seconds just until mixed. Season to taste with salt and pepper.

Note: For thinner, crispier latkes, add 1 or 2 additional eggs.

Heat 1/4 inch oil in large skillet. Drop potato mixture in oil by tablespoonfuls. Flatten latkes with back of spoon. Fry until lightly browned on both sides. Drain on paper towel.

To reheat, place latkes in a single layer on an ungreased, foil-lined baking sheet. Bake uncovered at 450 degrees 7 to 8 minutes, or until crisp and hot.

Yield: 36 latkes   *Selma Streicher*

DAD'S WAFFLES

3 eggs
2 cups buttermilk
2 cups flour
1 teaspoon baking soda
1 teaspoon salt
1 teaspoon sugar
1 teaspoon baking powder
7 tablespoons salad oil

Place eggs in large mixing bowl and beat 1/2 minute with electric mixer. Add buttermilk and beat an additional 1/2 minute.

In a separate bowl, sift together flour, baking soda, salt, sugar, and baking powder, and add gradually to egg mixture, beating until smooth. Add oil, mix well.

Bake in preheated waffle iron.

Tastes even better if batter is made the day before serving.

Serves 4 to 6   *Mary Lou Nizetich*

WHOLE WHEAT BLUEBERRY WAFFLES

In a large bowl, sift together flour, baking powder, and salt.

In another bowl, mix eggs, oil and milk. Gradually add to the dry ingredients while stirring. Measure out about half cup of this mixture into a small bowl, and add to it 1/3 cup of blueberries. Mix. Pour the blueberry mixture onto the preheated waffle iron and bake for about 5 minutes.

Yield: 6 large round waffles   *Carol Flaherty*

1-1/2 cups plus 2 tablespoons whole wheat flour, sifted
2 tablespoons baking powder
1/2 teaspoon salt
3 eggs
7 tablespoons vegetable oil
1-1/2 cups milk
2 cups fresh or frozen (undefrosted) blueberries

BUTTERY CELERY DRESSING

In large bowl, combine bread crumbs with poultry seasoning, salt, and pepper.

Slowly cook celery, onion and parsley in butter until tender, but not brown. Add to crumbs. Add water (or broth) and egg. Mix well.

Yield: stuffing for 5-pound bird

Margaret Gwartney

7 cups day-old bread crumbs or 1/2-inch squares lightly packed
1/2 teaspoon poultry seasoning or sage
1 teaspoon salt
1/4 teaspoon pepper
1-1/2 cups finely diced celery
1/4 cup minced onion
3 tablespoons snipped parsley or parsley flakes
1/3 to 1/2 cup butter or margarine
1/3 cup boiling water or broth
1 egg

SPICY TURKEY STUFFING

Simmer livers in water, salt and garlic until tender. Remove livers and chop fine.

Brown pork with livers in oil in a large frying pan. Combine in a large bowl with remaining ingredients.

Rub turkey cavity with salt and pepper. Stuff loosely. Roast as usual. Baste occasionally with sherry.

Yield: stuffing for 16-pound turkey

Jacqueline P. Smith

1 cup chicken or turkey livers
4 cups water
1 teaspoon salt
1 clove garlic
1/2 pound ground pork
1/2 cup slivered, toasted almonds
1/2 cup raisins, softened in hot water
1/2 cup chopped green olives
3 tablespoons chopped onion
3 tablespoons chopped green pepper
2 tablespoons chopped parsley
3 tablespoons chopped celery
1/4 teaspoon basil
1 cup tomato sauce
1 cup sherry
salt and pepper
1 large package bread cubes

On Bread

"There is no one thing upon which health and comfort in a family so much depend as bread. With good bread the coarsest fare is tolerable; without it, the most luxurious table is not comfortable."

—*The Young Housekeeper's Friend*, 1845

~ Pasta ~

PASTA

LASAGNA GASPER

Meat Sauce:

Heat oil. Add chopped onions, garlic, and parsley, and fry lightly. Add tomatoes, tomato paste, bay leaves, salt, and pepper and stir until well mixed. Toss in ground beef, and break up with a fork or spoon. Cook over low heat, stirring occasionally, at least 45 minutes or until it has that "done sauce" look. Since I use very lean meat, I toss a pat of butter on top while it stands waiting to be assembled.

Cheese Sauce:

While meat sauce is cooking, melt butter in medium size skillet and lightly sauté onion. Mix in the flour smoothly; add grated cheese and a dash of salt. Gradually stir in milk, and continue cooking over low heat, stirring continuously, until sauce is as thick as heavy cream.

Beat egg yolks slightly; add to them a little of the hot cheese mixture, and then add to remaining hot cheese mixture, but not enough to cook the egg yolks. Stir; then add eggs to remaining hot cheese mixture. Cook over low heat for 10 minutes, stirring regularly. Remove from heat and set aside.

Cook lasagna noodles according to directions on package. When done, remove from pot and drain thoroughly.

Preheat oven to 325 degrees.

Grease a 9 x 13-inch baking dish. Layer with noodles on bottom, then meat/tomato sauce, then cheese sauce. Repeat layers, ending with cheese on top. Bake 20 minutes, or until it bubbles in the center.

Slip under broiler briefly. Don't take your eyes off it as it can burn very quickly—after all this work, you don't want a catastrophe!

Serves 6 to 8   *Blossom Gasper*

Meat Sauce:

1/4 cup olive or salad oil
1 large onion, chopped
1 clove garlic, minced
6 sprigs parsley, minced
1 can (1 pound 12 ounces) tomatoes
1 can (4 ounces) tomato paste
2 bay leaves
1 teaspoon salt
1/4 teaspoon pepper
1 pound lean ground beef
1 pat butter (optional)
1 package (8 ounces) lasagna noodles

Cheese Sauce:

4 tablespoons butter, melted
1 small onion, finely chopped
3 tablespoons flour
3/4 cup grated Parmesan cheese
dash of salt
2 cups milk
2 egg yolks

LASAGNA RYAN

2 to 2-1/2 cans Italian-style peeled
　　tomatoes
2 cans (8-ounce) tomato paste
　　(with two cans of water)
2 teaspoons salt, or to taste
3 teaspoons dried oregano
1/4 teaspoon pepper
2 teaspoons onion salt
1/3 cup salad oil
2 cups minced onions
2 cloves garlic, minced
2 pounds ground chuck or round
2 teaspoons salt, or to taste
1 pound lasagna noodles
2 pounds Ricotta cheese
1-1/2 pounds Mozzarella cheese,
　　thinly sliced
1 cup grated Parmesan cheese

In a large saucepan or kettle, combine tomatoes, tomato paste, water, salt, oregano, pepper, and onion salt; start simmering, uncovered.

In a skillet, sauté onion and garlic in oil until lightly browned; add ground meat and salt. Cook until meat loses red color; add to tomato sauce; simmer 2-1/2 hours, or until thickened.

Meanwhile, cook lasagna noodles according to directions on package, stirring occasionally. Drain, separating noodles.

Preheat oven to 350 degrees.

Use half of the noodles, Ricotta, Mozzarella, Parmesan, and sauce in each of two 12 x 8 x 2-inch baking dishes: In bottom of each dish place several spoonfuls of sauce; top with a crisscross layer of noodles, then with half of this dish's Ricotta. Top with one-third of this dish's Mozzarella and half of its Parmesan. Repeat again, ending with sauce. Top with remaining Mozzarella and bake 50 minutes or until bubbly.

Allow to stand 15 minutes before serving.

Serves 8　　　　　　　　　　　　　　　*G. Ryan*

QUICK LASAGNA AL FORNO

2 tablespoons oil
1 small onion, diced
1 clove garlic, minced
1 pound ground beef
2 cans (15-ounce) marinara sauce
salt and pepper to taste
1 package lasagna noodles
1 pound Mozzarella cheese,
　　sliced thinly
1 pound Monterey jack cheese,
　　sliced thinly
1/2 pound sharp cheddar cheese,
　　sliced thinly
1/4 cup grated Parmesan cheese

In a large skillet, brown onions and garlic in 2 tablespoons oil. Add ground beef and brown. Add marinara sauce, simmer 15 minutes. Salt and pepper to taste.

Cook lasagna noodles per package instructions.

Preheat oven to 375 degrees.

Arrange in buttered 9 x 13 x 2-inch baking dish a layer of noodles, a layer of sliced cheese (all Mozzarella, or jack or cheddar), a layer of sauce. Sprinkle with grated cheese. Repeat, building up layers until all noodles and sliced cheeses are used. Top with sauce and grated Parmesan cheese.

Bake at 375 degrees for 20 minutes.

Serves 6　　　　　　　　　　　　*Helen Homen*

BUFFET MANICOTTI

Combine chicken, cottage cheese, beaten egg, onion, parsley, and Italian seasoning in a bowl.

Cook manicotti per package directions. Remove manicotti from water one at a time with slotted spoon. Drain well and pat dry with paper towel. Fill manicotti with chicken mixture. Set aside.

Make the Cheese Sauce and the Buttered Crumbs.

Spoon 3/4 cup Cheese Sauce into greased 13 x 9 inch baking dish and arrange stuffed manicotti in single layer over sauce. Spoon remaining sauce over manicotti and sprinkle with Buttered Crumbs. Bake at 350 degrees about 30 minutes or until heated through and crumbs are lightly browned.

Cheese Sauce:

Melt butter in a large skillet. Stir in flour and cook, stirring, 1 minute. Add milk and cook and stir until sauce comes to a boil and thickens. Stir in remaining ingredients and cook over low heat, stirring, until cheese melts. Do no allow to boil after adding cheese.

Buttered Crumbs

Melt butter in a small skillet and stir in paprika. Pour over bread crumbs and toss to mix evenly.

G. Ryan

1-1/2 cups chopped cooked chicken
    or turkey
1 cup small curd cottage cheese
1 egg, beaten
1/4 cup minced onion
2 tablespoons minced parsley
1/2 teaspoon Italian seasoning
manicotti shells

Cheese Sauce:

3 tablespoons butter or margarine
3 tablespoons flour
2 cups milk
1/4 teaspoon Worcestershire sauce
1-1/2 cups shredded Muenster, jack
    or cheddar cheese
1/4 teaspoon salt

Buttered Crumbs

2 tablespoons butter or margarine
1/8 teaspoon paprika
1 cup bread crumbs

STUFFED MANICOTTI

Cook manicotti as directed on package, drain, and set aside.

Chop fresh spinach (or use frozen chopped spinach), cook, and drain.

Combine all ingredients except sauce and shells, mix well, and stuff shells.

Place in 9 x 13-inch baking dish. Spoon sauce on top. Additional grated cheese may be sprinkled on top, if desired.

Bake at 350 degrees for 45 minutes. Uncover and let stand 5 to 10 minutes, before serving.

Serves 7

Ida Tandy

8 ounces manicotti shells (14)
24 ounces creamed cottage cheese
8 ounces shredded Mozzarella cheese
1/2 cup Parmesan cheese
1 cup fresh spinach, or 10-ounce
    package of frozen chopped
    spinach
1 large egg
1 teaspoon garlic powder
1 teaspoon oregano
1/2 teaspoon salt
1/2 teaspoon basil
1 jar Prego meat spaghetti sauce

BAKED NOODLES WITH MUSHROOMS

4 tablespoons butter
1 pound mushrooms, sliced
1/4 cup minced parsley
salt and pepper to taste
12 ounces medium wide egg noodles
1/3 cup soft bread crumbs

In a large skillet, sauté mushrooms in 3 tablespoons butter for 6 minutes.

Add parsley and season with salt and pepper.

Cook and drain noodles as directed on package.

Add noodles to mushrooms. Add 1 tablespoon butter and correct seasoning.

Melt 1 tablespoon butter in a small skillet and pour over bread crumbs. Toss to mix evenly.

Put noodle/mushroom mixture in a greased casserole and sprinkle top with buttered bread crumbs.

Bake at 350 degrees for 20 minutes or until hot and brown.

Esther Quinn

FABULOUS NOODLE KUGEL

Jewish

1 pound broad noodles
7 eggs
3 cups milk
1 pint sour cream
1 pound cottage cheese
1 cup sugar
1-1/2 teaspoons vanilla
4 ounces melted butter or margarine
1 cup white raisins
additional butter or margarine for
     dotting

Topping:

2/3 cup cornflakes, crumbled
1 tsp cinnamon
1 teaspoon sugar

Cook noodles according to instructions on package, then drain.

In a very large pot, place all eggs and beat lightly. Beating each ingredient in well, add milk, sour cream, cottage cheese, sugar, vanilla, and melted butter. Mix in raisins. Add cooked noodles and mix thoroughly.

Pour into two greased 9 x 13-inch glass baking dishes, and refrigerate 3 hours or overnight. Consistency will be loose before refrigeration, but will set when chilled.

When ready to bake, mix topping ingredients in a small bowl and sprinkle over pudding. Dot with butter and bake at 350 degrees for 1-1/2 hours.

Selma Streicher

FETTUCCINE ALFREDO

Prepare noodles per package directions. Drain.

While noodles are cooking, beat egg yolk lightly with fork, then add cream.

Melt butter.

Place drained, hot noodles in warm serving bowl or platter. Pour over the noodles, egg and cream mixture, melted butter and one-half of the cheese. Toss noodles with fork and spoon until well blended, adding balance of cheese a little at a time while tossing.

Top with remaining cheese and serve immediately.

Serves 4

G. Ryan

1 package egg noodles, (medium or wide)
1 egg yolk
1/3 cup light cream or sour cream
1/4 pound butter, unsalted
1/2 cup grated parmesan cheese

GRANDMA'S NOODLES

Combine flour and salt. Add eggs and mix. Add cold milk or water and mix with wooden spoon until dough forms a ball. Roll out into a thin sheet on a lightly floured surface. Cut with a noodle cutter or roll ligfhtly around rolling pin. Slip out rolling pin. Cut dough crosswise into 1/8-inch strips for narrow noodles or 1/4-inch strips for wide noodles. Shake out strips.

Drop into boiling chicken broth. Cook for 10 to 12 minutes. Add cooked chicken pieces and cook for 3 to 4 minutes more.

Note: Noodles can be dropped into boiling salted water instead of broth. Cook 12 to 15 minutes, or until done.

Margaret Gwartney

1 cup flour
1/2 teaspoon salt
3 eggs
2 tablespoons milk or water (enough to form dough in ball)
boiling chicken broth or water
chicken pieces (optional)

ILIANA'S PASTA

vegetable oil
1 pound lean ground meat
1 medium onion, chopped
1 clove garlic, crushed
1 can (8-ounces) spaghetti sauce
1 can (8-ounces) tomatoes
1 can sliced mushrooms
8 ounces shell macaroni
1-1/2 cups sour cream
1/2 pound Provolone cheese,
    thinly sliced
1/2 pound Mozzarella cheese,
    thinly sliced

Brown beef in oil, breaking with a fork as it cooks. Drain off excess fat. Add chopped onions, crushed garlic, spaghetti sauce, tomatoes, and undrained mushrooms. Simmer 20-30 minutes.

Cook macaroni according to instructions on package. When done, rinse and drain.

Place half of macaroni in a large, greased casserole. Cover with half the meat mixture, then half the sour cream. Top with thin slices Provolone. Add rest of macaroni, meat, and sour cream, and top with thin slices of Mozzarella.

Cover and bake for 40 minutes at 300 degrees.

Remove cover and bake till cheese browns slightly and bubbles.

Emmy Ruud

PASTA PRIMAVERA

2 tablespoons salad or olive oil
1/2 cup sliced onion
1-1/2 cups quartered mushrooms
1 cup sliced yellow squash
1/2 cup sliced zucchini
1 small green pepper, cut in strips
2 cloves garlic, minced
1 jar (15-1/2 ounces) spaghetti sauce
1/2 pound spaghetti

In a 10-inch skillet, over medium heat, in hot oil, cook sliced onions, quartered mushrooms, sliced squash, green pepper strips, and minced garlic until tender, about 10 minutes.

Stir in spaghetti sauce; heat through, stirring occasionally.

While sauce is cooking prepare spaghetti according to package directions. Drain.

Spoon sauce over hot spaghetti and serve.

Variations: Any of the following fresh vegetables may be substituted: broccoli, cauliflower, green or waxed beans, green peas, eggplant and green onions.

Serves 5   *G. Ryan*

PIROHI
Ma Geist's Famous Recipe

Filling:

Boil potatoes. When done, drain and mash in a large bowl.

Cook sauerkraut according to instructions on container. When done, drain and squeeze out all of the juice, and add to potatoes.

Chop onion and sauté in butter until they are golden. Add to potatoes and sauerkraut. Mix well and season with salt and pepper.

Dough:

In a large bowl, combine flour, salt, and egg. Add warm water to make a soft dough, not too sticky or too stiff. Roll out dough to pie crust thickness. Cut out circles about 4 inches in diameter, and accumulate on a lightly floured surface.

Sauce:

Chop onion and sauté in butter, then add cream. Season with salt and pepper to taste.

Place 6 quarts of salted water in a large pot and heat so that it will be boiling when you are ready to drop the pirohi in. Make filling, dough, and sauce.

Fill each circle of dough with 1 teaspoonful of the sauerkraut/potato mixture. Fold over and pinch edges to seal.

Drop pirohi into 6 quarts of boiling, salted water. When they float to the top, continue a slow boil for 10 minutes. Do not allow to boil rapidly.

Fill a large pan with cool water. Take pirohi out of the boiling water and place in the cool water to remove the starch. Then drain.

While pirohi are draining, make sauce.

Place pirohi on a greased cookie sheet to cool at room temperature. Be careful not to let them stick together.

When cooled, arrange pirohi in a medium-sized roasting pan, cover with sauce, and heat in 300-degree oven until heated through.

Serve with extra sauce if desired.

Yield: 30 pirohi   *Lynda Kalinczok*

Filling:

2 quarts potatoes, boiled, drained
    and mashed
1 quart sauerkraut
4 ounces butter
1 medium onion, chopped

Dough:

3 cups flour
1 egg
1 teaspoon salt
1/8 cup (approximately) warm water

Sauce:

1 medium onion, chopped
4 ounces butter
2 pints cream
salt and pepper to taste

KYNUTE KNEDLIKY
Raised Dumplings

1-1/2 slices white bread
1 tablespoon butter
1/2 cake yeast
3/4 cup milk, lukewarm
1 egg, beaten
1 teaspoon salt
2 cups flour

Dice bread and brown slightly in butter; then cool.

In a large bowl, crumble yeast into lukewarm milk. Let rise for approximately 20 minutes. Beat egg and add to yeast mixture; then add salt and flour. Beat thoroughly with wooden spoon until smooth. Add cooled bread cubes and mix. Let rise until double in bulk, about 1 hour.

Dust your hands with flour and make dumplings about the size of tennis balls. Let these rise again on floured board (about 15 to 20 minutes) until, when you press lightly with your thumb, the dough springs back into shape.

Bring water to a full boil in a large, deep kettle. Lower each dumpling gently into the boiling water, using a large spoon. Cover for 5 minutes. Cook for 10 to 12 minutes longer after water starts to boil constantly.

When done, remove each dumpling with a slotted spoon. Split each dumpling in half, using 2 forks.

Note: These can be made omitting bread cubes. Delicious with sauerkraut and duck.

Velma Erro

LINGUINI AND CLAMS A LA CARMELA

1 pound linguini
1/2 cup chopped parsley
3 or 4 large cloves garlic
1/2 cup olive oil
1/4 pound butter
3 cans (7-ounce) clams
Parmesan cheese, grated

Cook linguini per package instructions. Drain. Put in serving dish.

While linguini is cooking, mince parsley and garlic and sauté in olive oil and butter. Add clams and reheat (do not cook or clams will be tough).

Pour sauce over cooked linguini in serving bowl. Sprinkle with grated Parmesan cheese.

Serve with additional Parmesan cheese on the side.

Carmela Castagnola

LINGUINI AND CLAMS

Cook linguini per package instructions.

In a heavy saucepan, sauté garlic in olive oil until almost brown, and remove from heat. Add butter, clams, clam juice, and parsley. Simmer for 5 minutes. Do not overcook. Drain linguini, then add to sauce and cook 2 minutes longer.

Serves 2   *John Trani*

1/2 pound linguini
5 cloves garlic, chopped
2 tablespoons olive oil
2 tablespoons butter
1 can (6-1/2 ounces) minced clams
1 bottle clam juice
3 tablespoons parsley, minced

POLISH PIEROGI
Dough and Cheese or Sweet Cabbage Fillings
Poland

Make cheese filling, cabbage filling, and dough.

Pinch off small pieces of dough and roll into circles. Fill with cheese or cabbage filling. Fold over and pinch edges to seal well.

Drop into boiling water and cook 10 to 15 minutes. They will float in water when done. Remove and drain thoroughly.

Pan fry in butter until golden brown just before serving.

These pierogis can be made up days ahead of time and frozen until needed.

Cheese Filling:

Boil potatoes. When done, drain and mash in a bowl. Add grated cheese while potatoes are hot, then salt and pepper to taste. Set aside.

Sweet Cabbage Filling:

Core and shred cabbage and drop in a large pot of rapidly boiling water. Cook for 8 to 10 minutes. Then drain and place in a large bowl.

Fry onion in a little margarine until cooked. Add to cabbage. Season to taste with salt and pepper. Set aside.

Dough:

In a large bowl, cut margarine into flour until the size of rice. Add milk, water, eggs and salt. Knead in bowl. If too dry, add more water.

                            Karen Brickner

Cheese Filling:

5 medium potatoes, cooked and
    mashed
1 pound sharp cheddar cheese, grated
salt and pepper to taste

Sweet Cabbage Filling:

1 large head cabbage, shredded
1 large onion, chopped
salt and pepper to taste

Dough:

3/4 stick margarine
4 cups flour
1 small can evaporated milk
1 small can water (2/3 cup)
2 eggs
2 teaspoons salt
butter for pan frying

NJOKI
Potato Dumplings

5 medium russet potatoes
boiling salted water
1 teaspoon salt
1/2 teaspoon white pepper
3 tablespoons grated Parmesan
    cheese
2 tablespoons soft butter
1 tablespoon shortening
1 whole egg
2 egg yolks
1 cup flour, approximately
spaghetti sauce
additional Parmesan cheese, if desired

Cook potatoes in boiling salted water until tender. Remove from water and peel while still hot. Work through a potato ricer into a large bowl. Add salt, pepper, grated cheese, butter, shortening, egg, and egg yolks. Mix to blend. Add flour a little at a time. The trick to making the njoki light and fluffy is to add only enough flour to keep dough together, but not to add so much that they become heavy. Work mixture to blend.

Flour a pastry cloth or board. Cut off a ball of dough and roll into a finger-sized cylinder.

Cut cylinder into 1 to 1-1/2 inch pieces. Roll each lightly in flour. Press against a cheese grater to make a pattern on top.

Drop into boiling salted water, 12 to 18 at a time. Boil until njoki float to the top. Remove with a wire slotted spatula and place in a 10 x 13-inch baking dish; lightly cover with spaghetti sauce. Sprinkle with additional Parmesan cheese, if desired.

Add more njoki and sauce (and cheese). Continue layering until all njoki are cooked.

Place casserole in a 250-degree oven for 12 to 15 minutes to allow flavors to blend.

Serves 6 to 8   *Jermina Ursich*

RICOTTA LASAGNA SWIRLS

Cook lasagna noodles according to package instructions. When done, rinse and drain.

Make sauce.

Wash and chop spinach finely. Steam until quite limp, but not mushy, for approximately 7 minutes. Place in a large bowl (there is no liquid). Add cheeses, salt, pepper, and nutmeg, and mix.

Coat each noodle with 2 to 3 tablespoons of spinach mixture along its entire length. Roll up and turn on end so spiral shows at top, and place in a shallow, 10 x 12-inch casserole.

Pour sauce over rolled up noodles and bake at 350 degrees for 20 minutes.

Sauce:

Sauté garlic and onion in oil. Mix in tomato sauce, basil, salt, and pepper.

Pat Trutanich

8 lasagna noodles
1 pound fresh spinach, washed and
    finely chopped
2 tablespoons grated Parmesan
    cheese
1 cup ricotta cheese
1/2 teaspoon salt
dash of pepper
1/4 teaspoon ground nutmeg

Sauce:

2 cloves garlic, minced
1 medium onion, chopped
2 tablespoons oil
2 cans (8-ounce) tomato sauce
1/2 teaspoon basil, crumbled
1/2 teaspoon salt
dash of pepper

WAUSETTI

Brown onion and pork until done. Add tomato sauce and mix. Simmer for 20 to 30 minutes.

In a large pot, cook noodles according to instructions on package, then drain. Add cheese while noodles are hot; add mushrooms; combine with meat mixture and place in a 9 x 12-inch casserole. Top with crumbs.

Bake at 350 degrees for 20 minutes.

Serves 6 to 8   *G. Ryan*

2 onions, diced
2 pounds ground pork
2 cans (8-ounce) tomato sauce
8 ounces noodles
1/2 ounces sharp cheddar cheese,
    grated
1 can (8-ounce) mushrooms, drained
bread crumbs for topping

RAVIOLI

Filling:

1/2 bunch fresh spinach (tops only),
    or 5 ounces frozen chopped
    spinach
1/2 cup lightly salted boiling water
12 to 14 ounces chicken breasts,
    boned, skinned, and cubed
1 tablespoon olive oil
1 tablespoon butter
1/2 onion, chopped
salt and white pepper, to taste
1 large clove garlic, pressed
5 sprigs parsley, minced
1/8 teaspoon nutmeg
1/8 teaspoon thyme
pinch dried oregano
1 slice bread, broken into pieces
1 egg
2 tablespoons ricotta cheese
2 tablespoons Parmesan cheese,
    grated

Processor Ravioli Dough:

2 large eggs
1 tablespoon olive oil
2 tablespoons cold water
2 cups sifted all-purpose flour

Egg Roll Wrappers as "Dough":

Ravioli mold and small rolling pin
    that comes with it
1-1/2 to 2 packages egg roll wrappers
1/2 cup cold water
corn meal

Filling:

Cook spinach in salted boiling water for 5 minutes, drain, press out all water. Set aside.

Skin chicken breasts and cut meat into cubes (about 1 inch).

In a large skillet, heat oil and butter, add onions, and sauté lightly. Add chicken, sprinkle with salt and pepper, and sauté until chicken loses pink color. Add garlic and parsley. Stir to combine evenly over medium heat.

Add drained spinach, mix thoroughly, sprinkle with nutmeg, thyme, and oregano, and sauté for an additional 3 to 5 minutes. Allow to cool.

In a food processor, use a steel blade to process bread to fine crumbs. (Can use a meat grinder with fine blade, or other method to make fine crumbs.) Add chicken/spinach mixture by the spoonfuls; process using pulse action.

Using pulse action add egg, ricotta and Parmesan cheese until combined. Place in a bowl, chill in refrigerator, 1/2 hour or overnight.

Processor Ravioli Dough:

Egg roll skins, obtainable at supermarkets, may be used instead of Processor Ravioli Dough. See instructions on next page.

Place metal chopping blade in work bowl of food processor. Break the eggs directly into the bowl; add olive oil and water and blend lightly by snapping the motor on and off twice. Add 1 cup of the flour; turn motor on and let run 5 seconds nonstop. Add the remaining cup of flour and process for 10 seconds nonstop. The dough will form a ball and ride up on the chopping blade's spindle.

Remove dough from processor and divide in half. Shape each half into a round ball, set on a lightly floured board, and cover with a bowl turned upside down. Let stand for 20 minutes.

Roll one ball of the dough on a lightly floured pastry cloth with a lightly floured, stockinette-covered rolling pin. Work with quick strokes, from the center outward. Roll the dough as thinly as possible into a rectangular shape. Repeat with second ball of dough.

RAVIOLI (Continued)

Leaving about a 1-inch margin around the edges, place a 1-teaspoon mound of filling on one of the pieces of dough at about 2-inch intervals. Brush water between the mounds. Lay the second pasta strip over the first. Press the pasta around each mound of filling so that the two moistened strips stick together firmly. Using a fluted pastry wheel, cut carefully along and across the pasta dough midway between the rows of filling to separate the ravioli.

Fill a large pan about two-thirds full of water; add salt and 1 tablespoon oil. Bring water to a boil, then lower ravioli into it a few at a time. Cook ravioli in batches to avoid overcrowding. Check ravioli after about 3 minutes; they should be tender, yet firm. If not, let them boil for another minute or so, then test again. Remove with slotted spoon and drain.

Butter lightly a shallow platter; arrange on it the drained ravioli, and top with your favorite sauce, or simply butter, and grated Parmesan cheese.

Egg Roll Wrappers as Dough:

Moisten with cold water all edges of ravioli mold; place one wrapper over mold. Place 1 teaspoon of filling in center of each ravioli. Moisten edges again and cover with another wrapper. Roll rolling pin over ravioli several times until they are cut apart. Place on cookie sheet that has been lightly sprinkled with corn meal. *May be frozen at this point.* Cook as above, cooking time is shorter, 1 to 2 minutes.

Dolores Lisica

ANCHOVY and BREAD CRUMB VERMICELLI

2 cans (2-ounce) anchovies
2 to 3 tablespoons olive oil
2 small cloves garlic, pressed
1 cup bread crumbs
8 to 10 ounces vermicelli
salt and pepper, to taste

Drain, then mince anchovies, reserving the oil in a small skillet.

Add 1 tablespoon olive oil to reserved anchovy oil in skillet and heat; add minced anchovies and pressed garlic. Sauté lightly for 1 or 2 minutes. Pour out of skillet and set aside.

Wipe skillet with a paper towel, then add 2 tablespoons oil; heat and add bread crumbs. Brown lightly, stirring constantly. Crumbs can burn very quickly. Remove from skillet and set aside.

Cook vermicelli per package instructions; drain thoroughly.

In saucepan in which pasta was cooked, place half of anchovies and half of bread crumbs; add half of cooked vermicelli and toss with 2 forks. Add remaining anchovies, bread crumbs, and pasta. Toss with forks until all pasta is coated with crumbs and anchovies. Heat lightly, taste, and adjust seasonings.

Serves 2 to 4   *Chris Lisica*

PEAS AND PASTA

2 tablespoons olive oil
1 medium onion, chopped
1 pound lean ground beef
2 large cloves garlic, minced
1 tablespoon sugar
salt and pepper to taste
1 can (16-ounce) tomato sauce
1 pound frozen petite peas
2 tablespoons butter
1/2 pound fresh mushrooms, sliced
2 tablespoons sherry wine (optional)
1/2 pound macaroni, shells or
    elbow size
1/2 cup Parmesan or Romano
    cheese, grated

Heat oil in a large saucepan and add chopped onion, ground beef, 1 clove garlic, sugar, and salt and pepper to taste. Sauté lightly for 10 to 15 minutes.

Add tomato sauce, and simmer for 20 minutes.

Add peas and cook another 10 minutes.

Sauté the mushrooms in butter, add 1 clove garlic, and sherry. Set aside.

Cook the macaroni according to package directions, drain and set aside.

To assemble: butter a 9 x 12-inch casserole dish. Layer the macaroni on the bottom; spread meat and tomato mixture on top. Sprinkle with grated cheese and top with sautéed mushrooms.

Bake in a 350 degree oven for 10 minutes, just long enough to heat through and melt cheese.

Serves 4 generously   *Virginia Manzella*

Desserts

DESSERTS

APPLE RICE PUDDING

Combine all ingredients except rice and walnuts.

For microwave, place in a 1-1/2 quart casserole. Cover and cook for 5 to 6 minutes. Stir in rice and walnuts.

For conventional stove, cook in saucepan on top of stove until mixture bubbles. Stir in rice and walnuts, then place in a 1-1/2 quart casserole.

For both methods, cover and let sit for 10 minutes to absorb liquid. Fluff mixture with a fork. Let cool.

Refrigerate and serve chilled.

Note: For tiny tots, omit nuts.

Betty Spence

1 cup apple juice or cider
3/4 cup chopped apple, unpeeled
1/4 cup white raisins
1 tablespoon butter or margarine
1/4 teaspoon salt
1/2 teaspoon cinnamon
2/3 cup Minute rice
1/3 cup chopped walnuts

CHOCOLATE BREAD PUDDING

Add chocolate to milk in a double boiler and heat. When chocolate is melted, beat with a rotary egg beater until smooth and blended.

In a bowl, beat eggs slightly. Mix in sugar and salt. Add chocolate mixture gradually, stirring vigorously. Add vanilla.

Cube bread and place in buttered 9 x 12-inch baking dish. Pour mixture over it.

Place dish in a pan of hot water and bake in moderate oven at 350 degrees for 50 to 60 minutes, or until pudding is firm.

Serve hot with hard sauce, or cold with cream.

Hard Sauce:

Cream butter until soft; add sugar gradually. Beat until well blended. Add salt, vanilla, and egg; beat until very smooth. Chill thoroughly.

This is a recipe my mother clipped from a "ladies' magazine" in 1929, when almost no one could afford to throw away stale bread.

Serves 6

Prudy Zorotovich

1-1/2 squares unsweetened chocolate,
   cut in pieces
3 cups cold milk
3 eggs, slightly beaten
1 cup sugar
1/2 teaspoon salt
1 teaspoon vanilla
1-1/2 cups bread, cubed

Hard Sauce:

2 to 5 tablespoons butter
1 cup powdered sugar, sifted
1/8 teaspoon salt
1 teaspoon vanilla or 1 tablespoon
   coffee, rum or brandy
1 egg

CHOCOLATE MINT RING

1 quart milk
1/2 cup sugar
3 squares unsweetened chocolate
2 tablespoons gelatin
1/4 cup water

Sauce:

3/4 cup sugar
6 tablespoons water
12 marshmallows, cut up
1 egg white, stiffly beaten
green food coloring
drop of oil of peppermint

Scald the milk and add sugar. Stir to dissolve.

Melt the chocolate and add to the hot milk mixture.

Soften gelatin in cool water, then add to chocolate mixture. Stir until dissolved.

Pour mixture into 1-quart ring mold. Refrigerate to set.

Make sauce. Unmold chocolate ring on a platter and pour the sauce in the middle.

Sauce:

In a medium saucepan, cook sugar and water to syrup. Add marshmallows and cook until melted. Pour over stiffly beaten egg white. Add food coloring and oil of peppermint. Mix well.

Serves 8   Jacqueline P. Smith

PUMPKIN PUDDING

3 eggs, beaten
1 can (32-ounce) pumpkin
1 cup milk
1/2 teaspoon salt
1/2 teaspoon ginger
1/2 teaspoon cloves, ground
1 teaspoon cinnamon
1 cup sugar
1 spice cake mix, dry
1-1/2 sticks butter, melted
3/4 cup chopped nuts
frozen whipped topping or
    whipped cream

In a large bowl, beat eggs. Mix in pumpkin, milk, salt, ginger, cloves, cinnamon, and sugar.

Pour into a 9 x 13-inch greased pan.

Sprinkle dry spice cake mix over top. Drizzle with melted butter, and sprinkle with chopped nuts.

Bake 1 hour at 350 degrees.

Top with frozen whipped topping or whipped cream.

Serves 16 to 20   Elise R. Huffman

BROWN SUGAR PEARS

1 can (29-ounce) sliced pears in syrup
2 tablespoons margarine
1/4 cup packed brown sugar
1 teaspoon grated lemon rind
1 tablespoon lemon juice
1/2 teaspoon rum flavoring
dairy sour cream for topping
nutmeg, grated

Drain pears. Save 1/2 cup of syrup.

Combine the syrup, margarine, brown sugar, grated lemon rind, and lemon juice in a small skillet. Add pears and heat, stirring gently. Stir in rum flavoring.

Serve warm, topped with sour cream and nutmeg.

Serves 4   Margaret Spangler

CHOCOLATE SOUFFLÉ

Melt butter in saucepan. Remove from heat and stir in flour.

In a separate pan, on low heat, melt chocolate in half and half and coffee, stirring frequently. Pour melted chocolate mixture into butter and flour mixture. Blend carefully. Return to heat and bring to a bubble. Allow to bubble for 1 minute. Remove from heat and scrape vanilla bean into mixture. Cool and cover.

Beat egg yolks with 3 tablespoons sugar until light and fluffy; add to chocolate mixture. Return to heat for 1 minute or until just warmed.

Beat egg whites until foamy. Add salt and cream of tartar and continue to beat until soft peaks form. Add remaining tablespoon of sugar and beat until stiff peaks form. Stir a large dollop of the egg whites into the chocolate mixture. Carefully fold in remaining whites.

Grease a 1 or 1-1/2 quart soufflé dish, then dust with granulated sugar. Pour soufflé mixture into dish.

Bake at 375 degrees for 30 minutes.

Remove and sprinkle with confectioner's sugar. Continue baking for an additional 5 minutes.

Bobbie Miller

3 tablespoons butter
3 tablespoons flour
6 ounces German sweet chocolate
1-1/4 cups half and half
1/4 cup coffee
1 vanilla bean
4 egg yolks
4 tablespoons sugar
6 egg whites
dash of salt
dash of cream of tartar
granulated sugar for dusting
confectioner's sugar

FLAN DE NARANJA
Caramelized Custard

Mexico

Heat 1/2 cup sugar in skillet over low heat until sugar is melted and turns golden brown, stirring to prevent burning. Pour at once into a round 1-1/2 quart baking dish, tilting dish to coat bottom.

Beat eggs with remaining sugar, stir in milk, orange juice and peel until well mixed. Pour over caramel layer in baking dish.

Place dish in a pan of boiling water 1 inch deep. Bake at 350 degrees until knife inserted near center comes out clean.

Cool to room temperature. Invert onto serving platter or use individual dishes.

Serves 6 to 8   *Lillian Peterson Drenckhahn*

3/4 cup sugar
6 eggs
1 cup milk
1 cup orange juice
grated peel of 2 oranges

FROZEN PINEAPPLE CRUNCH

2 eggs, separated
1/2 cup heavy cream, whipped
1/3 cup sugar
2 tablespoons lemon juice
1 can (14-ounce) crushed pineapple, drained

Topping:

2 tablespoons butter or margarine
1/4 cup packed brown sugar
2 cups cornflakes
1/2 cup chopped nuts

Beat egg white until stiff and set aside. Whip cream and set aside.

In top of double boiler, beat yolks until thick and lemon colored. Beat in sugar and lemon juice and cook over hot water, stirring frequently, until thickened (about 10 minutes). Fold in pineapple, egg whites and whipped cream. Turn into a 1-quart shallow container.

In a skillet, mix together topping ingredients. Heat, stirring, until butter is melted and sugar is caramelized slightly. Pour onto pineapple/cream mixture and freeze overnight.

Serve with additional whipped cream, if desired.

Serves 8   *Mrs. Oscar H. De Jerf*

FROZEN RAISIN TORTONI

1 egg, separated
1/2 cup milk
1/3 cup sugar
1 teaspoon unflavored gelatin
1/4 teaspoon salt
1/2 cup almond macaroon crumbs
1 cup heavy cream
1/2 cup seedless raisins, slightly chopped
2 tablespoons California medium sherry

In a saucepan, combine lightly beaten egg yolk and milk; stir in sugar mixed with gelatin and salt. Cook over very low heat, stirring constantly, until mixture coats spoon. Remove from heat and stir in macaroon crumbs. Cool.

Beat egg white until stiff, then with same beater, beat cream until stiff. Fold egg white and cream into cooled custard. Fold in raisins and wine. Turn into individual molds and freeze until firm.

Betty Di Masi

ENGLISH TRIFLE

2 cups cooked vanilla custard
1 dozen lady fingers, or sliced sponge cake
strawberry preserves
sherry
1/2 pint whipping cream
1/4 cup sliced maraschino cherries
1/4 cup slivered almonds

Make vanilla custard according to instructions on package. It should be of moderately thick consistency.

Place 4 lady fingers in a glass bowl. Spread each piece with strawberry jam. Soak each with sherry. Cover with custard. Repeat for at least 2 layers.

Let it "set and soak" in the refrigerator for several hours. Serve with whipped cream and maraschino cherries and top with slivered almonds.

Nita Scriven

~Cookies and Candies~

COOKIES AND CANDY

ANISE STICKS

In a large bowl, cream margarine and butter. Add sugar slowly. Add one egg at a time, beating well after each egg.

In another large bowl, sift flour, baking soda, and baking powder.

In a measuring cup, mix milk, water, and anise oil.

While stirring, add dry ingredients and liquids alternately to butter mixture. Add nuts and mix well.

Shape on ungreased cookie pan with spoon like a long flattened roll and bake at 350 degrees until a golden brown.

Remove from oven and slice in a slanted fashion with a wet steak knife. Lift cookies with a steel spatula and turn over on their sides on the cookie sheet. Bake a few minutes until golden brown. Remove from oven and turn cookies over on other side; bake a few more minutes until golden brown.

Remove from oven and let cool thoroughly before storing in air-tight container to retain freshness. A great Italian cookie!

Lucy DiMeglio

1/4 pound margarine
1/4 pound butter
2-1/2 cups sugar
4 eggs
6 cups flour
1 teaspoon baking soda
1 teaspoon baking powder
3/4 cup milk
1/4 cup water
2 teaspoons anise oil (available at pharmacies)
2 cups chopped walnuts or almonds

ABC DELIGHTS

In a bowl, mix sunflower seeds, oatmeal, and sesame seeds. Sprinkle carob powder over the mixture; add honey and stir. Add peanut butter and mix well.

Form into balls. Roll in coconut. Refrigerate before serving.

Vicki Boutté

1/2 cup carob powder
1/2 cup honey
1/2 cup crunchy peanut butter
1/2 cup hulled sunflower seeds
1/2 cup uncooked oatmeal
1/2 cup sesame seeds

BUTTERSCOTCH PEANUT BUTTER COOKIES
Refrigerator Cookies

6 ounces butterscotch bits
3 heaping tablespoons peanut butter
4 cups corn flakes

In a double boiler, melt together butterscotch bits and peanut butter.

Place corn flakes in a bowl and add butterscotch and peanut butter mixture. Mix until cornflakes are well coated.

Drop by spoonful on a cookie sheet.

Refrigerate.

Ruth E. Havens

CANDY CANE COOKIES

1/2 cup shortening
1/2 cup butter or margarine
   (softened)
1 cup sifted powdered sugar
1 egg, slightly beaten
1 tablespoon almond extract
1 tablespoon vanilla extract
2-1/2 cups all-purpose flour
1/2 tablespoon red food coloring

Cream shortening and butter until fluffy. Add sugar and mix well. Add slightly beaten egg and extracts, and mix. While stirring, gradually add flour. Mix well. Dough will be stiff.

Remove half of dough. Add red food coloring to the half of dough left in the bowl and mix well.

On a lightly floured surface, roll the plain dough and the red colored dough, separately, into long, thin cylinders. Then twist the cylinders around each other.

Cut into 3- to 4-inch lengths and form into the shape of candy canes.

Place cookies on an ungreased cookie sheet.

Bake at 375 degrees for about 9 minutes.

Frances DiMeglio

Cookies and Candy

CHOCOLATE MERINGUE COOKIES

Melt chocolate chips in oven or double boiler.

Add salt to egg whites and beat until foamy. Add sugar to egg whites, gradually, beating well after each addition. Continue to beat until stiff peaks are formed. Add vinegar and vanilla and beat well. Fold in melted chocolate, coconut, and nuts.

Drop by teaspoonfuls onto greased baking sheets.

Bake at 350 degrees for about 10 minutes.

Yield: 2-1/2 to 3 dozen   *Jacqueline P. Smith*

6 ounces chocolate chips
2 egg whites
1/8 teaspoon salt
1/2 cup sugar
1/2 teaspoon white vinegar
1/2 teaspoon vanilla
1/2 cup flaked coconut
1/4 cup chopped pecans

COCONUT-OATMEAL PUFFS WITH DATE FILLING
Finland

Sift flour with baking powder, baking soda and salt. Set aside.

Preheat oven to 375 degrees.

In a large bowl, cream shortening and sugar. Add beaten eggs. Add oatmeal and coconut. Stir in vanilla. While stirring, gradually blend in sifted flour mixture. Shape into balls the size of half-teaspoons. Place on greased cookie sheet. Bake at 375 degrees for 6 to 8 minutes. Cool.

Date Filling:

In a small saucepan, combine dates, water, orange rind, and sugar. Cook over moderate heat until thick and smooth.

Remove from heat and add orange and lemon juices and mix well. Cool.

After the puffs cool, press 2 of them together with some of the cooled date filling between them.

Yield: 5-1/2 dozen   *Veni Hill*

2-1/4 cups flour
1 teaspoon baking powder
1 teaspoon baking soda
1 teaspoon salt
2/3 cup shortening or margarine
1-1/2 cups sugar
1 cup brown sugar
2 eggs, beaten
1 cup oatmeal
1 cup coconut
2 teaspoons vanilla

Date Filling:

1 pound chopped dates
1 cup cold water
grated rind of 1 orange
1/4 cup brown sugar
1/4 cup orange juice
2 teaspoons lemon juice

203

COOKIE JAR GINGERSNAPS

2 cups flour
1 tablespoon ginger
1 teaspoon cinnamon
1/2 teaspoon nutmeg
2 teaspoons baking soda
1/2 teaspoon salt
3/4 cup shortening
1 cup sugar
1 egg
1/4 cup dark molasses
sugar to roll cookies in

Measure and sift flour, ginger, cinnamon, nutmeg, baking soda, and salt.

In a large bowl, cream shortening. Gradually add sugar. Add egg and molasses. Mix. While stirring, gradually add dry ingredients. Blend well.

Form into teaspoon-sized balls. Roll in granulated sugar.

Space 2 inches apart on cookie sheet.

Bake at 350 degrees for about 12 minutes.

Take cookies out when they look a little undercooked. Check bottom of cookies for indication of doneness.

Beverly Stockert

CRUNCHY NUT COOKIES

1/2 cup soft shortening
1 cup white sugar
1 cup brown sugar
2 eggs
1 teaspoon vanilla
3 cups flour
1 teaspoon baking soda
1/2 teaspoon salt
1 cup chopped nuts

In a large bowl, cream shortening. Add sugar and beat well. Add eggs and vanilla and mix thoroughly.

In another large bowl, sift together flour, baking soda, and salt. Gradually stir into the creamed mixture. Add nuts.

Shape 1 level tablespoon of dough into a ball. Place on ungreased baking sheet. Flatten with bottom of greased glass dipped in sugar. Repeat until all dough is used.

Bake 8 to 10 minutes at 375 degrees.

Cool and store in an air-tight container.

Lucy DiMeglio

CVITE
Puffy Cookies

Sift together flour, baking powder, and salt. Set aside.

In a large bowl, cream butter and shortening, and add sugar slowly. Beat together until creamy. Add eggs one at a time, beating well after each addition. Add vanilla, and anise if desired. Add flour mixture alternately with milk. Beat well.

Drop by spoonfuls on a well greased cookie sheet.

Bake at 400 degrees for 3 minutes.

Cool on rack covered with waxed paper. Sift powdered sugar over tops of cookies, if desired.

Maria Dorotich

3-1/2 cups flour
3-1/2 teaspoons baking powder
dash salt
1/4 cup butter
1/2 cup shortening
1 cup sugar
3 eggs
1 teaspoon vanilla
1 teaspoon anise (optional)
1 cup milk
powdered sugar (optional)

FRUIT 'N OATMEAL COOKIES

Here is a milk-free, egg-free cookie — a boon for moms with allergic children or those on a cholesterol-free diet.

In a large bowl, combine flour, oatmeal, salt, baking powder, sugar, and cinnamon. Add dates or raisins and oil; mix well. Stir in water or applesauce and vanilla.

Drop by teaspoonful onto greased cookie sheet.

Bake at 375 degrees for about 15 minutes.

Variation: For a wheat-free version, substitute oat flour or rice flour.

Yield: 4 dozen

Char Arno

1 cup flour
1 cup oatmeal
1/2 teaspoon salt
2 teaspoons baking powder
1/2 cup brown sugar, firmly packed
1/2 teaspoon cinnamon
1/2 cup chopped dates or raisins
4 tablespoons salad oil
1/2 cup water or thin applesauce
1 teaspoon vanilla

GRANOLA SPECIAL

2 cups rolled oats
1/2 cup coconut
3 tablespoons whole sesame seeds
1/4 cup butter or margarine
1 cup raisins
1 cup chopped nuts or sunflower seeds
1/2 cup wheat germ
1/4 cup honey

In a large heavy pan or dutch oven, combine oats, coconut, sesame seeds, and butter. Mix well and brown in a 350-degree oven for 10 to 15 minutes. Stir mixture to brown evenly.

Remove from oven and mix in raisins, nuts, and wheat germ. Pour honey over top and mix well.

Bake an additional 10 to 15 minutes in a 350-degree oven.

Cool and store in air-tight container.

This recipe is very flexible, and ingredients of your choice can be added or subtracted.

Jackie Morrison

SEVEN LAYER COOKIES

1/4 pound butter
1 cup graham cracker crumbs
1 cup coconut
6 ounces package chocolate chips
6 ounces package butterscotch chips
1 can sweetened condensed milk
1-1/2 cup chopped nuts

These cookies are so rich they are almost like a candy bar. They are good for camp or pot luck parties where no one has a chance to eat too many.

Melt butter in a 9 x 13-inch pan and stir in crumbs. Spread evenly on bottom of pan.

Sprinkle coconut and chocolate and butterscotch chips on crumbs. Drizzle half the milk on top. Add nuts and top with remaining milk.

Bake at 325 degrees for 30 minutes or more. *Be careful not to overbake or the chocolate will burn.*

Lauren Litman

FISH EYE COOKIES
Jam Shortbread Cookies

Sift together flour, cream of tartar, baking soda, and salt, and set aside.

In a large bowl, cream shortening, add white and brown sugars, and beat until fluffy. Add egg yolks, milk, and vanilla. Add flour mixture to creamed mixture; blend well. Chill dough for one hour.

Divide dough into 2 portions. On a well floured surface roll out each portion to 1/8 inch thickness. With a 2-inch cookie cutter, cut cookies in both portions of dough. Put cookies from one portion of dough on an ungreased cookie sheet, and place 1/2 teaspoon preserves in center of each cookie.

Using a small cutter, cut another hole (the eye) in center of all cookies in second portion of dough. Place these cookies on top of first portion cookies in such a way that the jam shows through the small holes. Seal edges of the cookies with fingers.

Bake at 350 degrees for 10 to 12 minutes.

Yield: 42 cookies   *Fran Henderson*

2-2/3 cups sifted flour
2 teaspoons cream of tartar
1 teaspoon baking soda
1/2 teaspoon salt
1 cup shortening
1/2 cup granulated sugar
1/2 cup brown sugar
2 egg yolks
3 tablespoons milk
2 teaspoons vanilla
1/2 cup raspberry preserves

SHORTBREAD COOKIES

Cream margarine and sugar until very smooth. Add corn oil and mix. Add flour and cornstarch and mix well.

Roll into balls the size of a large marble and place on an ungreased cookie sheet.

Press flat with the tines of a fork.

Bake in a 350-degree oven for 10 to 12 minutes.

Yield: 2 dozen   *Roselyn R. Egly*

1/4 cup margarine
1/4 cup brown sugar
1/4 cup corn oil
1 cup sifted flour
1/4 cup cornstarch

SPRITZ COOKIES

1 cup butter
3/4 cup sugar
1 egg plus 1 egg yolk (unbeaten)
2-7/8 cups flour
1/8 teaspoon salt
1 teaspoon vanilla
1 teaspoon almond flavoring

In a large bowl, cream butter; add sugar gradually and cream well. Add egg and yolk and beat well.

Sift flour; measure and add salt. Sift 3 times. Gradually add to first mixture. Add vanilla and almond flavorings.

Chill overnight.

Place a small amount of dough in a cookie press and press onto cookie sheet. Repeat until all dough is used.

Bake in a hot oven at 400 degrees for 10 to 11 minutes.

At holiday season, I often use green food coloring and use a disc to make small wreaths.

Emmy Ruud

RUM RUM BALLS

2 cups finely crushed chocolate wafers
1 cup sifted powdered sugar
1 cup chopped pecans or walnuts
1/4 cup light corn syrup
1 cup dark rum
1 cup flaked coconut

In a large bowl, combine chocolate wafers, sugar, nuts, corn syrup, and rum. Mix well.

Form into balls; roll in coconut and place on cookie sheet.

Refrigerate overnight.

Vicki Boutté

CHOCOLATE FUDGE

1 can (13 ounces) evaporated milk
4 cups sugar
6 ounces chocolate chips
1/8 pound butter
1 pint marshmallow cream
1 teaspoon vanilla
1 cup walnuts, chopped

Heat milk and mix in sugar. Add butter and cook to 238 degrees (use a candy thermometer).

Remove from heat and add chocolate chips; stir until melted. Add marshmallow cream and beat until creamy. Add vanilla and walnuts. Mix well.

Pour into a buttered pan.

When cool, cut into squares.

Mildred Davis

PERFECT FUDGE

In a saucepan, combine milk, sugar, cocoa, and salt. Bring to a boil slowly, stirring constantly. Boil slowly until it forms a firm ball in a cup of cold water.

Place the pan in cold water, being careful not to spill any water into the pan. Cool until thick, stirring occasionally to check consistency.

Add butter and vanilla, and beat until it is of spreading consistency.

Pour onto buttered plate.

Arthur Litman

3/4 cup milk
2 cups sugar
3 tablespoons cocoa
dash of salt
2 tablespoons butter
1 teaspoon vanilla

HONEYCOMB CANDY

New Zealand

Place sugar, vinegar, salt, and corn syrup in a large saucepan. Stir over medium heat until the sugar dissolves

Continue cooking without stirring until temperature reaches 300 degrees (use a candy thermometer) or a little of the mixture dropped into a saucer of water separates into hard brittle threads and breaks easily.

Remove from heat and add baking soda. Mixture will immediately puff up. *Don't get it on your skin—it's hot!*

Pour into a shallow, well greased, 9-inch metal pan (not glass). Place on a rack to cool.

When cold, break into pieces. May be frosted with firm chocolate before breaking.

Nita Scriven

1 cup sugar
1 tablespoon vinegar
1/4 teaspoon salt
1 cup dark corn syrup
1 tablespoon baking soda

PEANUT BUTTER FUDGE

1 cup undiluted evaporated milk
2 cups sugar
1/4 cup butter or margarine
1 cup miniature marshmallows or
    10 large marshmallows
1 jar (12-ounce) of chunk-style peanut
    butter (about 1-1/3 cups)
1 teaspoon vanilla extract

Combine milk, sugar, and butter in a heavy skillet. Set over medium heat and boil 4 minutes, stirring constantly.

Remove from heat and stir in marshmallows, peanut butter, and vanilla extract until evenly blended.

Turn into buttered 8-inch square pan and spread to corners. Chill before cutting into squares.

Note: This fudge can be prepared in an electric skillet. Set temperature at 280 degrees. Bring mixture to boiling and boil about 5 minutes.

Yield: 2 pounds   *Helen Homen*

WHITE FUDGE

3/4 cup evaporated milk
3/4 cup water
3 cups granulated sugar
3/4 teaspoon salt
3 tablespoons butter
1-1/2 teaspoons vanilla
3/4 cup marshmallow cream
1/3 cup chopped candied fruits

In a saucepan, combine milk and water with sugar, salt, and butter. Mix thoroughly. Cook to soft ball stage (236 degrees, using a candy thermometer). Stir constantly.

Remove from heat. Cool at room temperature, without stirring, until lukewarm (135 degrees).

Add vanilla. Beat until mixture holds its shape.

Add marshmallow cream and candied fruits. Beat again until mixture loses its gloss and is very stiff.

Spread into a buttered pan.

Mildred Davis

PEANUT BUTTER RAISIN CHEWS

1 cup peanut butter
1 cup light corn syrup
1 cup nonfat dry milk
1 cup confectioner's sugar
1/2 cup nuts (optional)
1/2 cup raisins
1/2 cup chocolate chips

In a large bowl, mix the peanut butter, corn syrup, dry milk, confectioner's sugar, and nuts. After these are well blended, add raisins and chocolate chips and mix thoroughly.

Press 1/2 inch thick in a buttered 9 x 11-inch pan. Cut into pieces approximately 1 inch square. Fresh candy may be cut with scissors.

May be eaten right away or chilled before serving to firm up candy.

Yield: 5 dozen   *Dottie Hill*

~Pies and Pastries~

PIES AND PASTRIES

PIE DOUGH ANY DUMMY CAN DO

Sift flour and salt into bowl. Take out 1/3 cup of the flour and mix it with water to form a paste.

Add shortening to remaining flour and, using a pastry blender, cut shortening into flour until small pea-sized balls are formed. Add flour/water mixture, mix thoroughly until dough comes together and can be shaped into a ball.

Divide into two parts; roll out each crust to a circle about 1/8 inch thick and 2 inches larger than the top of the pie pan.

If a 2-crust pie is desired, do not pre-bake crust.

If two 1-crust cooked pie shells are desired, place each crust in a 9-inch pie pan. Press it down lightly to eliminate any pockets. Cut off excess dough, leaving a one-inch overhang all around. Tuck overhang under to make a ridge, and crimp with fingers or fork all around. With a fork, prick the crust on the bottom and sides at about 1/2-inch intervals to prevent puffing while baking. Check while baking; if a puff appears, quickly reach in and prick it with the fork.

Bake at 425 degrees for 12 to 15 minutes.

Mary Lou Nizetich

2 cups flour
1 teaspoon salt
1/4 cup ice water
2/3 cup shortening

MOM'S APPLE PIE

Peel, core, and slice tart apples. Put in a large bowl and sprinkle with lemon juice.

In another bowl, combine sugar, flour, cinnamon, nutmeg, and salt. Mix with apples, blending evenly. Set aside.

Put pastry ingredients in food processor and mix until it forms a ball. Divide into 2 equal parts. Roll out each part between 2 sheets of waxed paper.

Line a 9-inch pie plate with one pastry. Fill with apple mixture and dot with margarine. Cover pie with top pastry and flute the edge. Prick the top crust 5 or 6 times to allow steam to escape during cooking. Brush with egg, then sprinkle with sugar. Bake at 400 degrees for 55 to 60 minutes, or until crust is browned.

Selma Streicher

6 cups sliced tart apples
1 tablespoon lemon juice
3/4 to 1 cup sugar
2 tablespoons flour
1/2 to 1 teaspoon cinnamon
dash nutmeg
dash salt
2 tablespoons butter or margarine
sugar for sparkle
1 egg, beaten

Pastry:

3 cups enriched flour
1 teaspoon salt
1 cup shortening
5 to 7 tablespoons ice cold water

CHERRY ELEGANTE

1-1/2 cups flour
3/4 cup butter or margarine
3/4 cup chopped nuts
1 package (8-ounce) cream cheese,
    room temperature
1 cup powdered sugar
3 cups whipped topping
2 small packages coconut cream
    pudding
1 can cherry pie filling
toasted coconut (optional)

Mix flour, butter or margarine, and nuts. Press into a 9 x 13-inch cake pan. Bake at 350 degrees for 20 minutes or until almost brown.

Cream the cheese. Gradually beat in the powdered sugar. Fold in 1 cup of whipped topping. Spread on the cooled crust.

Prepare the pudding as directed on the package. Cool, stirring occasionally. Do not chill. Carefully spread over the cheese layer.

Spoon the cherry pie filling over the pudding layer. Spread the remaining whipped topping over the cherry layer and top with toasted coconut.

Refrigerate for several hours or overnight before serving.

Serves 18   *Nancy Hedges*

CHOCOLATE CHIP PIE

1 cup broken pecans
1 cup chocolate chips (more, if
    desired)
2 unbaked, 9-inch pie shells
4 eggs, beaten
1 cup sugar
1/4 pound butter, melted
1 cup light corn syrup

Combine pecans and chocolate bits. Divide evenly and spread into pie shells.

Beat eggs. Beat in sugar, melted butter, and corn syrup. Pour over nuts and chocolate bits.

Bake at 350 degrees for 30 to 40 minutes.

Yield: 2 pies   *Rosemarie Powers*

CHOCOLATE LUSH

Preheat oven to 350 degrees.

Mix together crust ingredients and press into a 9 x 12-inch pan. Bake for 15 minutes and cool thoroughly.

For filling, beat cream cheese and powdered sugar until creamy. Fold in 1 cup whipped topping and spread mixture onto cooled crust.

For topping, mix milk and pudding mix, using an electric mixer or a rotary egg beater, and pour over cream cheese layer; set aside until thickened (5 to 10 minutes).

Top with remaining whipped topping and sprinkle with almonds.

Serves 8 to 10   *Rose Marie Castagnola*

Crust:

1/2 cup butter
1/2 cup chopped or slivered almonds
1 cup flour

Filling:

1 package (8-ounce) cream cheese, softened
1 cup powdered sugar
1 cup whipped topping

Topping:

3 cups milk
2 packages (4-ounce) instant chocolate pudding mix
1 cup whipped topping
slivered almonds

CHOCOLATE MOCHA PIE

Put vanilla ice cream, milk, chocolate pudding, and chocolate syrup into a mixing bowl and beat, using an electric mixer, until well blended.

Put mixture into a cooled graham cracker pie shell. Spread Cool Whip on top. Freeze.

Vi Kasner

1 graham cracker pie crust
4 cups vanilla ice cream
2 tablespoons milk
1 package instant chocolate pudding
1/4 cup chocolate syrup
1 carton (8-ounce) Cool Whip

FRENCH CHOCOLATE PIE

To make crust, combine finely crushed chocolate wafers and melted butter. Press into a 9-inch pie dish and bake 5 to 6 minutes at 350 degrees. Cool.

Combine butter, vanilla, and 1-1/2 cups sugar; then add melted chocolate. While stirring, add eggs, one at a time; then beat for 5 minutes.

Pour filling into pie shell and chill until firm.

Whip cream, gradually adding 2 tablespoons sugar and the vanilla. Whip until stiff. Spread on top of chilled pie.

Decorate with chocolate candy bar shavings. Chill thoroughly.

Lucy DiMeglio

Crust:

2/3 package chocolate wafers, finely crushed
3/4 stick butter, melted

Filling:

1/2 pound butter
2 teaspoons vanilla
1-1/2 cups sugar
2 squares baking chocolate, melted
4 eggs
1/2 pint whipping cream
2 tablespoons sugar
1 teaspoon vanilla
chocolate candy bar shavings

CRANBERRY PIE

1/2 pound cranberries
1/2 cup chopped nuts
1-1/2 cups sugar
1 cup flour
2 eggs, slightly beaten
1-1/4 stick butter, melted

Wash and dry cranberries and place evenly over bottom of a 10-inch pie pan. Sprinkle with nuts and 1/2 cup sugar.

Mix flour, remaining sugar, eggs, and butter. Mix throughly. Pour over cranberries.

Bake for 40 to 50 minutes at 325 degrees.

Really delicious! I hate cranberries, but I love this pie. Better make two—one won't be enough!

Scottie Gershon

LEMON PIE

1 8-inch baked pie shell
4 eggs, separated
1 can (14-ounce) condensed milk
2 tablespoons margarine
1/2 cup lemon juice
1/2 cup sugar
1/4 teaspoon vanilla

Preheat oven to 325 degrees.

Put egg yolks in bowl and add milk, margarine, and lemon juice. Beat until smooth.

In another bowl, beat egg whites until foamy. Gradually add sugar. Beat until meringue is stiff and glossy. Fold a few tablespoons of meringue into lemon filling. Turn into pie shell.

Stir vanilla into remaining meringue and spread over filling.

Bake 20 minutes at 325 degrees.

Anne Terry

LEMON LUSCIOUS PIE

1 baked 9 inch pie shell
1 cup and 2 tablespoons sugar
3 tablespoons cornstarch
1/4 cup butter
1 tablespoon grated lemon rind
1/4 cup lemon juice
3 egg yolks
1 cup milk
1 cup sour cream
1 teaspoon vanilla
1/2 pint whipping cream

Combine 1 cup sugar and cornstarch in saucepan. While stirring, add butter, lemon rind, lemon juice, and egg yolks. Stir in milk. Cook over medium heat, stirring constantly, until thick. Cool.

Fold in sour cream. Spoon into pie shell. Chill at least 2 hours.

Beat whipping cream until it thickens. While beating, slowly add 2 tablespoons sugar and vanilla. Beat until fluffy. Spread over top of pie.

Lucy DiMeglio

LEMON SQUARES

Preheat oven to 350 degrees.

Combine crust ingredients with fork or pastry blender and press into a greased 9 x 13-inch pan. Bake for 15 to 20 minutes, or until lightly browned.

Mix filling ingredients in large bowl with electric mixer. Beat on high speed for 5 minutes. Pour on hot crust.

Bake at 350 degrees for 15 to 20 minutes or until top is firm. Cool slightly and dust lightly with powdered sugar, if desired. Cut into squares.

Serves 9 to 12   *Vicki Boutté*

Crust:

2 cubes margarine or butter
2 cups flour
1/2 cup powdered sugar

Filling:

4 eggs
1/2 cup fresh lemon juice
2 cups sugar
4 tablespoons flour
dash of salt
powdered sugar

LEMONADE PIE

Place cream cheese in a bowl and let it come to room temperature. Then beat cheese until smooth.

Add Cool Whip, lemonade, and condensed milk, and beat until smooth. Spoon into pie crusts.

Chill at least overnight.

Yield: 2 pies   *Virginia Mulligan*

2 graham cracker pie crusts
1 package (8-ounce) cream cheese
1 small carton Cool Whip
1 small can frozen lemonade
1 small can condensed milk

PASTIERRA
Traditional Easter Wheat Pie

1/2 pound wheatberries*
1/2 teaspoon salt
rind of 1 lemon (not grated)
milk—unmeasured
1 lemon rind and 1 orange rind,
    finely grated
1/4 pound unsalted butter
1/4 cup citron, grated*
2 cups sugar
7 eggs
1 teaspoon vanilla extract
1 teaspoon rum extract
1 teaspoon lemon extract
1 drop milefiore extract*
1 pound ricotta cheese
1-1/2 cups milk

*These items may be found at an
    Italian grocery store.

Vanilla Custard:

2 cups milk
2 eggs, separated
8 level teaspoons flour
8 level teaspoons cornstarch
1 cup sugar
1/2 teaspoon vanilla extract
1/2 teaspoon lemon extract

Dough:

1 cup butter
1/2 cup sugar
4 eggs
1 teaspoon vanilla
4-1/2 cups sifted flour
2 teaspoons baking powder

Soak wheatberries for 3 or 4 days. Cover with water and boil with salt and lemon rind for about 15 to 20 minutes. Drain water and discard lemon rind.

Cover cooked wheat with as much milk as it will take (no need to measure). Add grated rinds and cook about 15 minutes, stirring constantly over low heat. Remove from heat and add butter, citron, sugar, eggs, and extracts.

In a separate bowl, beat ricotta and milk until smooth. Add to wheatberry mixture. Set aside.

Vanilla Custard:

In a double boiler, combine milk, 2 egg yolks, flour, cornstarch, 1/2 cup sugar, and extracts, and cook until thickened. Remove from heat and mix into wheatberry mixture.

Beat egg whites until soft peaks form. Add 1/2 cup sugar and beat until stiff. Fold into wheatberry/custard mixture.

Dough:

To make dough, cream butter and sugar. Add eggs, one at a time. Add vanilla, flour, and baking powder. Work in by hand. Roll out. Line two 9 x 13-inch glass baking dishes with dough, cutting off the excess. Pour in wheatberry/custard mixture and cover with strips of remaining dough to form lattice. Bake at 350 degrees for about an hour or until firm.

In Ischia, Italy, where I was born, this was always made for Easter Sunday dessert. All my fellow countrypeople have their various versions of the pastierra, but basically they are much the same. The real fun is to sample and critique each other's pies after Easter.

Caterina Cuomo

PECAN PRALINE CHOCOLATE PIE

Praline:

In a small heavy saucepan, combine sugar and water. Bring to a boil over moderate heat. Do not stir. Boil, swirling the pan, until syrup is just amber colored. Stir in pecans and return syrup to a boil. Pour onto a lightly oiled marble slab or baking sheet and let cool for 20 minutes in refrigerator. Break into pieces and set aside.

Crust:

Mix crust ingredients and press onto bottom and sides of a 10-inch glass pie plate. Bake in middle of oven at 375 degrees for 8 to 10 minutes, or until the edges are browned lightly. Cool on a rack.

Chocolate Layer:

In the top of a double boiler, set over simmering water, combine the chocolate, butter, corn syrup, and water. Cook, stirring, until chocolate is melted. Remove pan from heat. Dip pecans into this mixture, coating the bottom of each. Set them on waxed paper, chocolate down, and chill in refrigerator. Pour remaining chocolate mixture evenly over the pie crust and chill until chocolate is set.

Filling:

In a small bowl, sprinkle gelatin over 1/4 cup cold water and let it soften for 15 minutes. In top of double boiler, combine egg yolks, 2 tablespoons sugar, and milk. Cook, stirring constantly with a wooden spoon, until it thickens and coats the spoon. Stir in gelatin mixture until thoroughly mixed. Remove pan from heat and stir in creme de cacao and praline pieces. Transfer mixture to a large bowl and let it cool, stirring occasionally, until it begins to thicken.

In a bowl, beat egg whites with cream of tartar and a pinch of salt until they hold soft peaks. Beat in remaining 4 tablespoons sugar a little at a time, and beat until it holds stiff peaks. Stir 1/3 of the egg whites into the custard praline mixture, then fold in remaining egg whites gently but thoroughly.

In a chilled bowl, beat cream until it holds stiff peaks. Fold it into the praline mixture, and spoon the filling into the pie shell, mounding it. Chill for 2 hours. Before serving, stud top of pie with pecan halves you have dipped in chocolate.

Loa Sprung

Praline:

1/2 cup sugar
1 tablespoon water
1/2 cup coarsely chopped pecans

Crust:

1 cup graham cracker crumbs
1/2 cup finely chopped pecans
2 tablespoons sugar
1/3 cup unsalted butter, melted

Chocolate Layer:

4 ounces semisweet chocolate, chopped
1-1/2 tablespoons unsalted butter
3 tablespoons dark corn syrup
2 tablespoons water
8 pecan halves

Filling:

1 tablespoon unflavored gelatin
1/4 cup cold water
3 large egg yolks
6 tablespoons sugar
2/3 cup milk
2 tablespoons creme de cacao
3 large egg whites, at room temperature
1/8 teaspoon cream of tartar
1 cup well chilled heavy cream

RASPBERRY RIBBON PIE

1 9-inch pie shell, baked and cooled
1 package (3-ounce) raspberry gelatin
1/4 cup sugar
1-1/4 cup boiling water
1 package (10-ounce) frozen red
    raspberries
1 tablespoon lemon juice
1 cup heavy cream, whipped
1 package (3-ounce) cream cheese,
    softened
1/3 cup sifted powdered sugar
1 teaspoon vanilla
dash salt

In a bowl, dissolve gelatin and sugar in boiling water. Add frozen berries and lemon juice. Stir until berries thaw. Chill until partially set.

Beat cream until it holds stiff peaks.

In a separate bowl, blend cream cheese, powdered sugar, vanilla, and salt. Fold in a small amount of whipped cream. Then fold in remaining whipped cream.

Spread half the white mixture over bottom of pastry shell. Cover with half the red mixture. Repeat layers. Chill until set.

Lucy DiMeglio

FRENCH RHUBARB PIE

4 cups rhubarb
3 eggs, slightly beaten
1-1/2 cups sugar
3 tablespoons milk
2 tablespoons flour
1/2 teaspoon nutmeg
1 tablespoon butter
1 unbaked 9-inch pie shell

Crumbs:

1/2 cup soft butter
1/2 cup sugar
1 cup flour

Wash rhubarb; dry and cut into 1-inch pieces. Place in a large bowl.

In another bowl, beat eggs slightly. Blend in sugar, milk, flour, nutmeg, and butter. Pour over rhubarb and toss.

Line a glass pie pan with pastry. Fill. Cover with crumbs.

To make crumbs: blend 1/2 cup each of butter and sugar with 1 cup flour.

Bake pie at 400 degrees for 50 to 55 minutes.

Serve at room temperature.

Eloise Knoll

STRAWBERRY CHEESE PIE

Divide berries into 2 equal portions, with smaller berries in one portion and larger berries in the other.

Place the half with smaller berries into a heavy saucepan. Mash them with a potato masher. Add 1 cup sugar, cornstarch, and lemon juice. Cook over low heat, blending well, until thick and translucent. Remove from heat and cool.

In a separate bowl, combine cream cheese, remaining sugar, orange rind and juice, and light cream. Cream until light and fluffy.

Spread the cream cheese mixture smoothly and evenly into the pie crust. Arrange the large berries over the cream cheese mixture and cover all the berries with the cooled strawberry glaze. Refrigerate for at least 2 hours before serving.

Serve with dollops of lightly sweetened whipped cream, if desired.

Serves 6   *Kathy Rogers*

1 9-inch pie shell, baked and cooled
4 cups fresh strawberries, stemmed
   and hulled
1-1/3 cups granulated sugar
3 tablespoons cornstarch
2 tablespoons fresh lemon juice
1 package (8-ounce) cream cheese,
   softened
1 teaspoon grated orange rind
2 tablespoons fresh orange juice
2 tablespoons light cream
whipped cream (optional)

STRAWBERRY SUNSHINE PIE

Soften sherbet and spread evenly in bottom of pastry shell. Freeze solidly for 4 to 5 hours, or overnight.

Preheat oven to 500 degrees.

Beat egg whites with vanilla and cream of tartar until soft peaks form. Gradually add 6 tablespoons sugar, beating until stiff and glossy.

In a separate bowl, lightly combine strawberries with 1 tablespoon sugar.

Remove pie shell from freezer. Working quickly, arrange strawberries over sherbet. Spread meringue over berries, being careful to seal to very edges of crust. Place pie on cookie sheet and bake in 500 degree oven for 3 minutes, or until golden.

With sharp knife, cut in wedges and serve immediately.

Serves 6 to 8   *Lucy DiMeglio*

1 pint lemon sherbet
1 9-inch pie shell, baked
3 egg whites
1/2 teaspoon vanilla
1/4 teaspoon cream of tartar
7 tablespoons sugar
1 quart fresh strawberries, sliced

GIBANICA
Egg and Cheese Custard Pie

Yugoslavia

12 phyllo pastry sheets
1/2 stick unsalted butter, melted
powdered sugar for garnish
dried apricots

Apricot Filling:

14 ounces dried apricots
2 cups dry white wine
1/4 cup Cointreau

Raspberry Filling:

8 ounces seedless raspberry preserves
3 tablespoons Kirsch

Egg Custard:

8 ounces cream cheese, room
    temperature
1 pound cream-style cottage cheese
1/2 cup sugar
finely grated peel of 1/2 lemon
6 eggs, separated
1/2 cup club soda

Make Apricot Filling, Raspberry Filling, and Egg Custard.

Preheat oven to 350 degrees. Generously butter a 9 x 13-inch baking dish.

Without cutting phyllo, lay 1/2 sheet into dish (let remainder drape onto work surface). Brush with some butter. Fold other half of phyllo over and brush top with butter. Repeat with 1 more sheet.

Lay half of another sheet over top in same manner. Spoon 8 to 10 tablespoons custard over phyllo. Fold other half over and spoon same amount of custard over top. Repeat procedure with 1 more phyllo pastry sheet.

Prepare 2 more full sheets in same manner, spooning 1/4 of apricot filling over each of the 4 layers.

Repeat with 2 more sheets, spooning 1/4 of raspberry filling over each of the 4 layers.

Prepare 2 more full sheets in same manner, spooning about 8 to 10 tablespoons custard over each layer.

Finish with remaining 2 sheets of phyllo, brushing each layer evenly with remaining melted butter.

Bake until top is golden and fillings are set, about 50 to 55 minutes.

To serve, sprinkle with powdered sugar and decorate with apricots. Cut into squares. This fruit soufflé is best assembled the day of serving.

Apricot Filling:

Combine apricots and wine in saucepan. Cover and simmer until fruit is soft. Transfer to processor or blender and purée until smooth. Turn into bowl. Stir in Cointreau. Set aside.

Raspberry Filling:

In a separate saucepan, combine preserves and Kirsch and warm over low heat. Set aside.

Egg Custard:

In a large bowl, beat cream cheese with electric mixer until smooth. Add cottage cheese and blend well. Gradually blend in sugar and grated lemon peel. Add egg yolks, one at a time, beating thoroughly after each addition. Blend in club soda.

In a separate large bowl, beat egg whites until stiff, but not dry. Fold into yolk mixture.

Serves 12 to 16   *Jean Miner*

APPLE WALNUT COBBLER
Grandmother's "Quick" Company Recipe
British Isles

Mix 1/2 cup sugar, cinnamon, and 1/2 cup walnuts; set aside.

Peel, core, and slice apples thinly; place in bottom of a greased 9 x 9-inch pan. Sprinkle with cinnamon mixture.

In a large bowl, sift together flour, 1 cup sugar, baking powder, and salt.

In another bowl, beat egg, and add milk and margarine, and mix well. Add all at once to dry ingredients; mix until smooth. Pour over apples. Sprinkle remaining nuts over top.

Bake in slow oven at 325 degrees about 50 minutes; cut into squares. May be served with cinnamon topped whipped cream.

Donna Long

1/2 cup sugar
1 teaspoon cinnamon
3/4 cup coarsely chopped walnuts
4 cups peeled apples, sliced thin
1 cup sifted flour
1 cup sugar
1 teaspoon baking powder
1/4 teaspoon salt
1 egg, well beaten
1/2 cup evaporated milk
1/2 cup margarine
whipped cream (optional)
cinnamon (optional)

APPLE PITA
Yugoslavia

Make filling.

Sift flour, salt, and baking powder, set aside.

In a bowl, cream butter; add sugar and beat well. Add eggs, one at a time, beating well after each addition. Add dry ingredients and vanilla.

Grease a 10 x 12-inch baking pan. Place half of batter in pan and spread evenly.

Spread filling on top of batter. Sprinkle with remaining half of grated rinds. Top with remaining batter. Spread evenly. Bake at 300 degrees for 1 hour and 15 minutes.

Cut in squares or diamond shapes when cool.

Filling:

Peel, core, and grate apples into a bowl. Blend in walnuts, sugar, cinnamon, and nutmeg. Sprinkle half of grated rinds over filling (reserve half for topping).

Maria Dorotich

1-1/2 cups flour
1/4 teaspoon salt
1 teaspoon baking powder
1/4 pound butter
1 cup sugar
4 eggs
1 teaspoon vanilla

Filling:

7 green apples, peeled and grated
1 cup ground walnuts
2 to 3 tablespoons sugar
1 teaspoon cinnamon
1 teaspoon nutmeg
rind of 1 small orange, grated
rind of 1 small lemon, grated

223

APPLE STRUDEL

Yugoslavia

1 box filo dough
melted butter

Filling:

6 Pippin apples, peeled and grated
juice of one lemon
1/2 cup crushed graham crackers or
    vanilla wafers
1/4 cup brown sugar
1/4 cup sugar
1 teaspoon cinnamon
1 cup light raisins
1/4 cup ground almonds
1/4 cup ground walnuts
1 teaspoon vanilla
2 tablespoons dark rum
1 tablespoon grated orange rind
1 small can pineapple, well drained
    (optional)

Make filling and set aside.

Brush 3 filo sheets generously with melted butter, laying one on top of the other. Place a third of fruit mixture on top of the 3 layered sheets of filo. Roll jellyroll style, sealing the ends with melted butter. Place on greased cookie sheet. Repeat for each strudel.

Bake at 350 degrees for 35 to 45 minutes, or until golden brown.

Note: Strudel may be frozen unbaked if wrapped tightly in aluminum foil.

Filling:

Peel, core, and grate apples into a large bowl, sprinkle with lemon juice. Add remaining ingredients and mix well to blend.

Yield: 3 strudels   *Bonnie Mihovilovich*

CREAM PUFFS WITH CREAM FILLING

1 cup water
1/4 pound butter
1 cup flour
1/2 teaspoon salt
4 eggs

Filling:

1 large package vanilla pudding
1/2 pint whipping cream

To make shells, bring water and butter to a rolling boil. Add flour and salt all at once. Mix to form a ball. Cool slightly.

Then add 4 eggs, one at a time, beating well after each.

Drop on greased cookie sheet, using 1 teaspoon for small shells, or 1 tablespoon for large shells.

Bake at 450 degrees: 30 minutes for small shells or 45 minutes for large shells.

Make filling.

Cut baked shells in half. Fill one half with pudding and top with remaining half.

Filling:

To make filling, cook pudding according to package directions, but using only 2 cups of milk. Cool thoroughly. Whip cream and fold into pudding.

Yield: 30 small or 20 large   *Bernadette Trani*

THREE LAYER LEMON SQUARES

Mix flour, butter, and nuts. Press into a 13 x 9-inch, lightly greased pan. Bake 15 minutes at 375 degrees. Let cool completely.

In a medium sized bowl, mix sugar and cream cheese. Beat until fluffy. Fold in 5 ounces of whipped topping and spread on completely cooled crust. Refrigerate 1 hour.

Beat together lemon pudding and cold milk. Pour over the cream cheese layer. When this has set a short time, spread the remaining whipped topping over lemon pudding. Sprinkle with coconut, if desired.

Serves 16   *Elise R. Huffman*

1 cup flour
1/4 pound butter
1/2 cup chopped pecans
1 cup powdered sugar
8 ounces cream cheese, softened
1 carton (13-ounce) whipped topping
2 packages instant lemon pudding
3 cups cold milk
coconut, if desired

PAVLOVA

New Zealand

Pour sugar into mixing bowl. Add egg whites. Mix with electric mixer until combined. Mix on high speed for about 18 to 20 minutes until stiff.

Grease a sheet of waxed paper and place on cookie sheet. Sprinkle with water. Pile meringue mixture onto cookie sheet in a 10 inch circle. Bake at 300 degrees for 45 minutes. Turn off oven and leave meringue in until the oven cools. Remove from paper gently and put on a plate.

Whip cream into soft peaks. Pile onto meringue. Ring outer edge of cream with almonds and then a circle of chocolate. Sprinkle almonds in center.

Jackie Morrison

1-3/4 cup powdered sugar
4 egg whites
1 cup whipping cream
1/4 cup sliced almonds
2 tablespoons grated semi-sweet
    chocolate

HROSTULE

6 eggs
6 rounded tablespoons sugar
1/4 pound butter, melted
4 tablespoons whiskey
1 teaspoon anise (optional)
1 tablespoon vanilla
4-1/2 cups flour
salad oil for frying
granulated sugar for sprinkling

Beat eggs well. Add sugar gradually. Continue beating until fluffy. Add butter, whiskey, anise, and vanilla. Beat until well-combined.

Add flour gradually until dough is easy to handle. Knead and cut into small balls. Roll until very thin. Cut in strips. Tie into a bow shape.

Fry in a deep pan in medium hot salad oil. Remove from oil and drain in colander.

Prepare a large box lined with foil or waxed paper. Place hrostule in box and sprinkle with granulated sugar.

Minnie Cvitanich

CANNOLI

1 box cannoli shells (6 in a box)
12 ounces ricotta cheese
4 ounces sifted powdered sugar
2 ounces bittersweet chocolate chips
1 tablespoon candied fruits, diced
1/4 teaspoon vanilla
dash of cinnamon
1/4 cup chopped nuts

To make the filling for the cannoli shells, combine cheese with powdered sugar; mix well by hand. Add chocolate chips, candied fruits, vanilla, and cinnamon. Mix thoroughly and refrigerate.

Warm the shells slightly (just to soften them) in the oven before putting in the filling. Fill the shells and put chopped nuts into the ends of each shell.

Cover loosely with wax paper (do not use plastic wrap, which would make them soggy) and refrigerate before serving.

Variations: The shells may also be filled with cream, custard, ice cream, whipped cream, or yogurt.

Frances DiMeglio

PRŠURATE CVITANICH
Fruit Fritters

Cut up potatoes, yam, and apples, and add handful of raisins and the salt. Place in a covered saucepan with 3 cups of water and simmer over low heat until well cooked. When cooked, strain. Reserve liquid and mix it with whiskey.

Mash potato mixture; add flour and sugar. Slowly add the reserved liquid. Beat well. Add chopped walnuts, pine nuts, raisins, lemon rind and juice, orange rind and juice, vanilla, cinnamon, nutmeg, and cloves. If the batter is thin, add more flour in small amounts.

In a separate bowl, place 3 cups of batter. Add 1/2 teaspoon baking powder and 1/2 teaspoon baking soda. Beat well.

Drop dough by teaspoonfuls in deep hot oil. Fry until golden brown. Drain in collander, then place on paper towels. Repeat with next 3 cups of batter until all is used.

Serve immediately.

Minnie Cvitanich

2 medium potatoes
1 red yam
2 apples, cored and peeled
handful of raisins
1/2 teaspoon salt
3 cups water
4 ounces whiskey
3 cups flour, sifted
1-1/2 cups sugar
1-1/2 cups walnuts, chopped
2 ounces pine nuts
1-1/2 cups raisins
1 lemon, rind and juice
1 orange, rind and juice
1 tablespoon vanilla
1 teaspoon cinnamon
1/4 teaspoon nutmeg
1/8 teaspoon cloves
baking powder
baking soda
salad oil for deep frying

PRŠURATE TORBARINA
Fruit Fritters

Boil potatoes. Drain and mash.

Peel, core, and slice apples. Cook in water, together with sugar, until very soft. Place apples and remaining ingredients in a large stainless steel pot and beat vigorously for 15 minutes.

Drop batter by teaspoonfuls into hot oil in a deep fryer. Cook until lightly browned. Remove and drain on paper towels. Cool slightly and sprinkle with sugar, if desired.

Tastes best if eaten while still warm. These are prepared during Christmas season to serve with coffee, slivovitz, and other liquors.

Franka Torbarina

3 boiled potatoes, mashed
2 green tart apples, peeled, cored
    and sliced
1 cup sugar
1 egg
3 cups flour
2 tablespoons baking powder
1/2 teaspoon salt
1 cup raisins
1 cup chopped walnuts
1 orange rind, grated
1 lemon rind, grated
3 tablespoons vanilla
3 tablespoons rum
4 ounces whiskey
salad oil for deep frying

~ Cakes ~

CAKES

APPLE KUCHEN

Preheat oven to 350 degrees.

Cut butter into dry cake mix until crumbly. Mix in coconut. Pat mixture slightly into ungreased 13 x 9 x 2 inch oblong pan, building up sides slightly. Bake 10 minutes.

Arrange apple slices on warm crust.

Mix sugar and cinnamon. Sprinkle on apples.

Blend sour cream and egg yolks. Drizzle over apples. Topping will not completely cover apples.

Bake 25 minutes or until edges are light brown. Serve warm.

Variations:

Pear Kuchen:

Substitute 2 cans sliced pears, drained on paper towels, for the apples and 1 package devil's food cake mix or German chocolate cake mix for the yellow cake mix.

Peach Kuchen:

Substitute 1 can sliced peaches, drained, for the apples, and 1 package white cake mix or sour cream cake mix for the yellow cake mix.

Serves 12 to 15   *Helen Homen*

1/2 cup butter or margarine, softened
1 package yellow cake mix
1/2 cup flaked coconut
1 can (20 ounce) pie-sliced apples, drained,
  or 2-1/2 cups sliced and pared baking apples
1/2 cup sugar
1 teaspoon cinnamon
1 cup dairy sour cream
2 egg yolks or 1 egg

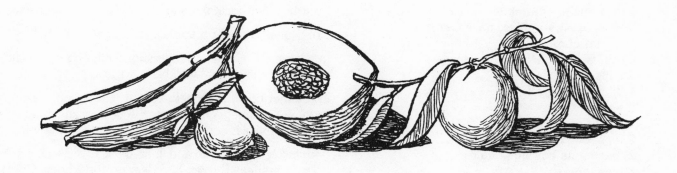

APPLE CAKE

Apple Mixture:

5 green tart baking apples
4 tablespoons fresh lemon juice
2 tablespoons sugar
1-1/2 teaspoons cinnamon

Batter Mixture:

3 cups unsifted flour
2-1/2 cups sugar
1/2 teaspoon salt
1-1/2 teaspoons baking soda
1-1/2 teaspoons baking powder
1 cup vegetable oil
1/3 cup orange juice
2 teaspoons vanilla
4 eggs

Glaze:

2 tablespoons soft butter
1-1/2 cups powdered sugar
1-1/2 teaspoons vanilla
1 to 2 tablespoons milk

Preheat oven to 350 degrees. Grease and flour a 10-inch tube pan.

Apple Mixture:

Peel and core apples. Slice into large bowl and sprinkle with lemon juice. Add sugar and cinnamon and toss lightly to cover evenly. Set aside.

Batter Mixture:

Place all the ingredients of the batter mixture into a large bowl of an electric mixer. Blend together on low speed for one minute. Increase to medium speed and beat for 3 minutes; should be a very thick batter.

Fill pan with alternating layers of batter and apples—3 batter layers and 2 apple layers. Start and finish with batter.

Bake at 350 degrees for 1-1/2 to 1-3/4 hours.

Cool on rack for 10 minutes. Remove from pan and allow to cool.

Glaze:

Glaze if desired. Mix glaze ingredients with electric mixer until fluffy. Spread on top of slightly warm cake.

Dolores Lisica

BRANDY APPLESPICE CAKE

1 cup raisins, plumped
4 cups baking apples, pared, cored
     and chopped
6 tablespoons brandy
2 cups sugar
1/2 cup salad oil
2 eggs
2 cups flour
2 teaspoons ground cinnamon
2 teaspoons baking soda
1 teaspoon salt
1 teaspoon ground nutmeg
1 teaspoon ground cloves
1 cup chopped walnuts

Pour hot (not boiling) water over raisins and set aside.

Core, peel, and chop apples; then soak in brandy.

In a large bowl, beat together sugar, oil, and eggs with an electric mixer until well blended.

In another bowl, sift together flour, cinnamon, baking soda, salt, nutmeg, and cloves. Stir flour mixture into oil mixture until blended. Fold in apples, nuts, and raisins.

Pour batter into greased and floured 9 x 13 x 2-inch pan. Bake in preheated oven 325 degrees for 1 hour. Cool in pan on rack.

Serve warm or cool with whipped cream.

Giovanna Mannino

APPLE CAKE MAROVICH

Core, peel and slice apples.

In a large pot, bring 1 cup of water to a boil, drop in apples, and boil for 6 to 7 minutes, or until just tender.

Remove from heat and add sugar and butter. Let cool.

Add 1 teaspoon vanilla, spices, baking soda, raisins and nuts. Mix well.

Sift flour and baking powder together and add gradually to mixture. Add lemon and orange rinds and salt.

Fill greased 10-inch tube pan and bake at 325 degrees for 1-1/2 to 1-3/4 hours. Cool on rack for 10 minutes before removing from pan.

Esther Marovich

6 apples (red or green), peeled
   and sliced
1 cup water
2 cups sugar
1/4 pound butter
1 teaspoon vanilla
1 teaspoon combined of allspice,
   nutmeg and cinnamon
2 teaspoons baking soda
1 cup raisins
1 cup chopped nuts
3 cups flour
2 teaspoons baking powder
1/2 grated lemon rind
1/2 grated orange rind
pinch of salt

CARROT CAKE

This cake is lighter in texture than most carrot cakes.

Sift together the flour, baking powder, baking soda, cinnamon, and salt.

Grate carrots and chop walnuts and set aside.

In a large bowl, mix sugar and oil. Add eggs and beat. Add carrots and walnuts, and mix well. Gradually stir in flour mixture.

Pour into greased 9 x 13 x 2-inch baking pan. Bake at 350 degrees for 50 to 60 minutes, or at 325 degrees for 1-1/2 hours.

Cream Cheese Frosting:

Cream butter and cream cheese. Add sugar, vanilla, and salt, and beat until smooth. Frost cake when cool.

Tracy Litman

2-1/2 cups flour
2 teaspoons baking powder
1-1/2 teaspoons baking soda
2 teaspoons cinnamon
1 teaspoon salt
3 cups grated carrots
1/2 cup chopped walnuts
2 cups sugar
1-1/2 cups cooking oil
4 eggs

Cream Cheese Frosting:

1/8 pound butter or margarine
1 package (8-ounce) cream cheese
1 pound powdered sugar
1 teaspoon vanilla
dash salt

CARROT TORTE

2 cups sifted flour
2 teaspoons baking powder
1-1/2 teaspoons baking soda
1 teaspoon salt
2-1/2 teaspoons cinnamon
2 cups sugar
1-1/2 cups oil
4 or 5 medium eggs
2-3/4 cups coarsely grated carrots
1 teaspoon salt
1 can (8-1/2 ounce) crushed
    pineapple, drained
1 cup chopped walnuts or pecans
1 cup shredded coconut

In a medium size bowl, sift together flour, baking powder, baking soda, salt, and cinnamon.

In a large bowl, combine sugar, oil and eggs. Add flour mixture a little at a time, mixing well after each addition.

Add carrots, pineapple, nuts and coconut and blend thoroughly.

Turn into 3 greased and floured 9-inch round baking pans. Bake at 350 degrees for 45 minutes.

Cool about 10 minutes before removing from pans.

Cool completely and frost between layers and top, leaving sides unfrosted.

Use Cream Cheese Frosting with previous recipe.

Lucy DiMeglio

CHEESE CAKE BERTRAM

1/8 pound butter, melted
7 or 8 double graham crackers
few drops almond extract (optional)
1 package (8 ounce) cream cheese,
    room temperature
1/2 cup sugar
2 large eggs, room temperature

Topping:

1 small carton sour cream
3 tablespoons sugar
1 teaspoon vanilla

Melt butter in oven at 300 degrees. Add to finely crumbed graham crackers (a few drops of almond extract may be added, if desired). Press firmly and evenly into 8-inch or 9-inch pie plate for crust.

Cream together cream cheese and 1/2 cup sugar. Add eggs and beat until creamy.

Pour cream cheese mixture into pie crust, and bake at 325 degrees for 25 minutes. Allow to cool.

When cool, refrigerate several hours.

Note: Recipe may be doubled and baked in greased and crumb-lined, 9-inch spring pan if desired.

Topping:

Mix sour cream with 3 tablespoons sugar and vanilla. Spread over baked pie, covering to edge. Return to oven and bake 10 minutes longer.

This pie is best if baked the day before serving. Before serving, you may top with frozen raspberries, strawberries, or blueberries.

Estelle Bertram

CHOCOLATE MARBLED CHEESECAKE

Pre-heat oven to 400 degrees.

Crust:

Combine flour, salt, and sugar. With pastry blender or fork, cut in butter until mixture resembles coarse crumbs. Add melted chocolate. Press over bottom of 9 inch spring-form pan. Bake at 400 degrees for 10 minutes.

Remove from oven. Turn oven heat up to 500 degrees.

Filling:

Place cream cheese in a large bowl. With electric mixer at slow speed, blend cream cheese with the sugar, adding sugar slowly. Beat until smooth. Add flour and vanilla. Add eggs one at a time, beating well after each addition. Beat in sour cream.

In a small bowl, combine 1 cup of cheese mixture with melted chocolate.

Pour half of plain cheese mixture over baked crust. Drizzle half of chocolate mixture over top. Cover with remaining plain mixture. Then drizzle remaining chocolate mixture. Cut through batter gently with knife and swirl to marbelize.

Bake at 500 degrees for 12 minutes. Lower oven to 200 degrees and bake for 45 to 50 minutes.

Cool, away from drafts, 2 to 3 hours. Refrigerate at least 6 to 8 hours.

Remove side of pan; use 2 spatulas to gently lift the cake from the bottom of pan to cake plate to serve.

Serves 12   *Dolores Lisica*

Crust:

3/4 cup flour
1/4 teaspoon salt
2 tablespoons sugar
1/4 cup butter
1 square unsweetened chocolate, melted

Filling:

3 packages (8-ounce) cream cheese, at room temperature
1-1/4 cups sugar
1/4 cup flour
2 teaspoons vanilla
6 eggs
1 cup sour cream, at room temperature
1 square unsweetened chocolate, melted

LOW CALORIE CHOCOLATE CHEESECAKE

6 graham crackers, crushed
3 ounces cream cheese, softened
1/2 cup cocoa
1/4 cup skim milk
1/2 cup Sugar Twin, or 8 packets
    Sweet & Low
1 teaspoon vanilla
1 envelope D-Zerta whipped topping,
    prepared per package directions

Line 8-inch pie pan with graham cracker crumbs.

Combine cheese, cocoa, skim milk, sugar substitute, and vanilla. Stir until smooth.

Prepare topping, whip, and combine with cheese mixture.

Pour into crumb-lined pie pan. Chill until set.

Serves 6, only 168 calories per portion.

Doris Berg

CHOCOLATE CAKE HAVENS

Batter:

1 package devil's food or chocolate
fudge cake mix
2 eggs
1-3/4 cups canned apple sauce

Frosting:

1 package (6 ounce) semi-sweet
    chocolate bits
4 ounces sour cream

Batter:

Ignore box instructions and mix all batter ingredients together.

Pour batter into greased and floured 13 x 9 x 3-inch baking pan.

Bake in 350-degree oven for 30 to 35 minutes until done. Test with a toothpick (when stuck in the center of the cake, toothpick should come out dry). Cool on rack.

Frosting:

Melt chocolate in double boiler or over hot water. Remove from heat and mix in sour cream. When thoroughly blended, spread on cooled cake.

Batter Variation: Instead of apple sauce, use 1 can (21-ounce) cherry pie filling and add 1 teaspoon almond extract.

Ruth E. Havens

DOLORES' CHOCOLATE CAKE

Bring egg, butter, and buttermilk to room temperature.

Grease and flour an 8 x 10-inch glass pan. *Using a glass baking pan is a must*—the cake doesn't rise or bake properly in a metal baking pan.

Preheat oven to 375 degrees.

Sift sifted flour with salt twice and set aside.

Add baking soda to 1/2 cup buttermilk, stir, and set aside.

In a large bowl, and using an electric mixer, cream butter until soft. Gradually add sugar, then egg. Beat well. Add flour alternately with soda/buttermilk and plain buttermilk. Mix at low speed until blended. Add chocolate and vanilla and beat well.

Pour into *glass* pan. Bake for 25 to 30 minutes, or until cake leaves the sides of pan. Cool completely before frosting.

Use Fluffy White Frosting on page 252 and drizzle with Chocolate Glaze.

Chocolate Glaze:

Melt chocolate in oven in small pyrex dish or measuring cup. Add shortening and Karo syrup, and stir to combine. Drizzle on top of frosting.

Serves 6 to 8   *Dolores Lisica*

1-1/4 cups cake flour, sifted
1 teaspoon salt
1 teaspoon baking soda
1 cup buttermilk
1/4 pound butter
1 cup sugar
1 egg
2 squares unsweetened chocolate, melted
1 teaspoon vanilla

Chocolate Glaze:

1 ounce unsweetened chocolate, melted
1 tablespoon shortening
1 tablespoon dark Karo syrup

CHOCOLATE BROWNIE CAKE

2 cups sugar
2 cups flour
1 teaspoon baking soda
1 cup margarine
4 tablespoons cocoa
1 cup water
2 eggs
1/2 cup buttermilk
2 teaspoons vanilla

Chocolate Frosting:

1/2 cup margarine
4 tablespoons cocoa
6 tablespoons milk
1 pound powdered sugar
1 teaspoon vanilla
1 cup chopped nuts

Bake and ice it and it's ready to travel!

Preheat oven to 400 degrees.

Combine sugar, flour and soda in a large mixing bowl.

Place margarine, cocoa and water in a saucepan and bring to a boil. Remove from heat and pour over dry ingredients. Add eggs, buttermilk, and vanilla; mix well.

Pour into a greased 9 x 13 x 2 inch pan.

Bake at 400 degrees for 45 minutes.

Cool slightly and frost with Chocolate Frosting.

Chocolate Frosting:

Combine margarine, cocoa, and milk and bring to boil. Remove from heat and add powdered sugar, vanilla and nuts.

Serves 10 to 18   *Elise R. Huffman*

FUDGY MARSHMALLOW CAKE

1/4 pound margarine
1 cup sugar
4 eggs
1 large can chocolate syrup
1 cup flour
1 teaspoon baking powder

Spread:

2 cups miniature marshmallows
1/2 cup chopped pecans

Chocolate Frosting:

1/2 stick margarine, melted
2 squares semi-sweet chocolate
1-1/2 cups sifted powdered sugar
1 egg
1 teaspoon vanilla

In an electric mixer, cream margarine and sugar. While stirring, add eggs one at a time. Add chocolate syrup. Add flour gradually. Add baking powder and beat for 2 minutes.

Bake in greased and floured 9 x 13 inch glass or metal pan for 30 minutes at 350 degrees.

Spread:

While cake is still warm, spread miniature marshmallows and then nuts on cake.

Chocolate Frosting:

Melt and combine margarine, chocolate and powdered sugar. Add egg and vanilla and mix until smooth. Drizzle over cake.

Lucy DiMeglio

GOLDEN CREAM CHOCOLATE CAKE

Sift flour, baking powder, baking soda, and salt together 3 times.

In a large bowl, cream shortening and sugar together. Add eggs, one at a time; add chocolate; blend. Add flour alternately with milk. Add vanilla.

Pour into two greased 8-inch cake pans and bake at 350 degrees for 30 minutes. Cool on racks.

Spread Golden Cream Filling between layers. Frost with Chocolate Fluff Frosting.

Golden Cream Filling:

Combine sugar, flour and salt in top of double boiler. Add milk gradually. Place over boiling water and cook 10 minutes.

While stirring, pour small amount of mixture over 2 slightly beaten egg yolks and return egg mixture to double boiler.

Cook 2 minutes; add vanilla and cool.

Chocolate Fluff Frosting:

In a bowl, cream margarine and add half of sugar. Blend. Add vanilla, melted chocolate, and salt.

Beat 2 egg whites until stiff. Add remaining sugar gradually to egg whites, beating after each addition. Add egg white/sugar mixture to chocolate mixture, folding gently.

Mildred Davis

2 cups sifted cake flour
2 teaspoons baking powder
1/4 teaspoon baking soda
1/2 teaspoon salt
1/2 cup shortening
1-1/4 cups sugar
2 eggs
3 squares unsweetened chocolate, melted
1 cup milk
1 teaspoon vanilla

Golden Cream Filling:

1/2 cup sugar
3 tablespoons flour
1/4 teaspoon salt
1-1/2 cups milk
2 egg yolks
1 teaspoon vanilla

Chocolate Fluff Frosting:

4 tablespoons margarine
1-1/2 cups powdered sugar
1 teaspoon vanilla
3 squares unsweetened chocolate, melted
pinch of salt
2 egg whites

MILKY WAY CAKE

8 large Milky Way candy bars
1/2 pound margarine
2 cups sugar
4 eggs
1/2 teaspoon baking soda
1-1/4 cups buttermilk
2-1/2 cups flour
1 cup chopped pecans

Icing:

2-1/2 cups sugar
1 cup evaporated milk
6 ounces semi-sweet chocolate chips
1 cup marshmallow creme
1/4 pound margarine

Melt together candy bars and 1/4 pound of margarine.

In a large bowl, cream remaining margarine and sugars together. Add eggs, one at a time, to sugar mixture.

Mix baking soda with buttermilk; add flour and buttermilk mixture alternately to the creamed sugar mixture. Stir in candy and nuts.

Pour into three greased and floured 9-inch cake pans or a tube pan.

Bake at 350 degrees for about 30 minutes.

Cool on rack.

Chocolate Marshmallow Icing:

To make icing, cook sugar and milk to soft ball stage (with a spoon, drop a tiny bit of mixture into a cup of cool water; before done it will form strings; when done it will form a soft ball).

Add remaining ingredients and stir until all ingredients are melted.

Lucy DiMeglio

SUSIE'S CHOCOLATE CAKE

2 cups flour, sifted
2 cups sugar
1/4 pound butter
2 eggs
3/4 cup cocoa
1 cup hot coffee
1 cup milk
2 teaspoons baking soda
1 teaspoon baking powder
1/4 teaspoon salt

Sift flour into a large bowl.

In a pan on the stove, mix all other ingredients. Turn on heat and melt. Add to flour in large bowl. Beat until well blended.

Pour into greased and floured 9 x 13-inch cake pan.

Bake at 325 degrees for 25 minutes.

Sharon E. Hand

SWISS CHOCOLATE CAKE

Sift flour, sugar, baking powder, baking soda, and salt into mixing bowl.

In a large bowl, mix shortening, melted chocolate, evaporated milk, and vanilla. Add flour mixture to chocolate mixture and beat 200 strokes, or 2 minutes on mixer. Add eggs; beat 200 strokes or 2 minutes with mixer.

Pour into two 8- or 9-inch pans. Bake at 350 degrees for 30 to 35 minutes, or until cake tests done.

Chill layers in refrigerator until thoroughly cold.

Split each layer in half horizontally.

Whip cream until stiff. Add sugar and vanilla to taste. Spread cream evenly between layers and on top of cake. Decorate top with curls of chocolate.

Refrigerate until firm—overnight is ideal.

Cut in inch-thick slices for serving. Keep refrigerated.

Ludy DiMeglio

1-3/4 cups sifted cake flour
1-1/3 cups sugar
2 teaspoons baking powder
1/4 teaspoon baking soda
3/4 teaspoon salt
2/3 cup shortening
2 ounces chocolate, melted
1 cup undiluted evaporated milk
1 teaspoon vanilla
2 eggs
2 cups heavy whipping cream
sugar and vanilla to flavor
    whipping cream
curls of shaved milk chocolate

DATE NUT COCOA TORTE

In a large bowl, pour boiling water over dates. Add soda, stir and cool.

In another bowl, cream shortening and sugar. Add eggs. Mix well.

Sift together flour and cocoa, then add to creamed mixture with vanilla. Add creamed mixture to dates. Mix well.

Pour into 9 x 13-inch greased and floured pan. Top with mixture of nuts, brown sugar and butterscotch or chocolate chips.

Bake at 350 degrees for 1/2 hour.

Serve with whipped cream or ice cream.

Elise R. Huffman

1-1/2 cups boiling water
1 cup dates, chopped
1 teaspoon soda
3/4 cup shortening
1 cup sugar
2 eggs
1-3/4 cup flour
1 or 2 tablespoons cocoa
1 tablespoon vanilla

Topping:

1/2 cup chopped nuts
1/2 cup brown sugar
1/2 cup butterscotch chips or
    chocolate chips

Ireland

COFFEE AND RUM CREAM CAKE

Batter:

3/4 cup unsalted butter
3/4 cup extra fine granulated sugar
   (bartender's sugar)
3 eggs
3/4 cup self-rising flour

Coffee and Rum Syrup:

1 cup sugar
1-1/2 cups water
2 tablespoons rum
3 tablespoons coffee essence or
   powdered instant coffee

Cream Topping:

1/2 pint whipping cream
few drops vanilla extract
walnut halves or chocolate chips

Preheat oven to 375 degrees. Grease an 8-inch cake tin and line bottom with a circle of greased waxed paper or parchment.

Cream butter and sugar together until light and creamy. Gradually beat in eggs, adding 1 tablespoon of flour with the last egg. Fold in remaining flour.

Pour into prepared pan and bake for 45 to 50 minutes.

Coffee and Rum Syrup:

Dissolve sugar in water over low heat. Remove from heat, add rum and coffee essence.

Place baked cake in a deep serving platter. Allow cake to cool. Pierce all over with a skewer, then pour coffee rum syrup all over the cake. Leave to soak for several hours. Refrigerate before serving.

Cream Topping:

Whip cream, add vanilla and beat until just stiff. Cover the top of cake with whipped cream and garnish with walnut halves or chocolate chips.

Serves 6 to 8

Chef William Lane
Innishannon Hotel
County Cork, Ireland

On Cake

"When cake or pastry is to be made, take care not to make trouble for others by scattering materials, and soiling the table or floor, or by the needless use of many dishes."

—*The Young Housekeeper's Friend, 1845*

DANA'S COFFEE CAKE

In a large mixing bowl, combine flour, sugars, salt, nutmeg, and oil. Mix with fork until crumbly. Set aside 1-1/2 cups of crumb mixture. Add cinnamon to reserved crumb mixture.

Combine remaining flour mixture with soda, baking powder, eggs and buttermilk. Blend gently. Do not over mix.

Grease and flour two 9 x 13-inch baking pans. Pour batter into greased pans. Sprinkle evenly with reserved crumb mixture.

Bake at 350 degrees for 25 to 30 minutes or until cake tests done.

Cut into squares to serve.

Serves 24   *Dolores Lisica*

4 cups flour
2 cups dark brown sugar, packed
1-1/2 cups granulated sugar
3/4 teaspoon salt
2 teaspoons nutmeg
1-1/2 cups salad oil
2 teaspoons cinnamon
2 teaspoons baking soda
1 tablespoon plus 1 teaspoon
    baking powder
3 large eggs
2 cups buttermilk

DUMP CAKE

Dump all ingredients into a large bowl. Stir with spoon until well mixed.

Spread in greased and floured 9 x 13 inch baking pan.

Bake at 350 degrees for 45 to 60 minutes or until toothpick comes out clean when inserted in middle of cake.

Cool on rack. Cut into squares and serve.

Lucy DiMeglio

1 can (1 pound 4 ounces) sliced
    apples, cherries or peaches
2 eggs
2 cups sugar
1/2 cup oil
1 teaspoon cinnamon
1 cup chopped nuts
1 teaspoon vanilla
2 cups flour
1 teaspoon salt
2 teaspoons soda

FLORIDA CAKE

Crust:

6 egg whites, room temperature
2 cups sugar
1 teaspoon vanilla
40 Ritz crackers
1/2 to 3/4 cups chopped nuts

Filling:

1/2 cup cocoa
1/2 cup margarine
2 cups powdered sugar
2 eggs
1 teaspoon vanilla

Topping:

1 carton (8 ounce) whipped topping
finely chopped nuts

Crust:

Beat egg whites until stiff. Add 1 cup sugar and vanilla. Beat again and set aside.

Crush crackers until very fine. Add remaining sugar and chopped nuts to crackers. Mix well and add to egg whites. Spread entire mixture on buttered 9 x 13-inch baking pan.

Bake at 350 degrees for 30 minutes.

Cool thoroughly.

Filling:

Combine all filling ingredients and beat well. Spread on cooled crust.

Topping:

Spread whipped topping on top and garnish with nuts.

Refrigerate at least 24 hours before serving.

Lucy DiMeglio

FROZEN STRAWBERRY MERINGUE TORTE

Crust:

1 cup graham cracker crumbs
3 tablespoons sugar
1/4 cup melted butter
1/2 cup chopped nuts

Filling:

2 cups sliced strawberries
1 cup sugar
2 egg whites
1 tablespoon lemon juice
1 teaspoon vanilla
1/8 teaspoon salt
1 cup whipping cream

Crust:

Combine all crust ingredients and press into bottom of a 10-inch springform pan.

Bake at 325 degrees for 10 minutes.

Filling:

In an electric mixer, combine all filling ingredients, except whipping cream, and beat at low speed to blend. Then beat until peaks form.

In another bowl, beat whipping cream until peaks are firm. Fold into berry meringue.

Pour into baked crust, cover and freeze about 12 hours.

To serve, remove pan sides and serve immediately.

Serves 8 to 10   *Giovanna Mannino*

FRUIT CAKE

The Finnish people serve coffee like the English serve afternoon tea. It consists of open-faced sandwiches, cookies, cake and raw vegetables. My mother-in-law introduced me to this custom and tradition when I was a young bride.

Dredge raisins, currants, lemon peel, maraschino cherries, pineapple, citron, and nuts in 1/3 cup flour.

Sift 1-1/2 cups flour with soda, cinnamon, allspice, and nutmeg.

In a large bowl, cream butter, add sugar and cream until light and fluffy. Add well beaten egg yolks and beat well. Add fruit juice, brandy, and preserves. Blend thoroughly.

Fold in dry ingredients. Add fruit and nuts.

Beat egg whites until stiff, but not dry, and fold in.

Bake in five 9 x 5-inch loaf pans. Bake at 250 degrees for 1 hour, then at 275 degrees for 2 hours, and, if necessary, at 300 degrees for 1/2 hour more.

Veni Hill

2 cups raisins
1 cup currants
6 ounces lemon peel
8 ounces maraschino cherries
8 ounces glazed pineapple
8 ounces citron
1 cup nuts
1/3 cup flour for dredging
1-1/2 cups flour for mixing
1/4 teaspoon soda
1 teaspoon cinnamon
1 teaspoon allspice
1/4 teaspoon nutmeg
2/3 cup butter
2/3 cup brown sugar
4 eggs, separated
3 tablespoons fruit juice, any kind
3 tablespoons brandy or cider
2/3 cup strawberry preserves

HOLIDAY CAKE

In a large bowl, cream butter or margarine, and add sugar and eggs. Beat well.

In a separate bowl, mix together flour, salt, soda, and cinnamon. Stir into egg mixture. Add vanilla, apples, bananas, chopped nuts, and chocolate chips, and mix well.

Bake in 9 x 13-inch metal pan at 325 degrees for 1 hour. Cool.

This cake tastes best if baked ahead and stored for a while.

Lucy DiMeglio

1 cup butter or margarine
2 cups sugar
2 unbeaten eggs
2 cups flour
1 teaspoon salt
1 teaspoon baking soda
1 teaspoon cinnamon
1 teaspoon vanilla
2 grated apples
2 bananas, mashed thoroughly
1 cup chopped nuts
1 cup chocolate chips

GOLDEN ANGEL CAKE

12 eggs, separated
2 teaspoons cream of tartar
1-1/4 cups sugar
1 cup flour, sifted 3 times
1 teaspoon vanilla

Beat egg whites until frothy, adding cream of tartar gradually. Continue beating until stiff. Beat in sugar using a wire whisk. Fold in 1 cup sifted flour. Then fold in beaten yolks. Add vanilla, mix well.

Bake in 10-inch angel food cake pan one hour or longer at 300 degrees.

Frost with favorite frosting.

Mildred Davis

ITALIAN CREAM CAKE

5 eggs, separated
1/2 cup margarine
1/2 cup vegetable shortening
2 cups sugar
1 teaspoon baking soda
1 cup buttermilk
2 cups flour, sifted twice
1 can (3-1/2 ounce) coconut
1 cup chopped nuts
1 teaspoon vanilla
1 teaspoon coconut flavoring

Cream Cheese Frosting:

1 package (8-ounce) cream cheese, softened
1/2 cup butter or margarine
1 pound box powdered sugar
1 teaspoon almond extract

Preheat oven to 350 degrees. Grease and flour three 9-inch cake pans.

Separate eggs and beat whites until stiff. Set aside.

In a large bowl, cream margarine and vegetable shortening, and then sugar. Add egg yolks one at a time, beating well after each addition.

Dissolve soda in buttermilk; add to shortening mixture alternately with flour. Beat well. Add coconut, nuts, and flavorings.

Fold in stiffly beaten egg whites. Pour into three greased and floured cake pans, using 2 cups batter for each pan.

Bake in preheated 350-degree oven for 25 minutes.

Cool on rack. Then frost.

Cream Cheese Frosting:

Combine all frosting ingredients and beat well.

Spread between layers and on top of cooled cake.

Lucy DiMeglio

JEAN'S PUMPKIN CAKE

Measure 1 cup cake mix and set aside.

Blend remaining cake mix with 1 cube melted butter and 1 beaten egg. Press into bottom of 11 x 8-inch baking dish.

For filling, mix together pumpkin, milk, brown sugar, cinnamon, nutmeg, cloves, ginger, pumpkin spice, and 3 beaten eggs; pour over bottom layer in baking dish.

For topping, blend with your fingers the remaining butter with 1 cup cake mix (previously set aside), 1/2 cup granulated sugar, and chopped nuts. Sprinkle over batter.

Bake at 350 degrees for 50 to 60 minutes.

Jackie Morrison

1 box yellow cake mix
1-1/2 sticks butter
4 eggs, beaten
1 can (29-ounce) pumpkin
2/3 cup evaporated milk
1/2 cup brown sugar
1-1/2 teaspoons cinnamon
1-1/2 teaspoons nutmeg
1/4 teaspoon cloves
1/4 teaspoon ginger
1/4 teaspoon pumpkin spice
1/2 cup granulated sugar
1/2 cup chopped nuts

NUTRITIOUS CAKE

Add 1 teaspoon baking soda to can of tomato soup and set aside. In a large bowl, cream shortening. Add sugar, flour, baking powder, salt, nutmeg, cinnamon, and cloves. Mix well. Stir in tomato soup, raisins, and nuts.

Pour into greased and floured 5 x 9-inch loaf pan. Bake at 350 degrees for 30 to 35 minutes.

Icing:

Cream together icing ingredients and spread over cooled cake.

Ruth Shannon

1 teaspoon baking soda
1 can tomato soup
1/2 cup shortening
1 cup sugar
2 cups flour
2 teaspoons baking powder
1/4 teaspoon salt
1 teaspoon nutmeg
1 teaspoon cinnamon
1 teaspoon cloves
1 cup raisins
1 cup chopped nuts

Icing:

3 ounces cream cheese, softened
1-1/2 cups powdered sugar
1 teaspoon vanilla

HELEN SMITH'S MILLION DOLLAR CAKE

1/2 pound butter or margarine
2 cups sugar
6 eggs
1/2 cup milk
1 package (12-ounce) vanilla wafers, crushed
1 package (7-ounce) pecan or walnut pieces
1 package (7-ounce) angel flake coconut

In a large bowl, using electric mixer, cream butter and sugar, and add eggs, one at a time, stirring well after each.

Add milk, crushed vanilla wafers, nut pieces, and coconut. Mix well.

Pour into greased and a floured angel food cake pan or a 9 x 13-inch cake pan.

Bake at 350 degrees for 1 hour and 15 minutes.

Sue Inouye

NUTTY GRAHAM PICNIC CAKE

2 cups all-purpose flour
1 cup (14 squares) graham cracker crumbs
1 cup firmly packed brown sugar
1/2 cup granulated sugar
1 teaspoon salt
1 teaspoon baking powder
1 teaspoon baking soda
1/2 teaspoon cinnamon
1 cup butter or margarine, softened
1 cup orange juice
1 tablespoon grated orange peel
3 eggs
1 cup chopped nuts

Glaze:

2 tablespoons brown sugar
5 teaspoons milk
1 tablespoon margarine or butter
3/4 cup powdered sugar
1/4 cup chopped nuts

Heat oven to 350 degrees. Generously grease and flour a 12-cup fluted tube pan or a 10-inch tube pan.

Lightly spoon flour into measuring cup; level off.

In a large bowl, combine all cake ingredients except nuts. Using an electric mixer, beat 3 minutes at medium speed. Stir in nuts.

Pour into prepared pan.

Bake at 350 degrees for 45 to 50 minutes or until toothpick inserted in center comes out clean.

Cool upright in pan for 15 minutes. Invert onto serving plate. Cool completely.

Glaze:

In a small saucepan, heat brown sugar, milk, and butter until just melted.

Remove from heat. Add powdered sugar and blend until smooth. Drizzle over cake. Sprinkle with nuts. *This is my original recipe that won the $25,000 grand prize in the Pillsbury Bake Off a few years ago.*

Esther Tomich

GLAZED LEMON CAKE

Preheat oven to 350 degrees.

Beat eggs in medium bowl; add cake mix, oil, and water. Blend in gelatin and rind.

Pour into a greased and floured tube pan.

Bake for 30-40 minutes. Remove from oven and cool briefly.

While still warm, make about 15 two-inch slashes in top of cake and drizzle with lemon glaze.

Lemon Glaze

Sift powdered sugar and then add to lemon juice until desired consistency is reached. Glaze should be thin.

Beth Litman

4 eggs
1 yellow or lemon cake mix
3/4 cup cooking oil
3/4 cup water
1 package (3-ounce) lemon gelatin
1 teaspoon grated lemon rind

Lemon Glaze

3 tablespoons lemon juice
1-1/2 to 2 cups powdered sugar

PASSOVER CAKE

Jewish

With mixer at high speed, beat egg whites until stiff. Set aside.

Beat egg yolks and sugar until lemon colored. Add lemon juice and mix. Add potato starch and mix again. Add cake meal and mix for 6 to 7 minutes. Then fold in egg whites, gently but thoroughly.

Pour mixture into an ungreased 10-inch tube pan and bake at 350 degrees for 1 hour, or until toothpick comes out clean.

Turn out onto rack immediately and cool.

Serves 12

Shirley Pike

12 eggs, separated
2 cups sugar
2 tablespoons lemon juice
2 tablespoons potato starch
1 cup cake meal

ORANGE CRUNCH CAKE

Crunch Layer:

1 cup graham cracker crumbs
1/2 cup firmly packed brown sugar
1/2 cup chopped walnuts
1/2 cup margarine or butter

Cake:

1 package yellow cake mix
1/2 cup water
2/3 cup orange juice
1/3 cup salad oil
3 eggs
2 tablespoons grated orange peel

Orange Frosting:

1 can ready-made vanilla frosting
1 cup frozen whipped topping, thawed
3 tablespoons grated orange peel
1 teaspoon grated lemon peel
1 can (11-ounce) mandarin oranges,
    drained, or 1 orange, sectioned
    and drained
mint leaves (optional)

Crunch Layer:

Preheat oven to 350 degrees. Grease and flour two 9- or 8-inch round cake pans.

In a small bowl, combine crunch layer ingredients until crumbly. Press half of crunch mixture into each prepared pan.

Cake:

In a large bowl, blend all cake ingredients at low speed until moistened. Beat 2 minutes at high speed. Pour batter evenly over crunch layer.

Bake at 350 degrees for 30 to 35 minutes, or until toothpick inserted in center comes out clean. Cool 10 minutes. Remove from pans. Cool completely.

Orange Frosting:

In a small bowl, beat frosting until fluffy. Add whipped topping and continue beating until light and fluffy. Fold in orange and lemon peels.

Place one layer, crunch side up, on serving plate. Spread with 1/4 of frosting. Top with remaining layer, crunch side up. Spread top and sides with remaining frosting. Arrange orange sections on top. Garnish with mint leaves.

Store in refrigerator.

Serves 16   *Giovanna Mannino*

PINEAPPLE CAKE

Mix pineapple and soda until foamy. Add cake mix and eggs; blend well.

Put batter into a greased and floured 13 x 9 x 3-inch pan. Sprinkle brown sugar evenly over the batter. Sprinkle chopped nuts evenly over the sugar.

Bake in a 350 degree oven for 40 to 45 minutes.

Ruth E. Havens

1-1/2 cups crushed pineapple
2 rounded teaspoons baking soda
1 package yellow cake mix
2 eggs
1 cup brown sugar
1/2 cup chopped nuts (optional)

7-UP CAKE

Preheat oven to 350 degrees.

Using an electric mixer, blend butter and sugar together for 10 minutes. Add eggs one at a time. Add flour. Mix in vanilla and lemon juice. Remove from mixer and fold in 7-Up gently by hand.

Bake in a tube pan at 350 degrees for 1-1/2 hours.

Jean Allen

3/4 pound butter
3 cups sugar
6 eggs
3 cups flour, sifted
1 teaspoon vanilla
1 teaspoon lemon juice
3/4 cup 7-Up

SWEDISH NUT CAKE

Mix all ingredients together by hand.

Pour into a greased 8 x 11 inch or 9 x 13-inch pan.

Bake at 350 degrees for 45 minutes. (If bundt or angel food cake pan is used, bake at 300 degrees for 1 hour.) Test.

Let cool before icing.

Ice or sprinkle with powdered sugar. Makes a very moist cake. If icing is desired, use a cream cheese icing.

Scottie Gershon

2 cups sifted flour
2 cups sugar
2 eggs
1/2 cup chopped nuts
2 teaspoons baking soda
1 teaspoon vanilla
1 can (20-ounce) crushed, undrained pineapple

RED VELVET CAKE

1 cup shortening
1-1/2 cups sugar
2 eggs
1 ounce red food coloring
2 tablespoons cocoa
1 teaspoon salt
1 teaspoon vanilla
1 cup buttermilk
1-1/2 cups cake flour, sifted
1 teaspoon baking soda
1-1/2 teaspoons vinegar

Fluffy White Frosting:

5 tablespoons flour
1 cup milk
1 cup butter or margarine
1 cup sugar
1 teaspoon vanilla

Preheat oven to 350 degrees.

In a large bowl, cream shortening, sugar, and eggs.

Make a paste of food coloring and cocoa and add to creamed mixture.

Add salt and vanilla to buttermilk, then add, alternating with flour, to creamed mixture.

Add soda to vinegar and fold into batter.

Pour into two 9-inch greased and floured cake pans.Bake at 350 degrees for 30 minutes.

Cool completely before frosting.

Fluffy White Frosting:

Cook flour and milk until thick, stirring constantly. Cool until completely cold.

Cream butter or margarine, add sugar gradually beating well after each addition. Add cold flour/milk mixture and beat together untill light and fluffy. This frosting has a whipped cream consistency and stays soft.

Mildred Davis

PINEAPPLE UPSIDE DOWN CAKE

In a large bowl, cream 2 sticks of butter and sugar. Add eggs one at a time, mixing well.

Sift flour, baking powder, and salt; add gradually to butter/eggs mix. Stir in milk and pineapple and vanilla extracts. Set aside.

In a 13 x 9-inch baking pan, melt 1 stick of butter. Add brown sugar and smooth out all over pan. Add crushed pineapple. Place pineapple slices on top. Pour batter over pineapple slices.

Bake at 350 degrees for 35 to 40 minutes.

Let cool 10 minutes, then invert onto a plate. Pineapple will be on top.

Jean Allen

3 sticks (3/4 pound)butter
2 cups sugar
4 eggs
2-1/2 cups flour
3 teaspoons baking powder
1 teaspoon salt
1-1/2 cups milk
1 teaspoon pineapple extract
1 teaspoon vanilla extract
1 cup brown sugar
1 can (8-ounce) crushed pineapple, drained
1 can (8-ounce) can sliced pineapple, drained

WHISKEY CAKE

Grease and flour two 8-inch cake pans.

Boil raisins in water for 20 minutes. Cool, drain and reserve one cup raisin water.

Sift flour, cinnamon, nutmeg, allspice, and salt together and set aside.

Using an electric mixer, cream shortening and sugar together. Add eggs and beat well. Add raisins and nuts. Add flour mixture alternately with cooled raisin water.

Stir baking soda into bourbon and add to cake batter.

Pour into baking pans. Bake at 375 degrees for 35 minutes.

Allow cake to cool before frosting.

Bourbon Frosting

Cream margarine and sugar together. Add all remaining ingredients and beat until smooth.

Mildred Davis

1-1/2 cups seedless golden raisins
3 cups water
2 cups flour, sifted
1/4 teaspoon cinnamon
1/4 teaspoon nutmeg
1/4 teaspoon allspice
dash salt
1-1/2 cups shortening
1 cup sugar
2 eggs
3/4 cup chopped nuts
2 tablespoons baking soda
5 tablespoons bourbon whiskey

Bourbon Frosting:

1/2 cup margarine
1-1/4 boxes (20 ounces total) powdered sugar
1 egg
dash salt
1 teaspoon vanilla
5 tablespoons bourbon whiskey

~ San Pedro Menus ~

MENUS

GERMAN DINNER FOR SIX

GRANDMA STONER'S WIENER SCHNITZEL

HILLA'S RED CABBAGE   AUNT DOT'S HOT POTATO SALAD

GRANDMA KNOLL'S FASTNACHT KUCKA

AUNT FLORENCE'S SOFT SUGAR COOKIES

GRANDMA STONER'S WIENER SCHNITZEL
Breaded Veal Cutlet

Cut veal into 6 serving size pieces and coat with mixture of flour, salt and pepper. Dip into a blend of egg and milk. Coat with bread crumbs. Let stand 5 to 10 minutes to "seal" coating.

Melt the butter in a large, heavy skillet. Add the cutlets and cook over medium heat until browned and tender, about 20 minutes on each side.

Remove cutlets to a warm serving platter. Sprinkle with lemon juice, if desired.

Eloise Knoll

2 pounds veal round steak (cutlet)
    or pork cut 1/2 inch thick
1/4 cup flour
1 teaspoon salt
1/4 teaspoon pepper
1 egg, slightly beaten
1 tablespoon milk
1 cup fine, dry bread crumbs
4 to 5 tablespoons butter

HILLA'S RED CABBAGE

3 pounds red cabbage
1 apple, peeled, cored and chopped
1 onion, minced
3 tablespoons chopped bacon or
    butter
1 tablespoon sugar
1/4 cup wine vinegar
1/2 teaspoon salt
pinch of ground cloves
pepper to taste
1 to 2 cups water or stock, as needed

Rinse, core, and shred cabbage.

Core, peel, and chop apple. Mince onion.

Heat bacon or butter in Dutch oven or enameled casserole. Add sugar to hot fat and sauté slowly until golden brown. Add apple and onion. Cover and braise over very low heat 3 to 4 minutes.

Add shredded cabbage and toss until coated with fat. Pour vinegar over cabbage and mix through. Cover pot and braise slowly about 10 minutes or until cabbage has turned bright purple.

Sprinkle with salt, add cloves, pepper, and 1 cup water. Cover and simmer slowly 1 to 2 hours, or until cabbage is tender. Add more liquid as needed. Taste cabbage for a sweet and sour flavor, adding vinegar or sugar as needed.

Eloise Knoll

AUNT DOT'S HOT POTATO SALAD

1/2 pound diced bacon, fried crisp
6 to 8 boiled potatoes, peeled and
    sliced while hot
6 eggs, hard cooked and diced
6 to 8 scallions, chopped (tops also)
salt and pepper to taste
4 tablespoons sharp vinegar

Fry bacon until crisp. Drain.

Boil potatoes. When done, peel and slice while still hot. Place in large bowl.

Hard-boil eggs. Shell and dice. Chop scallions.

To the potatoes, add salt, pepper, vinegar, scallions, bacon, and hot eggs. Mix lightly and serve at once.

Can be topped with knockwurst for a main dish.

Eloise Knoll

GRANDMA KNOLL'S FASTNACHT KUCKA
Doughnuts—A Shrove Tuesday Tradition

Soften yeast in warm water. Let stand 5 to 10 minutes.

Scald milk, then cool to lukewarm. Add 1 teaspoon sugar and 3 cups sifted flour and stir until smooth. Stir in the yeast. Cover. Let rise in a warm place until doubled.

Beat eggs, then stir into dough eggs, melted butter, 1 cup sugar, salt, nutmeg, and enough flour so that the mixture can no longer be stirred with a spoon (a soft dough). Cover and let rise until doubled.

Punch down dough and divide into two portions. On a floured surface, roll out each portion about 1/2 inch thick. Cut dough with a doughnut cutter. Cover dough and let rise.

When doubled, fry in deep fat heated to 370 degrees. Fry 3 to 4 minutes or until lightly browned, turning once or twice. Remove from fat and drain on absorbent paper (brown paper bags work great).

Can be covered in sugar.

Yield: 4 dozen

Eloise Knoll

1 package active dry yeast
1/4 cup warm water
2 cups milk, scalded and cooled
    to lukewarm.
1 teaspoon sugar
3 cups sifted flour
3 eggs, well beaten
1/4 cup melted butter
1 cup sugar
1-1/2 teaspoons salt
1/2 teaspoon ground nutmeg
3-1/2 to 4 cups sifted flour
sugar to cover (optional)

AUNT FLORENCE'S SOFT SUGAR COOKIES

Sift together flour, baking powder, salt, and cinnamon or nutmeg.

In a large bowl, combine the sugar and cooking oil or melted butter. Add eggs and vanilla, beating well after each addition. Add the flour mixture, all at once, and beat well.

Shape the dough into 1/2-inch balls. Dip the balls in granulated sugar. Sprinkle with sugar.

Bake 10 to 12 minutes on a lightly greased baking sheet at 350 degrees.

Eloise Knoll

2-1/2 cups flour
1-1/2 teaspoons baking powder
3/4 teaspoon salt
1 teaspoon cinnamon or 1/4 teaspoon
    grated nutmeg
1 cup sugar
3/4 cup cooking oil or melted butter
2 eggs
1 teaspoon vanilla
granulated sugar

GREEK DINNER

TZATZIKI
Cucumber and Yogurt Dip

SPANAKOPETES
Spinach Cheese Triangles

Greek Olives

SOUVLAKIA
Shish Kebob

ZESTI PATATO SALATA
Hot Potato Salad

Green Onions

YIAOURTOPETA
Yogurt Cake

Fresh Fruit in Season

Coffee

TZATZIKI
Cucumber and Yogurt Dip

2 cucumbers, peeled, seeded and
    diced
2 cups plain yogurt
3 cloves garlic, crushed
2 teaspoons red wine vinegar
2 teaspoons olive olive
salt and pepper, to taste

Peel cucumber. Cut in half lengthwise and scoop out seeds with a spoon. Dice and place in medium-sized bowl.

Add yogurt, crushed garlic, wine vinegar, olive oil, and salt and pepper to taste.

Mix together and serve with Greek sesame bread.

Thom Englezos

SPANAKOPETES
Spinach Cheese Triangles

Prepare spinach: wash, drain, and finely chop fresh spinach or, if using frozen chopped spinach, thaw and squeeze out moisture.

Sauté chopped onion in olive oil about 5 minutes; add spinach. Simmer over low heat, stirring occasionally, until most moisture is evaporated.

In a large bowl crumble feta; add pot cheese or Ricotta and blend well. Beat eggs, then add to cheese and mix.

Add crumbs to spinach mixture, mix, and add to cheese mixture. Stir well.

Cut phyllo, before unrolling, into 3 equal portions. Refrigerate 2/3 until needed. Cover 1/3, to be used immediately, with a slightly damp towel.

Take one sheet of phyllo and place on flat surface. Butter with pastry brush. Fold in long sides toward middle to form a strip about 2 inches wide and butter again. Place 1 tablespoon of the cheese mixture in the bottom right corner of strip and fold over into triangle shape. Continue folding, making sure that the bottom edge of each fold is parallel with the opposite edge (like a flag). Lightly butter finished triangle.

Fill remaining phyllo strips.

Place on baking sheet and bake at 425 degrees for 20 minutes, or until golden brown. Cool 5 minutes and serve warm.

Excess triangles can be frozen raw and baked unthawed 20 to 30 minutes or until golden.

Yield: 40 to 50 triangles   *Thom Englezos*

1 pound fresh spinach, washed, drained, and finely chopped, or 1 package frozen chopped spinach
1 medium onion, finely chopped
1/4 cup olive oil
1/2 pound feta cheese
6 ounces pot cheese or fresh Ricotta
3 eggs, beaten
1/4 cup dry bread crumbs
1/2 pound phyllo pastry sheets
1/2 cup melted butter

On Serving Dinner

"Among the little things which are worthy of the attention of a housekeeper, is that of having a dinner served HOT. It is often the case, that a well-cooked dinner loses much of its excellence, by a want of care in this particular."

—*The Young Housekeeper's Friend*, 1845

SOUVLAKIA
Shish Kebob

1/2 leg of lamb (4 or 5 pounds)
1/2 cup olive oil
1/4 cup lemon juice
1/4 cup wine
salt and pepper
1-1/2 teaspoons oregano
1 or 2 garlic cloves, chopped
1 or 2 bay leaves
tomatoes, quartered
onions, quartered
green pepper, cut into 1-inch squares
mushroom caps

Cut lamb into 1- or 2-inch cubes.

Combine oil, lemon juice, wine, salt, pepper, oregano, chopped garlic, and bay leaves. Add meat to marinade. Cover and refrigerate several hours or overnight.

Quarter tomatoes and onions; cut green pepper into 1-inch squares, and prepare mushroom caps.

Skewer meat, alternating with vegetables.

Cook over charcoal or in broiler, basting with marinade and turning occasionally, until cooked to taste.

Serves 4 to 6   *Thom Englezos*

ZESTI PATATO SALATA
Hot Potato Salad

4 potatoes
boiling, salted water
1 onion, sliced
cold water
1 to 2 teaspoons salt
1/2 cup olive oil
2 tablespoons red wine vinegar
salt and pepper
parsley, chopped

Cook potatoes in boiling, salted water until just tender. Drain and keep warm.

Slice onion into bowl. Cover with cold water and salt. Let stand 10 minutes, then drain well. Pat dry.

Slice potatoes and combine with onion. Add oil and toss to coat. Add vinegar, salt, and pepper, and toss well. If needed, season with more vinegar, salt, and pepper to taste.

Garnish with parsley and serve warm.

Thom Englezos

YIAOURTOPETA
Yogurt Cake

Sift flour, salt, and baking powder together and set aside.

In a large bowl, cream butter and sugar together about 10 to 20 minutes, or until pale yellow and fluffy and it does not stick to beaters. Add egg yolks, beating after each addition. Add yogurt and blend. Add flour mixture a little at a time and blend well.

Beat egg whites until stiff. Fold gently into other ingredients until thoroughly combined.

Pour into large greased and floured tube pan or angel food pan.

Bake at 325 degrees about 1 hour or until toothpick comes out clean. Cool on rack.

Sprinkle with powdered sugar.

Thom Englezos

3 cups flour, sifted
1/4 teaspoon salt
2 teaspoons baking powder
1/2 pound unsalted butter
2 cups sugar
5 eggs, separated
1 cup plain yogurt
powdered sugar

HUNGARIAN DINNER
for Six

CARAWAY SOUP WITH HOMEMADE CROUTONS

GYPSY-STYLE FRIED HAM SLICES

SUMMER SQUASH WITH DILL

PALACSINTA
Thin Crepes with Cottage Cheese Filling

CARAWAY SOUP WITH HOMEMADE CROUTONS

Soup:

1/3 cup butter
1/3 cup flour
1-1/2 teaspoons salt
1/8 teaspoon ground pepper
1-1/2 tsp caraway seeds
3/4 teaspoon paprika
1-1/2 quarts water
2 egg yolks, slightly beaten

Croutons:

2 tablespoons butter
2 slices bread

In a 2-quart saucepan, melt butter over low heat. Blend in flour, salt, pepper, and caraway seeds. Heat until mixture bubbles and is slightly brown, stirring constantly. Remove from heat and blend in paprika. Add water and bring rapidly to a boil, stirring constantly. Cover and simmer for 15 minutes.

To prepare croutons, melt butter in a large, heavy skillet. Toast 2 slices of bread and cut into 1/4- to 1/2-inch cubes. Place cubes in skillet until all sides are coated. Remove from heat.

When soup has simmered 15 minutes, vigorously stir about 3 tablespoons of hot soup into slightly beaten egg yolks, then blend egg mixture into soup. Cook over low heat for 2 to 3 minutes. Do not bring to a boil.

Remove soup from heat and pour through sieve to remove caraway seeds.

Serve with croutons.

Serves 6   *Katalin Petroczy*

GYPSY-STYLE FRIED HAM SLICES

Place ham slices in 12-inch heavy skillet. Cut fat at 1 inch intervals on the outside edges. Do not cut through to the lean. Cook slowly over medium heat 10 to 12 minutes. Turn occasionally until both sides are lightly browned. Remove ham to a heated platter. Cover and set aside.

Reserve 2 tablespoons of fat; heat and mix in breadcrumbs, stirring constantly. Add broth, vinegar, sugar, and pepper. Blend in parsley. Heat, but do not boil.

Cut each piece of ham into 3 pieces. Pour sauce over ham and serve immediately.

Serves 6   *Katalin Petroczy*

**2 large slices smoked ham,
    1/2 inch thick
2 tablespoons reserved fat
3 tablespoons breadcrumbs
1-1/2 cups meat broth
4 teaspoons vinegar
1 teaspoon sugar
dash of ground black pepper
1 tablespoon parsley, chopped**

SUMMER SQUASH WITH DILL

Choose young tender squash and pare only if the outside seems tough. Wash and trim squash and cut into thin, crosswise slices. Place into 3-quart heavy saucepan; add boiling water, salt, and dill. Cover and simmer about 15 to 20 minutes, or until squash is tender.

In a double boiler, mix sour cream, lemon juice, sugar, and paprika, stirring constantly. After sauce is heated through, carefully mix with squash and serve immediately.

Serves 6   *Katalin Petroczy*

**2 pounds summer squash
1/2 cup boiling water
1/2 teaspoon salt
2 teaspoons fresh dill, finely chopped
    or 1/4 teaspoon dill seeds
1 cup thick sour cream
1 tablespoon lemon juice
2 teaspoons sugar
1/2 teaspoon paprika**

PALACSINTA
Crepes

Batter:

1 cup sifted flour
1-1/2 teaspoons sugar
1/8 teaspoon salt
1 egg, slightly beaten
1 cup milk
1/2 teaspoon vanilla extract
powdered sugar

Fillings:

thick apricot or peach jam

Cottage Cheese Filling:

2 egg yolks, beaten
1/4 cup sugar
1/4 teaspoon salt
1 pound cottage cheese
1 ounce raisins
1/2 teaspoon vanilla extract
1/2 teaspoon grated lemon peel

Nut Filling:

1 cup grated walnuts
1 cup raisins
1/2 cup sugar
3 tablespoons lemon juice
2 teaspoons grated lemon peel

Sift flour, sugar, and salt together in a bowl. Mix in slightly beaten egg, milk, and vanilla. Beat mixture until smooth.

Heat an 8-inch skillet, lightly buttered, until moderately hot. Skillet is hot enough if drops of water form small beads on surface. Remove from heat.

Pour in 2 or 2-1/2 tablespoons of batter until bottom of skillet is covered. Tilt skillet back and forth to insure that batter spreads thinly and evenly. Batter should be very thin at all times. Add small amounts of milk if necessary.

Fry crepe over medium heat until slightly brown. Loosen edges with spatula. Turn crepe by inverting skillet onto a flat plate. Fry reverse side.

While one crepe is frying, spread cooked crepe with 2 tablespoons of filling of your choice (such as thick apricot or peach jam, cottage cheese filling, or nut filling). Roll, and sprinkle with powdered sugar.

Cottage Cheese Filling:

Beat egg yolks; add sugar and salt and beat together until thick. Add cottage cheese, raisins, vanilla, and lemon peel, blending after each addition.

Nut Filling:

Combine all ingredients and mix well.

Yield: 14 to 16 crepes   *Katalin Petroczy*

ITALIAN DINNER

MARITATA
Marriage Soup

FETTUCCINE ALLA CREMA

VEAL PICCATA

BROCCOLI ALL' AGLIO
Broccoli with Garlic

INSALATA DI POMODORO
Tomato Salad

DULCE DE MANDORLE
Almond Torte

Fresh Fruit

Zinfandel

MARITATA
Marriage Soup

In a food processor, or heavy mixer bowl, beat butter until soft. Beat in cheese, egg yolks, and cornstarch. Gradually mix in whipping cream. Set aside.

In a saucepan, heat chicken broth, water, and wine. Bring to boil; add pasta and boil gently for 8 minutes. Remove pan from heat. Mix a little hot broth into creamy cheese mixture, stirring constantly. Then stir cheese back into hot broth. Heat thoroughly and serve very hot.

Sprinkle each serving with parsley and Romano cheese, if desired.

Serves 8 to 10   *Lorette Rubino*

1 cup sweet butter, softened
2 cups grated Romano cheese
8 egg yolks
1 tablespoon cornstarch
2 cups whipping cream
4 cans (10 3/4-ounce) chicken broth
4 soup cans water
2 cups dry white wine
8 ounces coil vermicelli or other fine
    noodle, broken into 1/2-inch
    lengths
minced parsley

FETTUCCINE ALLA CREMA

1 cup unsalted butter or margarine
2/3 cup light cream
2 cups freshly grated Parmesan
1/8 teaspoon nutmeg
salt and freshly ground pepper
1 pound noodles

Melt butter or margarine in a saucepan. Add cream, 1 cup of the Parmesan, nutmeg, and salt and pepper to taste.

Cook the noodles al dente; drain and place in a large warm bowl.

Pour cream sauce over noodles and sprinkle with remaining grated cheese.

Serves 4 to 6   *Marilyn Walsh*

VEAL PICCATA

1 cup Italian bread crumbs
1 tablespoon fresh Italian parsley
    (flat), chopped
3 tablespoons Parmesan cheese,
    freshly grated
1/4 teaspoon powdered garlic
1 pound veal, cut for scallopini
    (6 servings)
flour for dredging
1 egg, beaten with 1 tablespoon water
2 tablespoons oil
2 tablespoons butter or margarine
juice of 1 lemon

Mix together bread crumbs, parsley, Parmesan cheese, and powdered garlic.

Lightly flour veal, shaking off excess flour, and dip into beaten egg, then bread crumbs.

Fry lightly in oil and butter. Turn just once. Remove to platter and keep warm.

Squeeze the lemon juice into the pan to deglaze and pour over the veal.

Serves 6   *Marilyn Walsh*

BROCCOLI ALL' AGLIO
Broccoli with Oil and Garlic

1 large bunch broccoli
boiling salted water
3 tablespoons olive oil
3 tablespoons butter
2 cloves garlic, chopped
salt and fresh ground pepper
3 tablespoons fresh lemon juice

Slice off and discard the tough ends of broccoli; split stalks into 2 to 4 lengths, with florets left on stalk. Steam in boiling, salted water until just fork tender.

Over medium heat in skillet, add oil, butter, and garlic. Sauté until transparent. Add drained broccoli and saute 3 to 4 minutes. Sprinkle with salt and pepper if desired. Arrange in vegetable bowl and drizzle with lemon juice.

Marilyn Walsh

INSALATA DI POMODORO
Tomato Salad

Place olive oil and minced garlic in a jar and let stand.

Slice tomatoes and arrange with alternate slices of cheese on a platter. Salt and pepper to taste, and sprinkle with basil. Drizzle with olive oil and garlic. Let stand 30 minutes before serving.

Giovanna Mannino

4 tablespoons olive oil
1 clove garlic, minced
5 large tomatoes sliced
1 pound ball Mozzarella cheese, sliced
**   1/4 inch thick**
salt and pepper to taste
2 tablespoons fresh basil

DULCE de MANDORLE
Almond Torte

Preheat oven to 350 degrees. Butter and flour an 8-inch cake pan.

In a mixing bowl, combine butter, sugar, and almond paste. Blend well. Beat in eggs, liqueur, and extract. Add flour and baking powder, beating just until mixed thoroughly. Do not overbeat.

Bake until tester comes out clean, 40 to 50 minutes.

Invert and dust with powdered sugar.

Serves 8   *Giovanna Mannino*

1/2 cup unsalted butter
3/4 cup sugar
7 ounces almond paste
3 eggs
1 tablespoon Triple Sec
1/4 teaspoon almond extract
1/4 cup flour
1/3 teaspoon baking powder
powdered sugar

MEXICAN DINNER

STACKED ENCHILADAS

REFRIED BEANS

CAPIROTADA
Mexican Bread Pudding

SPANISH RICE

AGUA de ARROZ
Rice Water Beverage

STACKED ENCHILADAS

1 pound ground beef
1/2 cup onions, diced
salt and pepper to taste
2 cans (16-ounce) red chili sauce
1 cup oil
9 corn tortillas
2 cups cheddar cheese, grated
2 cups shredded lettuce
2 small tomatoes, diced

In a skillet, cook meat and add onions. Season to your taste.

Heat red chili sauce to simmering point.

In a saucepan, heat oil. Dip one tortilla at a time into hot oil until tortilla is soft. Place soft tortillas on a plate.

Then, dip one soft tortilla into chili sauce and place in a 9 x 9-inch baking dish; spread about 2 heaping table-spoons of meat and about 1 heaping tablespoon of cheese on tortilla.

Dip a second tortilla into chili sauce and stack it on top of the first tortilla; spread same portions of meat and cheese on this second tortilla.

Continue layering tortillas, meat, and cheese until all have been used. Pour remaining chili sauce over and around the stacked enchiladas.

Bake in oven at 350 degrees for 20 minutes. Garnish each serving with lettuce and tomatoes.

Serves 4 to 6

Antonia Herrera

REFRIED BEANS

Clean the beans by removing dirt, stones, and foreign matter and rinsing in cold water.

Put into deep cooking pot with water. Add garlic and bacon. Bring to a boil. Cover and simmer on low heat. Cook for about 2-1/2 hours or until beans are tender. Drain.

In a large saucepan, heat oil and add the cooked beans and salt. Mash beans completely. Add cheese and cook, uncovered over medium heat, stirring often, until cheese melts.

Serves 8   *Antonia Herrera*

2 cups uncooked pinto beans
5 cups water
1 small clove garlic, sliced
1 strip bacon, diced
1/2 cup oil
1 teaspoon salt
1/2 cup shredded cheese

SPANISH RICE

In a cooking pot, brown rice lightly in cooking oil. Add onion and sauté.

Add water, tomato sauce, tomatoes, salt, and pepper. Bring to a boil and cover. Simmer on low heat for 20 minutes or until rice is done.

Serves 6 to 8   *Antonia Herrera*

2 cups uncooked white rice
1/2 cup cooking oil
1/2 onion, chopped
4 cups water
1 can (8-ounce) tomato sauce
1 cup tomatoes, chopped
1 teaspoon salt
1/4 teaspoon pepper

CAPIROTADA
Mexican Bread Pudding

Slice the bread in half and toast in the oven. Break the bread into bite-sized pieces with your hands.

In a saucepan, melt brown sugar and add water. Stir with cinnamon until mixed and discard cinnamon.

In a 9 x 13-inch greased baking dish, layer half of each ingredient in the following order: bread, raisins, apple, walnuts, cheese, and brown sugar syrup. Make sure the bread is soaked with the syrup. Repeat the layers and cover with remaining syrup.

Bake at 350 degrees for 10 to 15 minutes. Serve warm.

Serves 6 to 8   *Antonia Herrera*

1/2 loaf French bread
1 cup firmly packed brown sugar
1 cup water
1 cinnamon stick, 3 inches long
1 cup raisins
1 cup sliced apple
1 cup chopped walnuts
1/2 pound jack cheese, cut into
     1/2-inch cubes

AGUA de ARROZ
Rice Water Beverage

1 cup uncooked white rice
2 quarts water
1 stick cinnamon
sugar to taste

Wash rice and soak in water for about 3 hours in a deep pot.

Add cinnamon. Simmer for 1/2 hour on low heat.

Remove cinnamon and let the rice with the water cool.

Strain the rice mixture through a cloth napkin and squeeze to extract all the liquid. Add sugar to taste. Chill and serve with ice cubes.

Yield: 8 cups   *Antonia Herrera*

NEW ENGLAND DINNER FOR EIGHT

CLAM FRITTERS

YANKEE POT ROAST

SHORTBREAD
COOKIES

SYLLABUB

YANKEE POT ROAST

Heat Dutch oven over high heat and grease lightly. Dredge roast in flour and place in Dutch oven. Add 1 or 2 slices of onion. Lower heat to medium and brown well on all sides. This could take 1/2 hour.

Place meat on low rack in Dutch oven and add 1/2 cup liquid (water or tomato juice or a combination of the two). Cover, reduce heat and cook very slowly for 3 to 4 hours or until meat is fork tender, adding more liquid as needed.

During the last 2 hours, add small whole, peeled potatoes, tiny onions and carrots. Baste with pan liquids occasionally. Taste, add salt and pepper.

When meat is done, transfer meat and vegetables to warm platter and keep warm while making gravy using the pan juices and adding consommé to make a sufficient amount.

Serves 8 to 10   *Jacqueline P. Smith*

4 to 5 pounds beef pot roast
    (trimmed, rolled and firmly tied)
2 tablespoons flour
1 to 2 onion slices
1/2 cup water or tomato juice or
    combination of the two
1/4 teaspoon pepper
2 teaspoons salt
potatoes, small whole and peeled
tiny onions
carrots
consommé for gravy

CLAM FRITTERS

1 cup chopped, canned clams
milk
1 egg
2/3 cup flour
1 teaspoon baking powder
pinch salt
pepper
bacon fat (if desired)

Drain clams, pouring liquid into a measuring cup. Add enough milk to make 1/3 cup liquid.

In mixing bowl, beat egg and add clam juice and milk.

Sift together the flour, baking powder, salt, and pepper. Add to liquid and stir to blend. Add clams. Pat into 10 to 12 large fritters, or 30 cocktail size fritters.

Fry in bacon fat until hot, approximately 1 to 2 minutes on each side. Tartar sauce and/or catsup may be served on the side.

Jacqueline P. Smith

SHORTBREAD COOKIES

1 cup butter, not margarine
1/2 cup powdered sugar
2 cups flour
1/4 teaspoon salt
1/4 teaspoon baking powder

Cream butter. Gradually add sugar and beat well.

Mix flour, salt, and baking powder and add to butter/sugar mixture. Combine thoroughly.

Roll dough with rolling pin to 1/4-inch thickness. Cut in squares and place onto ungreased cookie sheets. Prick cookies with fork. Bake in preheated oven at 350 degrees for 20 to 25 minutes, until slightly brown on edges. Do not overcook.

Yield: 2 dozen   *Jacqueline P. Smith*

SYLLABUB

2 pints heavy cream
1 cup powdered sugar
1 teaspoon vanilla
1/2 cup sweet Madeira
2 tablespoons brandy

Whip cream until it begins to hold its shape. Gradually add the sugar. Add vanilla. Beat until very stiff. (This may be done an hour or two ahead of time and refrigerated at this point. If so, be sure to beat until stiff when removed from refrigerator before finishing).

Carefully fold in wine and brandy so it doesn't curdle.

Spoon into parfait or other attractive glass.

Serve immediately with shortbread or other dessert wafer.

Serves 8   *Jacqueline P. Smith*

NORWEGIAN DINNER

SPINATSUPPE
Spinach Soup

FISKGRATIN
Fish with Cheese Sauce

HIMMELSK LAPSKAUS MED EGGEDOSIS
Fruit Potpourri with Egg Sauce

SANBAKELSER
Almond Cookies

SPINATSUPPE
Spinach Soup

Thoroughly wash spinach, drain and chop coarsely. If frozen spinach is used, thaw it completely and drain.

Bring the soup stock to a boil in a 4-quart pot and add spinach. Simmer, uncovered, for about 8 minutes. Pour stock into another saucepan, straining out the spinach. Place spinach in a bowl and press with a spoon to remove most of the liquid. If desired, chop the cooked spinach even finer.

Melt butter in the soup pot, remove from heat and stir in flour. Add liquid stock, 1 cup at a time, stirring constantly. Return pot to heat and bring to a boil. Add spinach, salt, pepper, and nutmeg. Soup will thicken slightly. Simmer for about 5 minutes more.

Serve by garnishing each individual serving with a few slices of hard-cooked egg, if desired.

Ann Rumery

2 pounds fresh spinach or 2 packages frozen chopped spinach
3 quarts chicken stock
4 tablespoons butter
3 tablespoons flour
1 teaspoon salt
dash freshly ground pepper
1/8 teaspoon nutmeg
hard-cooked egg, sliced

FISKGRATIN
Fish with Cheese Sauce

2-1/2 to 2-3/4 pounds fresh fish fillets
1-3/4 teaspoons salt
1/2 teaspoon white pepper
1/4 cup lemon juice
11 tablespoons butter
6 tablespoons flour
3 cups light cream, heated
3 egg yolks
1 cup cooked, shelled and deveined
    shrimp, coarsely chopped
1 cup cooked lobster, chopped
1/4 cup grated Parmesan cheese

Preheat oven to 350 degrees. Place fish fillets in buttered baking dish. Sprinkle with 1 teaspoon salt, 1/4 teaspoon pepper, and lemon juice. Dot with 2 tablespoons butter. Cover with aluminum foil or lid and bake about 20 minutes. Bake until fish flakes. Do not overcook.

While fish is baking, heat 6 tablespoons butter and stir in flour. Cook until smooth, but do not let brown. Gradually stir in cream and cook over low heat until sauce is thick and smooth, stirring constantly. Remove from heat and beat in egg yolks, one at a time, and remaining 3 tablespoons butter. Sauce must be very smooth and hot. Remove cover from fish and drain off excess liquid. Top the fish with shrimp and lobster. Pour hot sauce over the fish and sprinkle with Parmesan cheese.

Place baking dish on broiler rack 4 or 5 inches away from element. Broil until golden brown and serve immediately.

You can probably make the cream sauce just before your guests arrive and reheat quickly when needed while you finish preparations, and brown the topping. I cannot over-emphasize the importance of serving this dish hot.

Ann Rumery

HIMMELSK LAPSKAUS MED EGGEDOSIS
Fruit Potpourri with Egg Sauce

1 cup chopped bananas
1 cup halved seedless grapes
1 cup chopped apples
1 cup chopped oranges
1/2 cup chopped walnuts or pecans

Eggedosis:

5 egg yolks
2 egg whites
5 tablespoons sugar
1 tablespoon brandy or rum

Toss the fruits and nuts together in a bowl and chill.

If using an electric mixer, set it on high speed, whip together the egg yolks, whites, and sugar. When thickened to a custard-like consistency, add the brandy or rum.

If using a wisk, whip the yolks and whites to a froth; add sugar gradually. Continue to beat vigorously until mixture thickens; beat in liquor. Chill. Serve fruit and sauce separately.

Ann Rumery

SANBAKELSER
Almond Cookies

Cream butter with sugar. Add eggs. Beat well after each addition.

Sift flour and add to mixture to make a stiff dough. Add almonds and extract. Blend in well. Chill overnight.

Press very thinly into cookie molds. Place molds on cookie sheet and bake at 400 degrees until a light brown.

Turn molds upside down immediately on tile or formica counter and then take off molds.

Shortly thereafter, place cookies on platters until cooled. Handle carefully at all times as these cookies are very fragile.

Store in closed tins in a cool spot for several weeks.

Emmy Ruud

3/4 pound sweet butter
1 cup sugar
2 eggs
3-1/2 cups flour
3/4 cup chopped, blanched almonds
1 teaspoon almond extract

SOUTHERN DINNER FOR SIX

SPARERIBS

OKRA CREOLE

BLACK-EYED PEAS

MIXED GREENS

CORNBREAD MUFFINS

SWEET POTATO PIE

SPARERIBS

4 pounds pork spareribs, separated
2 tablespoons flour
1 teaspoon salt
1/2 teaspoon pepper
3 tablespoons vegetable oil
2 small onions
1 cup chopped celery
1 clove garlic, minced
2 cups boiling water
1 cup chopped parsley

Dredge ribs in flour mixed with salt and pepper.

In a heavy skillet or dutch oven, sauté ribs in oil until brown.

Slice onions, chop celery, and mince garlic. Add boiling water, onions, garlic, and celery to ribs. Cover and simmer until tender.

Chop parsley and add.

Serve with rice, mashed potatoes, or noodles.

Serves 4 to 6   *Anne Terry*

OKRA CREOLE

2 pounds okra
1 medium onion, chopped
1 clove garlic, minced
1 medium green pepper, chopped
3 tablespoons butter
3 tomatoes, peeled, finely chopped
1 cup tomato juice
salt and pepper to taste
2 tablespoons chopped parsley

Wash okra and cut off ends.

In a skillet, sauté chopped onions, minced garlic and chopped green pepper in butter for about 10 minutes. Add peeled and chopped tomatoes and tomato juice. Add salt and pepper to taste. Add okra and chopped parsley. Cook 20 minutes.

Serves 6   *Anne Terry*

BLACK-EYED PEAS

Parboil meat 30 minutes or sauté in 2 tablespoons vegetable oil.

Wash peas thoroughly. In a large sauce pan or Dutch oven, cover peas with water; add meat or oil, chopped onion, garlic, parsley, pepper pods, salt, pepper, and bay leaf. Boil slowly, stirring occasionally, and adding more water if needed. Cook until peas are very tender.

Remove bay leaf and serve.

Serves 6   *Anne Terry*

1 pound smoked meat or bacon ends
   (2 tablespoons vegetable oil may
   be substituted for meat)
1 pound black-eyed peas
l large onion, chopped
1 clove garlic
several sprigs parsley
several red pepper pods (optional)
salt and pepper to taste
1 bay leaf

MIXED GREENS

Parboil meat in 2 cups water. If vegetable oil is used, reduce water to 1 cup; add vegetable oil and heat.

Add chopped green onions, minced garlic, baking soda, and salt and pepper to taste.

Wash greens thoroughly, making sure they are free of sand, cut into small pieces, and add to water.

Cook over moderate heat about 1-1/2 hours or until tender.

Serves 6 to 8   *Anne Terry*

1/2 pound bacon, ham, or salt pork;
   or 2 tablespoons vegetable oil
2 cups water, or 1 cup water if you
   use oil
1 bunch green onions
1 clove garlic, minced
pinch baking soda
salt and pepper to taste
1 bunch kale
1 bunch turnips
1 bunch mustard greens
1 bunch Texas mustard greens, or
   2 baskets brussel sprouts

CORNBREAD MUFFINS

1 cup corn meal
1/2 cup flour
2 teaspoon baking powder
1/2 teaspoon salt
1 tablespoon sugar
1 cup milk
2 eggs

Sift into a large bowl corn meal, flour, baking powder, salt, and sugar, and mix well.

Add milk and eggs and beat well.

Pour into a greased 8-inch baking pan or muffin tins.

Bake in 400 degree oven for 20 to 30 minutes.

Anne Terry

SWEET POTATO PIE

6 medium sweet potatoes or yams
1/2 stick margarine
1/2 cup sugar
3 eggs
1 cup milk
1 teaspoon allspice
1/4 teaspoon nutmeg
1 teaspoon vanilla
2 unbaked 8-inch pie shells

Boil potatoes until soft. Drain, peel, and mash. Add margarine and sugar. Mix well. Add eggs one at a time, beating well after each one. Add milk, allspice, nutmeg, and vanilla. Mix well.

Pour mixture into pie shells. Bake in 450-degree oven for 15 minutes. Reduce heat to 350 degrees for 30 minutes or until pies are firm and brown.

Anne Terry

YUGOSLAV DINNER FOR EIGHT

PILEĆA JUHA SA KNEDLIMA OD GRIZA
Chicken Soup with Cream of Wheat Dumplings

PEČENI GOLUBI SA KRUMPIRIMA
Roast Squab with Potatoes

PRŽENE TIKVICE
Sautéed Zucchini

ZELENA SALATA
Green Salad

TORTA
Walnut Torte

BAŠKOTINI
Sweet Biscuits

KRUŠKOVAC
Pear Liqueur

TURSKA KAVA
Turkish Coffee

PILEĆA JUHA
Chicken Soup

Using a large stock pot, bring salted water to a rolling boil; add chicken and vegetables. Bring to a rolling boil again; skim off fat regularly. Lower heat and cover. Simmer at medium heat for about 1-1/2 hours.

Remove potatoes and carrots when tender. May be reserved for later use.

Remove chicken and set aside. Strain soup, skim off fat. Reserved white meat of chicken may be diced and added to broth, if desired.

Soup may be served with Cream of Wheat dumplings, rice, capellini, or vermicelli, if desired.

Serves 6 to 8   *Dolores Lisica*

5 quarts water, approximately
salt to taste
1 chicken (3-pound), quartered
2 large onions, quartered
2 stalks celery
2 carrots
2 medium potatoes
1 medium fresh tomato

281

KNEDLIMA OD GRIZA
Cream of Wheat Dumplings

1-1/2 tablespoons soft butter
  (not melted)
2 eggs, separated
1/8 teaspoon salt
1/8 teaspoon white pepper
1/2 cup (scant) Quick Cooking
  Cream of Wheat
1 teaspoon minced fresh parsley

Place butter, egg yolks, salt, and pepper in straight-sided, 8-ounce low-ball glass.

Beat egg whites stiff and set aside.

Using handle of tablespoon, beat together egg yolks and butter until thoroughly mixed. Add Cream of Wheat, in spoonfuls, alternately with egg whites, to butter/egg mixture. Beat together until mixture is light and fluffy and slides off sides of glass. Add parsley and mix evenly.

Slide mixture into simmering broth (see previous recipe) by 1/2 teaspoonfuls. Dip spoon into broth and dumpling will slide right off.

The dumplings will more than triple in size when cooked. Cooking time varies from 6 to 12 minutes. Take one out and cut in half to test for doneness. Uncooked dumplings may be slipped onto foil and frozen.

Dolores Lisica

PEČENI GOLUBI SA KRUMPIRIMA
Roast Squab With Potatoes

Wrap squab in clean dish towel or paper towels to remove excess moisture.

Quarter onions and apples. Wrap 1 onion wedge and 1 apple wedge with slice of bacon and secure with toothpick. Set aside.

Lightly salt and pepper each squab on all sides and cavities. Place an apple/onion/bacon wedge into each squab and dredge squab lightly in flour.

Place olive oil in roasting pan and place in oven. Preheat roasting pan at 425 degrees. Place squab and potatoes in heated roasting pan. Brown on all sides, turning as necessary. Add sliced onions, garlic, and parsley. Roast for 30 minutes at 425 degrees.

Pour brandy and marsala over birds and potatoes. Lower oven to 325 degrees and roast for another 30 to 45 minutes. Check for doneness by moving drumstick. If it moves easily, the squab is done. Remove from roasting pan and arrange on serving platter.

De-grease pan juices. Place roasting pan on stove on high heat. Scrape pan, and add chicken broth. Reduce to 1/2 of volume. Taste and season, if necessary. Pour pan juices over squab and serve.

Squab became a family favorite back in the days when they sold for 25 cents each. Today they are served for very important birthdays and such.

Serves 8   *Dolores Lisica*

8 squab—giblets, neck, etc., removed, rinsed in cold water and drained
2 onions, quartered
2 apples, quartered
8 slices lean bacon
salt and pepper to taste
1/2 cup flour
3 tablespoons olive oil
8 to 12 small russet potatoes, peeled
2 onions, thinly sliced
4 cloves garlic, pressed
1/2 cup parsley, minced
1/2 cup brandy or bourbon
1/2 cup marsala or dry sherry
1 cup chicken broth

PRŽENE TIKVICE
Sautéed Zucchini

Cut zucchini into 1/4-inch slices. Slice onions. Peel tomatoes and cut into chunks. Mince parsley.

Heat oil in saucepan, add onions and sauté until golden. Add garlic, parsley, and tomatoes. Add zucchini, season, and stir gently to combine. Cover and cook 5 to 8 minutes.

Serves 4 to 6   *Chris Lisica*

1 large or 2 medium zucchini, cut into 1/4-inch slices
1 large onion, sliced thinly
2 medium tomatoes, peeled and cut into chunks
5 sprigs parsley, minced
2 tablespoons olive oil or butter
2 cloves garlic, pressed
salt and pepper to taste

BAŠKOTINI
Sweet Biscuits

1/4 pound butter
1/2 cup shortening
1-1/2 cups sugar
6 eggs
2 tablespoons vanilla
2 tablespoons rum
3 cups flour
pinch of salt
2 teaspoons baking powder

In a large bowl, cream butter and shortening, and add sugar slowly. Beat together until fluffy. Add eggs one at a time, beating well after each egg. Add vanilla and rum.

Sift flour, salt, and baking powder together. Add a little at a time to creamed mixture. Beat for another 2 to 3 minutes after all flour is added.

Line a cookie sheet with foil. Shape foil to form a corrugated shape—3 creases about 2-1/2 inches apart (creases stand up to separate the rows of biscuits). Fill with cookie batter dropped gently by the spoonful; smooth carefully with spatula or butter knife. Bake at 350 degrees for 15 to 20 minutes, just until firm.

Cool and cut carefully into 1-inch thick slices. Place on ungreased cookie sheet to make them crisp and dry. Bake at 350 degrees until golden. Turn and repeat until all sides are a golden color.
 Stored in a tin container, they can keep for months if kept dry and tightly closed. These are delicious with coffee or to accompany wine.

Franka Torbarina

TORTA
Walnut Torte

8 eggs, separated
8 tablespoons sugar
1/2 pound finely ground walnuts
1/2 cup fresh white bread crumbs

Frosting:

1/2 pound sweet unsalted butter
2 cups powdered sugar
6 tablespoons strong, black coffee,
    cold; Turkish recommended

Preheat oven to 350 degrees. Grease and flour two 9-inch cake pans.

Beat egg yolks and sugar together until smooth. Add walnuts and bread crumbs to egg yolk mixture and combine thoroughly.

In another bowl, beat egg whites until fluffy; add to yolk mixture, using mixer at low speed. Do not over-mix. Divide batter evenly into greased cake pans.

Bake at 350 degrees for 30 to 40 minutes, until an inserted toothpick comes out clean.

Allow to cool completely before frosting with Coffee Frosting.

To make the frosting, cream butter and sugar, adding coffee gradually. Beat together until smooth. Spread frosting over cooled cake.

Maria Čudić

TURSKA KAVA
Turkish Coffee

Turkish Coffee is made in the traditional way in a special long-handled copper pot with a lip but no lid, which has kept its Turkish name of dzezva. The American equivalent would be an enameled utensil used for melting butter.

Place water in the džezva, add sugar and bring to a boil. When the water boils, pour some into a demitasse cup to preheat cup. Add coffee to boiling water in džezva, stir, and return to a boil. Remove from heat, add reserved water from cup, cover for 30 seconds. Pour into demitasse cup and serve at once.

Yield: 1 serving   *Dolores Lisica*

1-1/2 demitasse cups cold water
1 teaspoon sugar
1-1/2 teaspoons very finely ground
   coffee

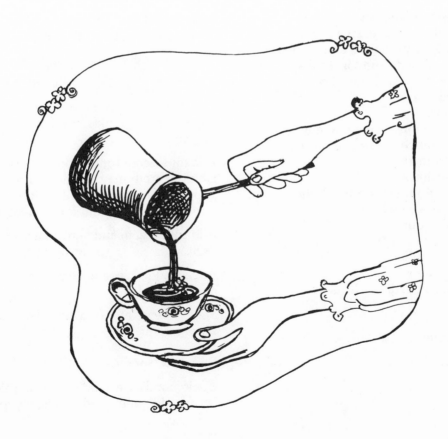

DINNER FOR TWENTY

BUTTER LEAF LETTUCE SALAD WITH POPPY SEED DRESSING

CHICKEN, SHRIMP, AND SCALLOPS IN WHITE SAUCE

Rice or Buttered Noodles

BROCCOLI AND CHEESE

Fresh Fruit Platter

CHICKEN, SHRIMPS AND SCALLOPS
In White Sauce

2 pounds cooked chicken, cut into
  bite-sized pieces; reserve broth
  (4 pounds raw skinned and boned
  chicken: breasts and/or thighs)
2 pounds raw shrimp, cleaned and
  deveined
2/3 stick butter
2 large white onions, chopped fine
1/2 medium bunch parsley, minced
3 tablespoons tarragon
3 tablespoons basil
3 cans (8-ounce) mushrooms, drain
  and reserve liquid
3 tablespoons flour
salt and pepper to taste
2 pounds raw scallops
3 pints sour cream
2 pounds sharp cheddar cheese,
  shredded

Buttered Noodles:

2-1/2 pounds noodles
butter

Boil chicken until done. Remove chicken (reserving broth), skin, and cut into bite-sized pieces. Set aside.

Clean and devein shrimp. Set aside.

Melt butter. Sauté onions until clear.

Add minced parsley, tarragon, basil, and drained mushrooms. Sprinkle with flour. Cook 3 minutes, stirring constantly.

Add mushroom liquor; cook until clear, adjusting liquid. Chicken broth may be added if needed. Add salt and pepper. Add chicken and seafood. Cook until shrimp turn bright pink, about 5 to 8 minutes.

Add sour cream and bring to a simmer. DO NOT LET BOIL.

Add shredded cheese, correct seasonings, correct thickening if needed.

Serve, refrigerate, or freeze. To reheat, use low heat, stirring frequently.

Buttered Noodles:

Cook noodles according to directions on package. Drain, add butter, and toss lightly together.

Serves 20   *Carrie Stock*

BUTTER LEAF LETTUCE SALAD
With Poppy Seed Dressing

Wash and dry lettuce. Store in tight container or damp pillowcase. Will keep 6 hours or more.

Drain oranges and store.

Slice onions; cover tightly.

Assemble salad. Add dressing.

Poppy Seed Dressing:

Use a food processor, or a mixer on medium speed.

Mix sugar, mustard, salt, and vinegar. Add onion juice and stir. Add oil slowly, beating constantly until thick. Add poppy seeds. Chill.

Serves 20   *Carrie Stock*

3 heads butter leaf lettuce
2 cans Mandarin oranges, drained
2 large red onions, thinly sliced
slivered almonds

Poppy Seed Dressing:

1-1/2 cups sugar
2 teaspoons dry mustard
2 teaspoons salt
2/3 cup red or white wine vinegar
3 tablespoons onion juice
2 cups salad oil
3 tablespoons poppy seeds

BROCCOLI AND CHEESE

Wash, stem, and remove leaves from broccoli. Cook in salted water until "tough" to the bite. Drain.

Mix soups together.

In a large greased 12 x 18 x 3-1/2 inch pan, layer broccoli, cover with soup, sprinkle dry onions, then a heavy hand of cheese. Repeat process until pan is filled (2 or 3 layers).

Cover tightly with foil and freeze or bake 30 to 40 minutes at 350 degrees.

Serves 20 to 25   *Carrie Stock*

10 pounds raw broccoli
salted boiling water
3 cans mushroom soup
3 cans celery soup
1/2 cup dry onion flakes
2 pounds sharp cheddar cheese,
    grated

RESTAURANTS

SARMA
Stuffed Cabbage Rolls

Yugoslavia

Cook rice according to instructions on package.

Mix together well: ground beef, cooked rice, eggs, bell pepper, onion, nutmeg, salt, and pepper, and set aside. Core cabbage; parboil it and remove larger outer leaves. Cut off the outer ribs of cabbage. Place filling in each cabbage leaf and roll it from the bottom of the leaf to the outer edge. Fold the side over the filling toward the center to hold the roll together. Repeat until filling is all used.

Slice any remaining cabbage into strips. Place 1/4 pound of sauerkraut and strips of cabbage into the bottom of a roasting pan, 3 inches or more in depth. Arrange cabbage rolls on top of sauerkraut and cabbage strips. Cover cabbage rolls with remaining sauerkraut.

Make sauce, then pour it over the cabbage rolls. Bake in oven for 1-1/2 to 2 hours at 400 degrees, or until beef is fully cooked.

Sauce:

To make sauce, sauté carrots, onion, and celery. Add tomatoes and tomato puree, water, sugar, vinegar, salt, and pepper. Bring to a boil, and thicken if desired.

Yield: 24 rolls

Ante Perkov
Ante's Restaurant

2 cups cooked rice
1 pound ground beef
4 eggs
1 bell pepper, finely chopped
1 onion, finely chopped
1/2 teaspoon nutmeg
salt and pepper, to taste
3 heads cabbage, cored
1/2 pound sauerkraut

Sauce:

2 cups chopped carrots
1 onion, chopped
1 cup celery, chopped
4 to 5 ripe tomatoes, chopped
1 can (1-1/2 pounds) tomato puree
4 cups water
3/4 cups sugar, or to taste
1/2 cup wine vinegar, or to taste
salt and pepper, to taste

BASTILLA
Moroccan Chicken Pie

Chicken amd Sauce preparation:

1 small chicken
1 medium onion, peeled and finely
    chopped
1/2 bunch parsely, chopped
1/2 bunch cilantro, chopped
1 tablespoon coriander
1 tablespoon ginger
1 teaspoon salt
1 pinch white pepper
1 pinch saffron
1/4 cup oil
2 cups water

Egg preparation:

6 eggs, well beaten

Pie preparation:

4 tablespoons butter
10 sheets filo dough (approximately)
1 tablespoon granulated sugar
1 tablespoon cinnamon
3 tablespoons almonds, crushed
    or sliced

Final preparation:

powdered sugar
1 tablespoon cinnamon

Bastilla is one of the most exquisite of all Moroccan entrees. Like many new experiences, the appearance and taste of this dish present initial confusion and surprise to the American diner.

This filling of chicken, spices and almonds, encased in a flaky, sugared pastry, is a delicious combination. The finished product, as it is served at Babouch, is a large golden brown pie, sprinkled with cinnamon and sugar and served on a beautiful porcelain platter. It is brought to the dinner table hot from the oven, and is properly eaten with the fingers.

To prepare the chicken and sauce, mix together all ingredients (except the chicken) in a roasting pan, to form a nice thick sauce. Place chicken into sauce and bake for 45 minutes at 350 degrees. When finished, remove chicken from sauce and remove all bones and skin. Chop chicken into small pieces and set aside to cool.

To make the egg preparation, place chicken sauce in a saucepan over medium heat. Fold eggs into sauce and stir continuously until soft curds form (approximately 20 minutes). Drain and dispose of all liquid remaining and set aside to cool.

To make the pie, melt 1 tablespoon butter in a 14-inch frying pan. Place filo dough into frying pan, completely covering the bottom of the pan and overlapping sides of pan approximately 2 inches. Sprinkle sugar over filo dough in pan. Sprinkle cinnamon evenly over sugar, and then sprinkle with almonds. Place chopped chicken evenly over almonds, and cover with egg mixture. Place 1 or 2 layers of filo dough over egg mixture and fold overlap filo to inside. Brush with 1 tablespoon melted butter and bake for 20 minutes at 350 degrees.

Remove from oven. Turn pie onto large platter and sprinkle with powdered sugar (enough to cover completely). Sprinkle 1 tablespoon cinnamon evenly over sugar and serve immediately.

Serves 10

Chef Youssef Keroles
Babouch Moroccan Restaurant

cigo's

OPEN 7 DAYS
BANQUETS AND CATERING
833-0949 • 833-2419
THE FINEST SEAFOOD
IN THE HARBOR

915 S. PACIFIC AVE., SAN PEDRO, CA. 90731

ČEVAPĆICI

Mix meats together, add remaining ingredients, mixing well. Roll mixture into sausages about 3 inches long and 3/4 inch in diameter. Grill, turning often, until done. Don't overcook. Serve with freshly chopped onion.

Serves 4 to 6   *Cigo's Restaurant*

1 pound lean ground beef
1/2 pound ground pork
1/4 pound ground lamb
2 teaspoons salt
1 teaspoon pepper
1 teaspoon garlic powder
chopped onion

CHEESE BUREK

In a large bowl, mix Feta cheese, Ricotta and pot cheese, eggs and sugar.

Top one sheet of filo dough with 1/4th of another sheet, centered. Sprinkle with melted butter, and fill with half of a handful of the cheese mixture. Loosely roll and brush with butter. Shape into a circle. Continue this procedure until all of the dough and filling is used. Place on ungreased cookie sheet and bake at 475 degrees for 8 to 9 minutes or until golden brown.

Cigo's Restaurant

3/4 pound Feta cheese, grated or
   crumbled
1/4 pound Ricotta cheese
1/4 pound pot cheese
2 egg yolks and 1 egg
1/2 cup sugar
2 pounds filo dough
melted butter

FETA SALAD

Slice tomatoes, bell peppers, and cucumbers in small pieces, chop onion, and place in bowl. Add olive oil, salt, and pepper, and mix together. Spoon into salad bowls, add crumbled Feta cheese on top. Add more salt and pepper, if necessary.

Serves 8   *Cigo's Restaurant*

5 firm tomatoes
4 bell peppers
3 cucumbers
1 onion, chopped
1/4 cup olive oil
1 teaspoon salt
1 teaspoon pepper
1/4 pound Feta cheese

809 South Grand Avenue
San Pedro, CA 90731
(213) 548-1240

PURÉE OF SQUASH WITH GINGER SOUP

2 pounds yellow crookneck squash
1/2 cup chicken stock
1 ounce sugared ginger (available at
    oriental grocery)
20 ounces heavy cream
1-1/2 ounces cognac or brandy
1/4 teaspoon mace
salt and white pepper, to taste

Chop squash coarsely (1- or 2-inch pieces) and boil for 10 to 15 minutes until tender. Drain.

Purée in food processor or blender together with chicken stock and sugared ginger.

Force through strainer.

Stir in remaining ingredients.

Heat and serve.

Serves 6 to 8

Chef Larry Hodgson
Grand House Restaurant

THE LEMON TREE CAFE AND CATERING
24416 Crenshaw Boulevard
Torrance, California 90505
(213) 530-3194

SPINACH MUSHROOM BRIE CREPES

Crepes:

In blender mix all ingredients until smooth. Cover and let stand 30 minutes. Heat a 7-inch or 5-inch skillet or crepe pan. Film with butter, pour in several tablespoons batter and tilt to spread thin. Cook until lightly browned, turn and lightly brown. Stack until ready to use. Makes 12 7-inch or 16 5-inch crepes.

Filling:

Wash, drain, and chop spinach, then; cook. Make roux from butter and flour. Add cream and stir. Cook until thick and flour is done. Add nutmeg, salt, pepper, and cheese and whisk together. Add to spinach and mix well.

Mushroom Sauce:

Cook mushrooms in butter until very soft. Remove from heat and add flour, mixing well. Add chicken broth and simmer until thickened. Add thyme and Kitchen Bouquet, then brandy.

Assembly:

In center of crepe, place a large tablespoonful of spinach mixture. Add a small piece of ripe Brie (about 1/2 inch wide and 3 inches long) and a bit of the mushroom sauce. Roll up crepe and put more mushroom sauce on top.

May be heated in microwave or moderate oven until warm and Brie melts. Two crepes make a good helping.

Joan Connor

The Lemon Tree Cafe

Crepes:

2 eggs
1 cup milk
1/2 teaspoon salt
1 cup flour
2 tablespoons melted butter

Spinach filling:

1-1/2 pounds spinach, cooked, chopped, and drained
1/2 stick butter
4 tablespoons flour
1-1/2 cups light cream
1/2 teaspoon nutmeg
salt and pepper
3 tablespoons Parmesan cheese

Mushroom sauce:

1/4 stick butter
1 teaspoon thyme
1 1/2 pounds mushrooms, sliced
3 tablespoons flour
3 cups chicken or beef broth
few drops Kitchen Bouquet if mushrooms are white
1/3 cup brandy
1/2 pound ripe Brie

Little Fisherman Restaurant

407 N. Harbor Blvd.
San Pedro
(213) 833-6059

•

Berth 73
San Pedro
(213) 547-5022

GARLIC SHRIMP FOR TWO

16 medium shrimp, peeled, deveined, and floured
1 ounce vegetable oil
1 ounce brandy
dash lemon juice
1 ounce white wine
1 teaspoon freshly chopped garlic
2 ounces fresh cream
salt to taste

Peel and devein shrimp, then flour them.

Heat skillet with oil. Sauté floured shrimp. When nearly cooked through, flame with brandy (warm brandy; pour over shrimp and light). Add dash lemon juice and wine. After flaming, add garlic.

Pour cream into skillet. Reduce liquid and salt to taste.

Divide shrimp on two plates. Pour cream sauce over shrimp.

Serve with rice, vegetables and your favorite wine. Our choice is Simi Valley Chardonnay 1982.

Little Fisherman II Restaurant

NIZETICH'S

A Dining Experience

1050 NAGOYA ST. • BERTH 80 • SAN PEDRO, CA 90731
(213) 514-3878

BREAD PUDDING WITH BRANDY SAUCE

In a large bowl, break bread up with hands, add scalded milk, then allow to cool.

Add remaining ingredients, except butter, to milk and bread. Pour into two 9 x 4-inch loaf pans, top with butter generously. Bake at 350 degrees for 45 minutes.

To make Brandy Sauce, blend all ingredients in sauce pan. Cook until thickened.

Serve bread pudding hot from pan and top with hot brandy sauce, or cool pudding and sauce completely, slice pudding in thin slices, and top with cool sauce.

Josephine Nizetich

Nizetich's Restaurant

1-1/4 loaves fresh white sandwich bread
1 quart plus 1 cup milk, scalded
2/3 cup sugar
7 eggs, beaten
1/2 cup white raisins
butter

Brandy Sauce:

1 pound butter
1-1/2 cups sugar
1 cup brandy
1 cup whipping cream
1 cup flour

SINCE 1938
COCKTAILS
LUNCHEONS
DINNERS

589 W. NINTH STREET
SAN PEDRO, CA 90731-3192
(213) 832-7437

LISBETH C. HOYT

CHOCOLATE MOUSSE

12 ounces semi-sweet chocolate chips
3 tablespoons water
4 eggs, separated
3/4 cup confectioner's sugar
1 cup whipping cream
few drops vanilla
cherries, strawberries, grapes
   (optional)

Melt chocolate with water in top of double boiler.

Beat egg yolks with sugar until creamy and light. Gradually blend into melted chocolate.

In another bowl, beat egg whites until stiff and stir into chocolate mixture.

In a small bowl, whip cream and flavor with vanilla.

Pour chocolate mixture into 8 wine glasses or dessert glasses. Chill for several hours and decorate with whipped cream and a cherry, strawberry, or grape.

Serves 8

Ingrid
Olsen's Restaurant

OYSTER WHARF
&
SAN PEDRO
MARINA

950 Sampson Way
San Pedro, Ca. 90731

OYSTER WHARF SAUTÉED CALAMARI

Pound calamari very lightly, salt and pepper and sprinkle with 1 tablespoon lemon juice. Cut steaks in half and set aside.

Heat oil in sauté pan to medium hot. Dredge calamari in flour, shake off loose flour and dip into beaten eggs. Brown each calamari steak on both sides, set aside on plate.

Discard oil from sauté pan and place butter in pan on low heat. Add parsley, 1 tablespoon lemon juice, and wine, and stir slowly.

Return calamari to pan briefly to heat and serve with sauce over steaks.

Serves 2

**2 calamari (squid) steaks, 4 to 5
  ounces each**
salt and pepper to taste
2 tablespoons lemon juice
oil
flour
3 eggs, beaten
1 tablespoon soft butter
1 teaspoon minced parsley
1 teaspoon white wine

Chef Tony Majuri

Oyster Wharf Restaurant

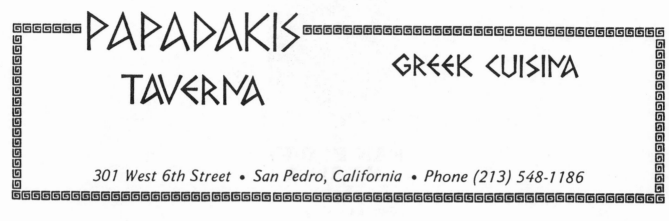

PAPADAKIS TAVERNA

GREEK CUISINA

301 West 6th Street • San Pedro, California • Phone (213) 548-1186

PSARI PLAKI
Fresh Sea Bass Greek Style

**10 Sea bass fillets, 8 ounces or larger,
1/2 cup flour for dredging fillets**

Sauce:

**1 cup light oil
8 cups onions, chopped
3 cups parsley
2 cloves fresh crushed garlic
1 #10 can whole tomatoes
4 cups white wine
small pinch rosemary
dash of salt, pepper, and oregano
3 bay leaves**

In a large pan sauté onions, parsley, and garlic until the onions become transparent. Add tomatoes, white wine, rosemary, salt, pepper, oregano, and bay leaves, and simmer for 1 hour at low heat.

Flour sea bass fillets and sauté quickly in light oil; transfer fillets to glass baking dish and cover with sauce. Bake at 350 degrees for 30 minutes.

Serves 10   *Papadakis Taverna*

P.O. Box 1619, San Pedro, CA 90733
Berth 94 Port of Los Angeles, San Pedro, CA • (213) 831-2351

BEEF TENDERLOIN EN CROUTE

Preheat oven to 350 degrees.

Season tenderloin with salt, pepper, and MSG, and quickly brown on all sides in oven or in skillet.

Roll pastry dough to 1/8 inch thickness and about 12 x 14 inch oblong. Trim edges. Brush pastry dough with half of egg and water mixture.

Slice liver paté; place half on center of dough. Place meat on top of paté and top with remainder of paté. Fold pastry over meat. Press dough firmly and roll edges. Punch a hole at both ends to release steam. Press with fork to seal edges.

Using trimmings of dough, form a criss-cross on top. Brush with remaining egg and water mixture, and place roast on top rack of oven for 10 minutes until pastry is slighly browned. Then place on lower rack.

Roast 35 to 40 minutes for medium rare meat.

Serves 6   *S.S. Princess Louise Restaurant*

2-1/4 pounds beef tenderloin
salt, pepper, and MSG
1 pound 2 ounces puff pastry dough
    (available at bakeries or frozen
    food departments in groceries)
1 egg, beaten, combined with 1/4
    cup water
1 can (2-3/4 ounces) liver paté or
    chicken liver paste

SPINACH SALAD

6 slices bacon, crumbled
1/2 cup chopped hard cooked eggs
    (2 small eggs)
2 bunches fresh spinach leaves,
    stems removed

Dressing:

1 egg
2 teaspoons Parmesan cheese
1 teaspoon total of salt, pepper,
    and MSG
2 tablespoons Dijon mustard
3 tablespoons fresh lemon juice
1 teaspoon sugar
1 capful Worcestershire sauce
1/4 cup safflower oil

Fry bacon. Drain on paper towels and crumble.

Hardboil eggs. Shell and chop.

Wash spinach leaves. Remove stems and place in large bowl. Sprinkle with crumbled bacon and chopped hard-cooked eggs.

In a separate bowl, mix all dressing ingredients except safflower oil. Then add oil and mix. Pour over spinach and toss until all ingredients are coated.

Serves 6   S.S. Princess Louise Restaurant

BANANAS FLAMBÉ

6 bananas
sugar
1/4 cup melted butter
1/3 cup brandy

Cut bananas in half lengthwise and sprinkle with sugar. Place in frying pan and sauté in butter and sprinkle with sugar.

Pour warmed brandy over bananas and flame.

S.S. Princess Louise Restaurant

JAPANESE
RESTAURANT
380 WEST SIXTH STREET   SAN PEDRO, CALIFORNIA 90731

AND
SUSHI BAR
213-832-5585

SENFUKU SUKIYAKI

Arrange all sukiyaki ingredients attractively on one or two platters.

Combine sauce ingredients in a 3-quart pan. Heat and bring to a boil. Keep hot.

Place suet in a large sukiyaki pan or cast iron skillet. An electric skillet may be used to prepare at the table. Melt suet over medium heat, stir to coat entire pan. The fat should smoke slightly before adding ingredients. Add all ingredients, except bean sprouts. Stir while frying, and until beef is browned. Add bean sprouts and fry a few minutes longer. Add sauce and serve while still cooking.

Serve with Japanese steamed rice, oshinko (mild pickles), hot or cold sake or Japanese green tea.

Serves 6 to 8   *Senfuku Restaurant*

beef suet
3 pounds sukiyaki beef, cut in strips
1 head cabbage, cut in 4-inch strips
1 pound mushrooms, sliced small
4 green onions, cut in 3-inch lengths
3 onions, sliced
2 packages tofu, cubed
1 package yam noodles (Shirataki)
l pound bean sprouts

Sauce:

3 cups water
3 cups cooking sake
3 cups soy sauce
2 cups sugar

Wallaby-Darned

An Authentic
Australian
CAFE/DELI

FEATURING
**Australian Wine - Beer
Meat Pies - Pasties
Souvenirs**

SPECIALIZING IN:
**Australian Cuisine
Gourmet Bar-B-Ques**
— All Occasions —

**John Lindfield • Proprietor
833-3629**
617 South Centre, San Pedro, CA 90731

SHEPHERD'S PIE

2 large onions, diced
3 pounds lamb shoulder, finely ground
1 pound peeled diced tomatoes
6 ounces tomato paste
1 teaspoon garlic, pressed
2 teaspoons ground pepper
salt to taste
3 cups mashed potatoes
sliced tomatoes
grated cheddar cheese

Sauté onion in large saucepan until soft. Add lamb and stir continually until cooked. Add diced tomatoes, tomato paste, and seasonings. (If there is a little fat, add a couple of tablespoons of flour to take it up.)

Place the mixture into a deep pie dish and cover with mashed potatoes, tomato slices, and cheddar cheese.

Bake at 375 degrees until crisp on top.

This recipe, which I use successfully in my cafe, is my mother's.

Serves 6 to 8

Executive Chef John Lindfield

Wallaby Darned

INDEX

Index

Index

Index

Index

Index